G000095672

MOVING BRITAIN FORWARD

Gordon Brown

MOVING BRITAIN FORWARD

SELECTED SPEECHES 1997–2006

with introductory comments by
Kofi Annan, Helen Clark, Linda Colley,
Lord Ralf Dahrendorf, Alan Greenspan, Al Gore,
Nelson Mandela, Wangaari Maathai, Trevor Phillips,
J.K. Rowling, Sir Jonathan Sacks, Sir Derek Wanless
and Sir Magdi Yacoub

edited by

WILF STEVENSON

BLOOMSBURY

First published in Great Britain 2006

Speeches of Gordon Brown Crown copyright © 2006

Selection, introduction and commentary copyright © Wilf Stevenson, 2006

Copyright in the introductory comments to each chapter and listed
in the contents page remains with the individual contributors.

All royalties are being donated to the Jennifer Brown Research Laboratory within
the University of Edinburgh's Research Institute for Medical Cell Biology.

The right of the author, editor and contributors to this
work has been asserted by them in accordance with
the Copyright, Designs and Patents Act, 1998.

Bloomsbury Publishing Plc
36 Soho Square
London W1D 3QY

www.bloomsbury.com

A CIP catalogue record for this book
is available from the British Library.

ISBN 0747588384
ISBN-13 9780747588382

10 9 8 7 6 5 4 3 2 1

Typeset by Hewer Text UK Ltd, Edinburgh
Printed in Great Britain by Clays Ltd, St Ives plc

The paper this book is printed on is certified by the © 1996 Forest Stewardship
Council A.C. (FSC). It is ancient-forest friendly. The printer holds
FSC chain of custody SGS-COC-2061

FSC
Mixed Sources
Product group from well-managed
forests and other controlled sources
Cert no. SGS-COC-2061
www.fsc.org
© 1996 Forest Stewardship Council

There is a golden thread which runs through British history, of the individual standing firm against tyranny and then of the individual participating in their society. It is a thread that runs from that long-ago day in Runnymede in 1215, on to the Bill of Rights in 1689 to not just one, but four great Reform Acts within less than a hundred years. And the tensile strength of that golden thread comes from countless strands of common continuing endeavour in our villages, towns and cities, the efforts and achievements of ordinary men and women, united by a strong sense of responsibility, who, long before de Tocqueville found civic associations to be at the heart of America, defined Britain by its proliferation of local clubs, associations, societies and endeavours – a Britain where liberty did not descend into licence and where freedom was exercised with responsibility.

Gordon Brown, Hugo Young Memorial Lecture
December 2005

CONTENTS

ACKNOWLEDGEMENTS

Gordon Brown has been unstinting in his support for this anthology, and without his agreement to quote from his speeches, there would be no book.

I am very grateful to Kofi Annan, Helen Clark, Linda Colley, Lord Ralf Dahrendorf, Trevor Phillips, Wangaari Maathai, Nelson Mandela, J.K. Rowling, Sir Jonathan Sacks, Sir Derek Wanless and Sir Magdi Yacoub for agreeing to contribute introductions to the various chapters of the book. Al Gore and Alan Greenspan kindly allowed me to quote comments made by them when speaking publicly about Gordon Brown.

Margaret Vaughan helped considerably with the introductory chapter. Shriti Vadera, Michael Jacobs, Spencer Livermore, Beth Russell and Damian McBride all helped to research the speeches, check dates and provide ancillary materials. I am particularly indebted to Cathy Koester for tracking down copies of the originals, and cross-referencing the dates on which the speeches were given, and I am also grateful to Sue Nye, Gil McNeil and Sarah Brown for their support of the project at various stages.

Liz Calder and Bill Swainson and the team at Bloomsbury have managed the publication process with great skill, and have been a pleasure to work with.

EDITOR'S NOTE

I am pleased that Gordon Brown's speeches have been collected for publication. Reading them gives an insight into the man behind the politician, and the values behind the policies. These are values we share: values of fairness and liberty and, above all, justice. Gordon Brown brings determination to the fight against international poverty, and it is rooted in a sense of justice that extends beyond Britain's shores. His speeches show a vision of a better world for all, a vision to which he is deeply committed.

Nelson Mandela

The speeches given by Gordon Brown often deal with ideas and political philosophy. The speeches on Britishness, for example, raise fascinating questions about our history and our place in the modern world; and some of the material around the question of how best to advance the public interest offers radical insights into the role and purpose of government. These have often not had the audience they deserve.

Gordon Brown is one of the few senior politicians on the contemporary British scene who has consistently given major speeches on topics which range across the political economy. His interests are broad, his scholarship used to great effect, and his passion and commitment come through on every occasion. But these speeches rarely get reported – it is almost as if the reporters sent to cover the speech are trained only to record the economic content of his speeches, whatever their actual focus.

Reading them again for this collection, it is hard not to be inspired by the passion of his convictions, the coherence of his vision and the rigour of his arguments. As a trained historian the Chancellor is clearly concerned to understand where ideas and policies come from and by whom they have been deployed in the past. He is always concerned to make explicit the connections between the guiding principles used by those of the democratic left and the policies which are derived from these writings. And he is anxious to show how policies will impact on present and future generations.

Some have questioned whether Gordon Brown makes one set of speeches for his Labour audiences and another for the City, but a close reading of them belies this rather trite criticism. Though varying in tone and style, the Chancellor's speeches stand as a coherent whole – as those of very few politicians do – because they reflect long thought and a coherent view of Britain, of our responsibilities to one another as citizens, and of Britain's role in the world. His vision is that of a Britain founded on liberty, responsibility and fairness: hence his interest in Britishness and British values, and the ideals and policies that flow from them. He starts from a dauntingly wide view of the individual in the changing global economy: men and women whose potential needs both encouragement and opportunity; men and women who are not alone, selfish or isolated, but living together in villages, towns and cities; living in communities within which we have responsibilities towards each other. It is a view that owes as much to the thinking of David Hume and Adam Smith – the two major figures of the Scottish Enlightenment – as it does to the growth of the concept of Britishness: a Britishness of liberty and civic duty that first flourished at around the same time, and in the twentieth century expanded to include a new fairness and opportunity for all.

And his vision of an opportunity-driven, dynamic market at one with a fair, open and responsible society is, he argues, more relevant in the age of the global economy than ever before. Globalisation, he says, brings both unrivalled opportunities and rising risks. To maximise opportunity and to minimise risk, people need both an open and enterprising economy where the creative, the dynamic and the hard working can prosper; and a fair society which offers proper insurance against what are even bigger risks. But he does not seek a 'handout society'. His emphasis on the potential of the individual makes poverty of aspiration one of his greatest concerns; young people must be both prepared and challenged to discover and achieve their full potential. The speeches gathered here reflect the work of a formidable and widely read intellect trained in the analytic skills of the historian but also – and far more importantly – inspired by a vision of what the political process can achieve for our society and our nation.

This collection of key speeches is drawn, with permission, from those given by Gordon Brown since he became the Chancellor of the Exchequer in May 1997 until April 2006. The book traces the development of Gordon Brown's thinking over nine years in government. It makes fascinating reading for anyone interested in the political process who wishes to understand how ideas developed in opposition have been modified and energised by the experience of government, and the unpredictable circumstances of a changing world.

Inevitably, in transforming what were live events into print, some of the colour and the texture of the original have been lost. I hope, however, that those who were present when these speeches were delivered will recognise what is included here, and that those who read them afresh will respond to the flow of ideas which spring from the text.

Wilf Stevenson
London, May 2006

1

BRITISHNESS

Twenty-first century Britain faces momentous change of a scale probably not encountered since the start of the nineteenth century. Then, the combination of the Industrial Revolution and the establishment of Britain as an unrivalled imperial power unleashed economic, social and cultural transformation. Today, the ocean of change created by three forces – globalisation, demography and technology – threaten to overwhelm us. But just as in the nineteenth century, it is the task of politics to offer a coherent account of these world-shaking movements; and to propose routes by which democratic societies can negotiate their own transformation, rather than being drowned by seemingly irresistible natural forces.

The response of many on the unrejuvenated left, shared by many on the far right, is what you might call the 'Canute' strategy: to stand on the shore of this sea of change and to try to command the waves to retreat. In this context that would mean attempts by governments to restrict flows of capital; efforts to throw up barriers to migration; and a retreat to narrow, nationalistic cultural norms. But as King Canute demonstrated, all that such a posture is likely to deliver is a severe soaking or worse. A second approach, favoured by the centre right, is simply to surrender to the ocean, to provide minimal protection against the storms and to wish everyone good luck. The strongest may survive; but I do not believe that even they can be sure of survival without a basic solidarity coming into play at the moments of greatest stress.

That is why Gordon Brown's appeal to the British people to think hard about the values that sustain our commitment to the common good is much more than an invitation to cheery flag-waving. It is why his speeches on Britishness should not be trivialised by cynics as just another canny Caledonian ploy. Nor should his exploration of national identity be seen as just a knee-jerk response to alarming outbreaks of interethnic conflict across Europe, or to the gathering strength of extremism in our own country.

The questions that Brown asks do encompass all of these events, but they are larger and more profound. And so is his answer. At the heart of his approach lies a simple but powerful proposition: 'The British way is not to fear change but to embrace it.' The important point about this statement is that it isn't just politician's optimism. It tells, first, that this is one politician who has grasped Bill Clinton's dictum that 'Globalisation isn't a policy; it's a fact. What matters is what we do about it.' And second that his response to the challenge, though it draws on universal values, is rooted in the traditions of these islands.

In these speeches, we see the emergence of a coherent left response to the challenge of identity politics. It may be that it is Brown's very Scottishness that has opened his mind to the value of an overarching national identity in cementing social solidarity. The Commission for Racial Equality's recent research on British identity showed that ethnic minority Britons find it easier to identify as Scots or Welsh than they do as English. That suggests that these are inclusive civic identities which do not pose ethnic hurdles for the Scottish Asians, or the black Welsh; it allows them to be just as Scottish and as Welsh as their white neighbours – and just as committed to the success of their nations. In the same way, it may be that a vital aspect of our response to the challenge of globalisation is a progressive assertion of British identity.

Finally, however, it is vital to distinguish that inclusive assertion of identity from the ethnically based exclusiveness put forward by the right. And here again, Brown offers a persuasive alternative; put simply, 'British is as British does'. In essence we define Britishness by our values, by our behaviour towards each other and by the nature of the institutions which define our community. No matter where you came from – or when – you too can be truly British. The route to the creation of an inclusive national identity could become, along with our language, our most valuable export in years to come. British experience and insight will be vital in a world desperately in need of the map across a sea of change.

Trevor Phillips

In the British Council 70th Anniversary Lecture, given on 7 July 2004, the Chancellor argues that on some of the bigger issues of our time, such as Europe, or the reform of the second chamber, or devolution, or asylum and immigration, there is still no consensus about what we should stand for as a country, or even how the British national interest is defined.

Early on in the speech, the Chancellor analyses the contributions of many writers, journalists and politicians who have written and spoken about Britishness over the years. He is hard on Thatcherism, and its stress on individualism over corporatism, arguing that it left unresolved all the big questions about Britain's future, including devolution, our constitution, and our relationship with Europe and the rest of the world. He quotes the views of many contemporary commentators, including Andrew Marr, Neil Ascherson, Tom Nairn, Norman Davies, Roger Scruton, Simon Heffer, Ferdinand Mount and Melanie Phillips and others representing all parts of mainstream opinion, and concludes that, beyond certain individual issues, some common ground does exist: 'the recognition of the importance of and the need to celebrate and entrench a Britishness defined by shared values strong enough to overcome discordant claims of separatism and disintegration.'

In this important speech, the Chancellor concludes that, for all the changes wrought by globalisation, national identity is still a vital force; and that only by understanding our Britishness, and the very things that bind our country together, will we be able to meet the challenges of the future. He argues that while the nation state must continue to represent our national interest, it is through a close constructive relationship with our European partners that Britain will not only enjoy greater prosperity but continue to have influence and continue to make a positive contribution on the world stage. As he says: 'The more influence we have in Paris and Berlin, the more influence we have in Washington. Equally, the less influence we have in the European capitals the less influence we have around the world.'

And his analysis of Britishness also leads the Chancellor to conclude that British values have much to offer Europe as it develops. Being in and leading in Europe means we can contribute British ideas to the development of the European Union. Our British qualities that will help Europe are openness to trade and our outward-looking and internationalist instincts and connections which stretch across the world; our creativity as a nation and our adaptability; our insistence on the importance of public service and openness in the running of institutions; and other values we share which stress the importance of hard work, self-improvement through education, fair play, and opportunity for all.

In the last half of the last century, post-imperial Britain came to be defined to the world by perceptions of national economic decline. In the first years of this new century we can begin to identify how:

- a once stop–go British economy is now stable;
- a once corporatist British business and industrial culture is seen now as more enterprising and more flexible;
- a country once characterised by high unemployment now enjoys record employment;
- a country on a rising tide of confidence can now aspire to become one of the great success stories of the new global economy.

But if we are to fully realise the economic potential of Britain my view is that we need something more. For the twelve years I have been Shadow Chancellor or Chancellor, I have felt that our country would be better able to meet and master the challenges of ever more intense global competition if we could build a shared sense of national economic purpose. Indeed, over half a century, Britain has been damaged by the absence of agreement on economic purpose or direction: lurching for narrow political reasons from one short-term economic panacea to another, often public sector fighting private, management versus worker, state versus market in a sterile battle for territory, that deprived British businesses and British workforces of confidence about the long term and held our country back.

So when in 1997 I made the Bank of England independent my aim was to build a consensus across all sections of society about the priority we all attached to economic stability. A shared purpose not just across macro-economic policy but across the whole range of economic questions is, I believe, even more essential now not just to face up to global competition from Asia as well as Europe and America but if we are to have the strength as a country to make the hard choices on priorities that will determine our success. Creating a shared national purpose also reflects a deeper need: to rediscover a clear and confident sense of who we are as a country. I believe that just about every central question about our national future – from the constitution to our role in Europe, from citizenship to the challenges of multi-culturalism – even the question of how and why we deliver public services in the manner we do – can only be fully answered if we are clear about what we value about being British and what gives us purpose and direction as a country.

Take the vexed question of Europe. I believe it has been a lack of confidence about what Britain stands for that has made it difficult for us to feel confident about our relationship with, and our potential role in, Europe. And as a result led many to believe – wrongly – that the only choice for Britain is between splendid isolation and total absorption. As with the debate over all international questions, the debate over Europe is, at root, about how the British national interest is defined and what we should stand for as a country.

Take our constitution and all the great and continuing debates about the nature of the second chamber, the relationship of the legislative to the executive, the future of local and central government. Our approach to resolving each of these questions is governed by what sort of country we think we are and what sort of country we think we should become.

Take devolution and nationalism. While the United Kingdom has always been a country of different nations and thus of plural identities – a Welshman can be Welsh and British just as a Cornishman or -woman is Cornish, English and British – and may be Muslim, Pakistani or Afro-Caribbean, Cornish, English and British – the issue is whether we retreat into more exclusive identities rooted in nineteenth-century conceptions of blood, race and territory, or whether we are still able to celebrate a British identity which is bigger than the sum of its parts and a union that is strong because of the values we share and because of the way these values are expressed through our history and our institutions.

And take the most recent illustration of what challenges us to be more explicit about these issues: the debate about asylum and immigration – and the debate about multi-culturalism. Here the question is essentially whether our national identity is defined by race and ethnicity – a definition that would leave our country at risk of relapsing into making a misleading 'cricket test' or, worse, colour the determination of what it is to be British. Or whether there are values which shape our national identity and which all citizens can share – thus separating citizenship from race – and which can find explicit expression so that they become a unifying and strengthening force.

And this is important not just for tackling these questions – central as they are – but for an even larger reason. In a growingly more insecure world people feel a need to be rooted and they draw strength from shared purpose. Indeed if people are to cope successfully with often bewildering change then a sense of belonging is vital. And that, in turn, depends on a clear shared vision of national identity. And I want to suggest that our success as Great Britain – our ability to meet and master not just the challenges of a global marketplace but also the international, demographic, con-stitutional and social challenges ahead – and even the security challenges facing a terrorist threat that has never been more challenging and demands upon those charged with our security never greater – depends upon us rediscovering from our history the shared values that bind us together, and on us becoming more explicit about what we stand for as a nation.

But if these issues around national identity are so impor-tant, my starting question must be: why over decades have we as a country singularly failed to address them and yet we see –

as Jonathan Freedland has so eloquently described – other countries, principally America, successfully defining themselves by values that their citizens share in common? The real answer, I believe, lies in our post-war history – in a loss of self-confidence and direction, even a resignation to national decline, a loss of self-confidence that is itself now becoming part of our history.

I was born in mid-century in what you might now call middle Scotland – in 1951. And while much was changing around us, Britain was still a country of fixed certainties that – echoing Orwell's *The Lion and the Unicorn* – were well understood, virtually unquestioned and barely stated. The early 1950s was the world of Sir Winston Churchill, a coronation that was reported with almost religious enthusiasm, an unquestionably United Kingdom, and around us symbols of an imperial Britain. I grew up in the fifties and sixties on maps of the world with a quarter of it pink and on British books and comics and then films which glorified the Blitz, the Spitfires, Sir Douglas Bader and endless reruns of *The Guns of Navarone.* This was, of course, a Britain whose confidence was built – unlike the USA – not on aspirations about the future but on real achievements of the past:

- the Britain that could legitimately make claim to be the first country in the world to reject the arbitrary rule of monarchy;
- the Britain that was first to make a virtue of tolerance and liberty;
- the Britain that was first in the Industrial Revolution;
- the Britain that was centre to the world's largest empire – the global economy of its day;
- the Britain that unlike continental Europe was never subject to revolution;
- the Britain that had the imperial mission which made us a world power and then a 'defence of the west' mission

which appeared to justify a continuing sense of ourselves as a world power;

- the Britain that – unlike America, which as a country of immigrants had to define itself by its belief in liberty and opportunity for all – did not feel its exceptionalism called for any mission statement, or defining goals, or explicit national ethos. Indeed we made a virtue of understatement or no statement at all.

This is a long way from the image of Britain of recent decades – what now goes for 'post-war Britain' – that long half century of uncertainty: the Britain of managed decline – at home and abroad; of failing corporatism; of sterile self-defeating struggles between public and private sectors, management and unions, state and market (in the fifties it was said we had managed decline, in the sixties mismanaged decline, and in the seventies we declined to manage); the Britain of doubts and hesitations about Europe; of the growth of secessionist movements in Scotland and Wales; of, as immigration rose, a retreat by some into defining Britishness through race and ethnicity, what was called the 'cricket test'; and then, as the sun set on the Empire, the failed attempts to root our post-1945 identity simply in the longevity of our institutions alone – indeed in the idea of unchanging institutions.

It was almost as if we looked backward with nostalgia because we could not look forward with hope. And so as the gap between imperial myth and reality grew, so too the view grew that Britain was not, in fact, underpinned by any strong sense of Britishness at all. And it led to a questioning of the very existence of Britain, right across mainstream opinion. Indeed Andrew Marr, now the political editor of the BBC, chose to entitle his 'state of the nation' book *The Day Britain Died*, writing: 'I have a profound belief in the likelihood of a British union dissolving within a decade.' For Neil Ascherson, from the liberal left, all that remains of

Britishness is 'a state, a flag and armed forces recruited from every part . . . just institutions . . . not social reality'. And with a similar eloquence his fellow Scottish writer Tom Nairn has argued that because there was little that is British left to underpin Britain, what he called 'the break-up of Britain' was inevitable.

Professor Linda Colley, whose ground-breaking historical research had demonstrated that the 'United Kingdom' was founded on great but ultimately transient historical forces – the strength of anti-French feeling, the bonds of empire and Protestantism – concludes:

> The factors that provided for the forging of the British nation in the past have largely ceased to operate. Protestantism, that once vital cement, has now a limited influence on British culture, as indeed has Christianity itself. Recurrent wars with the states of continental Europe have in all likelihood come to an end, so different kinds of Briton no longer feel the same compulsion to remain united in the face of the enemy from without. And crucially both commercial supremacy and imperial hegemony have gone. And no more can Britons reassure themselves of their distinct and privileged identity by contrasting themselves with the impoverished Europeans or by exercising authority over manifestly alien people. God has ceased to be British and providence no longer smiles.

And the historian Norman Davies even lists eighteen British institutions which according to him have defined Britishness and which he now suggests have lost their authority, putting the existence of Britain in doubt. And this view of decline and decay – and then a profound sense we have lost our way as a country – is, if anything, held more forcibly today by writers and thinkers from the right – Roger Scruton (whose highly challenging study of Englishness is entitled 'an elegy'), Simon Heffer and Ferdinand Mount. For them the final nails in the coffin of Great Britain are not just devolution but Britain succumbing to multi-culturalism and to Europe. For Mount, quoting Orwell that 'England is perhaps the only great country whose intellectuals are ashamed of their own nation-ality', our nation could become 'one giant cultural mall in which we would all wander, free to choose from a variety of equally valuable lifestyles, to take back and exchange pur-chases when not given satisfaction or simply to window-shop'. And Melanie Phillips concludes 'the big political divide in the country is now clear . . . it is over nothing less than the protection of liberal democracy and the defence of the nation itself'.

Yet as I read these writers and thinkers I detect that beyond the battleground on individual issues – our relationship with Europe, devolution and the constitution, asylum and immi-gration – some common ground does exist: it is the recogni-tion of the importance of and the need to celebrate and entrench a Britishness defined by shared values strong en-ough to overcome discordant claims of separatism and dis-integration. Take David Goodhart's recent contribution to the multi-culturalism debate. In questioning whether there is an inherent conflict between the need for social cohesion and diversity he argues that he wanted to emphasise that what we need is 'a core set of social norms . . . who are we does matter'. And while Melanie Phillips argues that a culture war is raging she has a remedy rooted in shared values of British-ness. There is hope, she says, because 'if citizenship is to mean anything at all, ministers must sign up to an overarching set of British values'. Interestingly, while Sir Herman Ousley, for-mer chairman of the Commission for Racial Equality, directly assails her views and indeed those of David Goodhart, he too returns to that same starting point – that there are British values all can share. Echoing Orwell's *'England, My England'*, his biographer Sir Bernard Crick argues that British 'people should have a sense of allegiance, loyalty, law and order, and political tolerance'. Even Tom Nairn writes of Britishness that 'there is a residual and yet still quite comfortable non-smallness about the term'.

But when we ask what are the core values of Britishness, can we find in them a muscularity and robustness that neither dilutes Britishness and British values to the point they become amorphous nor leaves them so narrowly focused that many patriotic British men and women will feel excluded? Of course, a strong sense of national identity derives from the particular, the special things we cherish. But I think we would all agree that we do not love our country simply because we occupy a plot of land or hold a UK passport but also because that place is home and because that represents values and qualities – and bonds of sentiment and familiarity – we hold dear. And it is my belief that out of tidal flows of British history – 2,000 years of successive waves of invasion, immigration, assimilation and trading partnerships that have created a uniquely rich and diverse culture – certain forces emerge again and again which make up a characteristically British set of values and qualities which, taken together, mean that there is indeed a strong and vibrant Britishness that underpins Britain. I believe that because these islands – and our maritime and trading traditions – have made us remarkably outward-looking and open, this country has fostered a vigorously adaptable society and has given rise to a culture both creative and inventive. But an open and adapting society also needs to be rooted and Britain's roots are on the most solid foundation of all, a passion for liberty anchored in a sense of duty and an intrinsic commitment to tolerance and fair play. The values and qualities I describe are of course to be found in many other cultures and countries. But when taken together, and as they shape the institutions of our country, these values and qualities – being creative, adaptable and outward-looking, our belief in liberty, duty and fair play – add up to a distinctive Britishness that has been manifest throughout our history, and shaped it. 'When people discard, ignore or mock the ideals which formed our national character, then they no longer exist as a people but only as a crowd,' writes Roger Scruton. And I agree with him.

For there is indeed a golden thread which runs through British history, of the individual standing firm for freedom and liberty against tyranny and the arbitrary use of power. It runs from that long-ago day in Runnymede in 1215 to the Bill of Rights in 1689 to not just one but four great Reform Acts within less than a hundred years. And the great tradition of British liberty has, first and foremost, been rooted in the protection of the individual against the arbitrary power of first the monarch and then the state. But it is a golden thread which has also has twined through it a story of common endeavour in villages, towns and cities – men and women with shared needs and common purposes, united as neighbours and citizens by a strong sense of duty and of fair play. And their efforts – and that sense of duty and fair play – together produced uniquely British settlements that, from generation to generation, have balanced the rights and responsibilities of individuals, communities and state and led to a deeply en-grained British tradition of public service.

First, liberty: it was Montesquieu who wrote in the eight-eenth century that ours was 'the freest country in the world'. I would suggest that it is because different ethnic groups came to live together in one small island that we first made a virtue of tolerance, welcoming and including successive waves of settlers – from Saxons and Normans to Huguenots and Jews and Asians and Afro-Caribbeans, and recognising plural identities. Today 85 per cent believe a strong sense of toler-ance is important to our country's success. And I would suggest that out of that toleration came a belief in religious and political freedom – illustrated best by Adam Nicolson's story of the creation of the King James Bible: different denominations coming together in a committee to create what was called 'irenicon', which means a symbol of unity for the whole nation.

Liberty meant not just tolerance for minorities but a deeply rooted belief – illustrated early in our history by trial by jury – in the freedom of the individual under the law and in the liberty of the common people rooted in constantly evolving English common law. When Henry Grattan – the eighteenth-century Irish politician – attempted to sum up our unique characteristics, he said that you can get a parliament from anywhere but you can only get liberty from England. Indeed so powerful were the ideas contained in the 1689 Bill of Rights which led to liberty associations all over Britain that both sides in the American War of Independence fought 'in the name of British liberty' and before America took the word to be its own, liberty was, in fact, identified with Britain.

Of course liberty is, in Matthew Arnold's words, 'a very good horse to ride, but to ride somewhere'. And history is strewn with examples of how we failed to live up to our ideals. But the idea of liberty did mean, in practice, that for half a century it was Britain that led the worldwide anti-slavery movement with engraved on the badge of the Anti-Slavery Society a figure of a black man and the quote, 'Am I Not a Man and a Brother'. Indeed at home no slave was ever permitted and abroad the Royal Navy searched the world to eradicate slavery.

And this view of liberty not only produced the Bill of Rights and the anti-slavery movement but caused Britain to lead the way in restricting the arbitrary power of monarchs and then onward to the far-reaching democratic reforms of the nineteenth and twentieth centuries. And at every point this British belief in liberty has been matched by a British idea of duty as the virtue that reinforces neighbourliness and enshrines the idea of a public realm and public service. A belief in the duty of one to another is an essential element of nationhood in every country but whether it arose from religious belief, from *noblesse oblige*, or from a sense of solidarity, duty in Britain – for most of the time an unwritten code of behaviour rather than a set of legal requirements – has been, to most people, the foundation of rights rather than their consequence.

And the call to civic duty and to public service – often impelled by religious convictions – led to the mushrooming of local and national endeavour, of associations and clubs, a rich tradition of voluntary organisations, local democracy and civic life. From the guilds, the charities, the clubs and associations – which bred amongst other things the City of London's unique structure – and from the churches, to the municipal provision of public amenities like libraries and parks and then to the mutual insurance societies, trades unions and non-governmental organisations, the British way is to recognise and enhance local initiative and mutual responsibility in civil affairs and to encourage and enhance the status of voluntary and community organisations – Burke's 'little platoons' – in the service of their neighbourhoods.

Alongside that passionate commitment to duty, Britishness has also meant a tradition of fair play. We may think today of British fair play as something applied on the sports field, but in fact most of the time it has been a very widely accepted foundation of social order: treating people fairly, rewarding hard work, encouraging self-improvement through education and being inclusive. In his last speech to parliament in March 1955 – the speech that urged the British people to 'never flinch, never weary, never despair' – Churchill described the essential qualities of the British people and at the forefront was fair play. For other nations, he said, 'The day may dawn when fair play, love for one's fellow men, respect for justice and freedom, will enable tormented generations to march forth triumphant from the hideous epoch in which we have to dwell.'

And this commitment to fair play – captured in Orwell's word 'decency' – has animated British political thought on both left and right over the centuries, right through to the passion for social improvement of the Victorian middle classes and the Christian socialists and trade unions who struggled for a new welfare settlement in the twentieth century. It was a settlement – making opportunity available to all, supporting the most vulnerable in society, inclusive, and ensuring what we would today call social justice – which over nearly half a century brought forth agreement across party and across social classes. So the British way has always been more than self-interested individualism. Even in the heyday of free-market philosophy society was always thought to rest on something greater than harsh organised selfishness. In his *Theory of Moral Sentiments* Adam Smith described the 'helping hand' that matched the 'invisible hand' of his *Wealth of Nations*. And he believed that the drive for economic success should be combined with traditions of social obligation, public service and a broad moral commitment to civic improvement. And this has brought forth tens of thousands of local neighbourhood civic associations, unions, charities, voluntary organisations – the space between state and markets in a Britain that has always rejected absolutism and crude selfish individualism – that together embody that very British idea – civic society – that was discovered in Britain long before 'social capital' ever entered our dictionary. And it is an idea that Chief Rabbi Jonathan Sacks captures eloquently for our times when he talks of British society and citizenship not in terms of a contract between people that, in legalistic ways, defines our rights narrowly on the basis of self-interest; but a British 'covenant' of rights and responsibilities born out of shared values which can inspire us to neighbourliness and service to others.

So while we talk in economics of the Anglo-Saxon model – the pursuit of economic individualism through free markets –

Britishness has always been more than just the 'freedom from' restraint but also stands for civic duty and fairness and these two qualities of British life – the notion of civic duty binding people to one another and the sense of fair play which underpins the idea of a proper social order – come together in the ethic of public service. And this gave rise to great British public institutions admired throughout the world, from the National Health Service and our army, navy and air forces to our universities, including the Open University, and the expression of civic purpose and social inclusion in culture and arts – our great national and municipal art galleries, museums and the BBC, not least the BBC World Service, and the British Council.

Alongside these values have been found what I regard as essentially British qualities: an ability to adapt, and an open-ness to new ideas and new influences which have made us, as a country, both creative and internationalist in our outlook. To have managed change for 300 years without violent revolu-tion is unique. I find it extraordinary that some appear to believe that it is somehow British to defend the idea of a constitution that never changes. It is precisely our ability to evolve our constitution that characterises the British way. So stability in our society does not come from rigidity: it comes from the ability to accommodate and master change: 'a state without the means of some change', Edmund Burke famously declared, 'is without the means of its conservation'. 'Change is inevitable', Benjamin Disraeli said in 1867: 'in a progressive society change is constant'. And a willingness and ability to adapt enabled Britain to embrace the opportunities of the Industrial Revolution with unprecedented vigour and success and, more than a century later, to mobilise from peace to war to survive and triumph in two world conflicts. And our very openness to new ideas and influences also means that at the heart of British qualities are a creativity and inventiveness – from the first agricultural revolution to the pioneering work of Babbage and Turing that made possible the computer and information revolution; in science, discoveries from DNA to cloning; in engineering, the work of Brunel and the inventions from the steam engine to the TV; and in medicine, from penicillin to interferon – an inventiveness that has ranged right across medicine and science to the arts and music. And so it is not surprising that as we rediscover these qualities, British dynamism is leading the world in some of the most modern and creative industries – communications, fashion, film, popular music, art, architecture, and many areas of science and the environmental technologies.

And out of that same openness to new ideas and influences, an outward-looking internationalism that made us not just the workshop of the world but as a country of merchant adventurers, explorers and missionaries the greatest trading nation the world has ever seen. Many people have made much of the fact that Britain was a set of islands. But unlike some other island nations Britain's history has never been marked by insularity. We are an island that has always looked outwards, been engaged in worldwide trade and been open to new influences – our British qualities that made us see, in David Cannadine's words, the Channel not as a moat but as a highway. An island position that has made us internationalist and outward-looking and not – as other islands have become – isolationist and inward-looking.

Of course all nations lay claim to uniqueness and exceptionalism and many would choose or emphasise the qualities of the British people in a different way from me. And in highlighting this view of British history – one which places what I regard as intrinsically British values and qualities at its centre – I do not want to claim moral superiority for Britain nor romanticise the past. And I do not gloss over abuses which also characterised our past. Nor do I claim the values and qualities I have described are not to be found in other nations. But I believe that they have shaped our institutions and together they have been responsible for the best of our past – creating a distinctive British identity that should make us proud of, and not reticent or apologetic about, our history. But most of all these values and qualities should inform any discussion of the central questions affecting our future. In fact the two ideologies that have characterised the histories of other countries have never taken root here. On the one hand an ideology of state power – which choked individual free-dom, making the individual slave to some arbitrarily defined collective interest – has found little or no favour in Britain. On the other hand an ideology of crude individualism – which leaves the individual isolated, stranded, on their own, detached from society around them – has no resonance for a Britain which has a strong sense of fair play and an even stronger sense of duty and a rich tradition of voluntary organisations, local democracy and civic life.

And this is my idea of Britain today. Not the individual on his or her own living in isolation 'sufficient unto himself' but a Britain of creativity and enterprise which is also a Britain of civic duty and public service. And in this vision of society there is a sense of belonging that expands outwards as we grow from family to friends and neighbourhood; a sense of belonging that then ripples outwards again from work, school, church and community and eventually outwards to far beyond our home town and region to define our nation and country as a society. And we should not only be explicit about our British values but express them fully in the way we organise our institutions. Let me suggest the agenda that flows from this.

First, start with Burke's 'little platoons', which reflect both a British desire for liberty and a strong sense of civic duty and fair play. If the British way is to encourage and enhance the status of voluntary and community organisations in the service of their neighbourhoods then we should recognise that aspects of post-war centralisation fell short of our vision of empowered in-dividuals and vibrant communities. The man in Whitehall never knew best; the woman in the WRVS and local community service usually knew much more. And so the question is how, from the foundation of British values, we refashion the settlement between individual, community and government. Today in Britain, there are more than 160,000 registered charities, more than 200,000 non-charitable voluntary and community organisations, around 400,000 in total, one for every hundred of the adult population – defining Britain as such a thing as society: an estimated 16 million people who do some kind of voluntary work – and nearly two adults in every five who give of their time to help others at least once in the year – and we best reflect our British traditions of civic duty and public service by strengthening our community organisations and making them more relevant to the challenges of today. Take community service by young people. If America has its Peace Corps and now its Americorps, South Africa its national youth service, France its 'Unis-cité', the Netherlands its 'Groundbreakers Initiative', Canada its Katimavik programme, should not Britain – with far greater and deeper traditions of voluntary and community service – be building on those traditions to engage a new generation of young people in service to their communities? And should we not be doing far more to provide nationally and locally the means by which young people find it easy to participate?

I am sure that, following the Russell Commission on young people, we will wish to consider establishing a National Youth Community Service; to ensure that poverty should not be a barrier to a gap-year option for a young person; to promote a range of opportunities nationally and internationally that back up the marvellous work already done by volunteering organisations; and to secure a business engagement in this that can translate the widespread social concern that exists among employers and employees alike into effective action for the common good. And I am sure we will also want to do more to translate community values into meeting new needs

through new means like the internet and community television and so carry on the British tradition of voluntary service
into the next generation. Take mentoring – underdeveloped
in Britain – where I can envisage a new initiative for the future
of Britain where through the internet, TV, local organisations
and personal contact, we could establish a new network of
mentors to befriend, advise, support and link those who need
help and advice to those who can help. And because sporting
activity is so important to defining our country's view of itself I
believe we should also look in detail at the proposal to revive
and expand participant sports in our country for a new
National Sports Foundation.

It follows secondly that if the British way is to restore and
enhance local initiative and mutual responsibility in civic
affairs we should be doing far more to strengthen not just
voluntary organisations but local institutions of government.
Rather than asking people to look upwards to Whitehall to
solve all their problems, the British way is surely to encourage
more and more people, from their own localities, to take
more charge of the decisions that affect their lives. Today,
with devolution, elected mayors and new local energy and
enthusiasm, many cities in England, Scotland, Wales and
Northern Ireland are undergoing a renaissance and, as they
become centres of initiative influencing our whole country,
the whole of Britain can learn and draw from the energy of
each of its parts. And a reinvigorated local democracy can, I
believe, emerge to empower people in their own neighbourhoods to deal with the challenges they face:

- anti-social behaviour, where the engagement of the
  whole community is paramount;
- schooling, where the participation of parents and the
  local community is vital;
- the health service, where the direct involvement of
  patients and prospective patients matters.

Third, a Britishness that thrives on a strong sense of duty and fair play and a commitment to public service means taking citizenship seriously. I would welcome a national debate on what the responsibilities and rights of British citizenship means in practice in the modern world. I believe strongly in the case for citizenship lessons in our schools but, for citizenship to matter more, these changes to the curriculum must be part of a far more extensive debate – a debate that, like the wide-ranging debate we see in America about what it is to be an American and what America stands for, includes our culture and history as well as our constitution and laws. And I believe we would be stronger as a country if there was, through new literature, new institutes, new seminars, new cross-party debate about our Britishness and what it means.

And what of the institutions and symbols that best reflect citizenship and thus give importance to national identity? These must be symbols that speak to all our citizens so I believe that we should respond to the undermining of an inclusive citizenship by the British National Party by not only fighting their racism but by asserting at every opportunity that the union flag does not belong to a vicious minority, but is a flag for all Britain – symbolising inclusion, tolerance and unity; and that England, Scotland and Wales – whose celebration of national identity is to be welcomed and encouraged – should also honour not just their own flags but the union flag for the shared values it symbolises. There is also a more substantive issue about the importance of integration set against respect for diversity. Of course we live in a multi-ethnic as well as multinational state but because a multi-ethnic Britain should never ever have justified a crude multi-culturalism where all values became relative, surely the common values that we all share should be reflected in practical measures to avoid religious hatred and to encourage – and in some cases require – the use of the English language. Take an economic example. Because many cannot find work because of language difficulties, it is surely right to pilot mandatory language training for those jobseekers whose language needs are preventing them from getting jobs. Upholding British values summons us to do far more to tackle discrimination and promote inclusion. And I believe that there should now be greater focus on driving up the educational attainment of pupils from ethnic minorities and a more comprehensive New Deal effort to tackle unacceptably high unemployment in areas of high ethnic minority populations.

If I am right, the British way is to develop a strong cohesive society in which in return for responsibility there is opportunity for all. And our British belief in fairness and our commitment to public service makes the NHS, founded on health care based on need not ability to pay, one of the greatest British institutions – an NHS that both reflects the values of the British people and is being modernised for our times in accordance with these very values. And we should never lose sight of the importance of the NHS not just to our view of Britishness but to the world's view of Britain. If, in the twenty-first century, we cannot make the NHS work in Britain we must ask what hope there is for millions in developing countries struggling with ill health and disease who cannot afford private health care. But if we can show that the NHS, health care based on need not ability to pay, is indeed the best insurance policy in the world then we give to the developing countries a model of modern health care – and hope.

Rediscovering the roots of our identity in our shared beliefs also allows us to address complex questions about our relationship with the rest of the world. This is not a subject for today but two observations follow from my remarks today. The first is that globalisation is fundamentally changing the nature of Europe. In the past, European integration was built on the idea of a European trade bloc dominated by European flows of capital, European-wide companies and European brands. Today we are in a completely different world of global movements of capital, global companies and global brands. As a result, the old integrationist project – the single market and single currency followed by tax harmonisation, federal fiscal policies and a quasi-federal state – the vision of a trade-bloc Europe – is fatally undermined. For to succeed econom-ically Europe must move from the old model – the trade-bloc or fortress Europe – to a new globally oriented Europe that champions economic liberalisation, a reformed social dimen-sion and a more open rather than protectionist approach to trade with the rest of the world.

The second observation is that while we must continue to learn from successes in other European countries, British values and qualities – particularly our outward-looking inter-nationalism that led us to pioneer free trade – have a great deal to offer in building the Europe of this new global era. Indeed British qualities and values can play a leading part in shaping a Europe that must reform, be flexible, be compe-titive, be outward-looking and build better trading and com-mercial relationships with the USA. So being fully engaged in Europe need not threaten Britain with subjugation inside an inward-looking trade bloc but can mean Britain and British values playing a full part in leading a global Europe. A Britain that thinks globally not only builds from our traditions of openness and outward-looking internationalism but builds upon huge British assets and strengths – the British Council itself, the BBC, the BBC World Service, our universities and our long-felt sense of obligation to the world's poor. And in addition to our well-known proposals for international devel-opment – including debt relief and the International Finance Facility for development – that represent a new deal between the richest and the poorest countries, I believe with you that we should build on the great success of the British Council internationally and do more to put one of our greatest assets – the English language, now the language of the internet and business – at the service of the world. One and a half billion people now speak English. Our aim should be that that no one in any continent is prevented by poverty, exclusion or educational disadvantage from learning the English language.

Thinking globally in an insecure world – and, more importantly, in the world since September 11th – requires us of course to take necessary steps to discharge a British government's first duty – the defence of its citizens, the people of Britain. And as we look forward to next week's Spending Review, I will make available the resources needed to strengthen security at home and take action to counter the terrorist threat at home and abroad. Those who wish to cut in real terms the Budget even for security will need to answer to the British people. We will spend what it takes on security to safeguard the British people.

I started this lecture by asserting that the British way is to embrace, not fear, reform and the challenge of the twenty-first century is not just to express our Britishness in the evolutionary reform of individual institutions but to continue to evolve towards a constitutional settlement that recognises both our rights and aspirations as individuals and our needs and shared values as a community. But as we discuss how our evolving British constitution can best reflect our British values, what is very clear to me is that even if a significant section of the Conservative Party has ceased to see itself as the Conservative and Unionist Party, our Labour Party must stand resolute as the party of the union. And indeed all decent-minded people should, I believe, stand for and champion a union that embodies the very values I have been discussing: a union that, because it reflects shared values, has achieved – and will in future achieve – far more by us working together than we could ever achieve separate and split apart.

So, in conclusion, there are good economic reasons for a new and rising confidence about the future of Britain. There are social and cultural reasons too for a new British optimism, a rising British confidence. We should think of Britain as a Britain discovering anew that its identity was never rooted just in imperial success or simply the authority of its institutions, nor in race or ethnicity. We should think of a Britain redis-covering the shared values that bind us together. Indeed the ties that today bind us are the same values and qualities that are at the core of our history . . . the values that should shape our institutions as they adapt, change and modernise to meet and master future challenges. So standing up for Britain means speaking up for British values and qualities that can inspire, strengthen and unify our country. And we can stop thinking about a post-war Britain of decline – the Britain that was – and start thinking about the Britain that we can become: Britain, a great place to grow up in; a Britain believing in itself; a new era of British self-confidence; not just a Britain that is a beacon for economic progress but a Britain proud that because of its values and qualities, progress and justice can advance together, to the benefit of all.

2

LIBERTY, RESPONSIBILITY
AND FAIRNESS

*For someone who is a historian and an academic to comment on
speeches by a major politician may seem strange. Politicians have to
work with the present; historians' chosen territory is the past. Politicians deal in power; academics generally possess none. Yet a keen
interest in academic history writings is one of Gordon Brown's
characteristic strengths. History is rarely a wholly reliable guide to
the future: but an instinctive sense and informed understanding of
the past can help politicians (and everyone else) to place contemporary
challenges and debates in a much broader context, and to move
beyond obscurantist myths, glib slogans and easy generalisations. As
Brown recognises, for instance, while its scale and many of the forms it
takes today are entirely new, globalisation itself is not, and neither is
Britain's exposure to it. Great Britain is a small island: but since the
seventeenth century, and for good as well as ill, its inhabitants have
had more to do with other continents than most other peoples. Extreme
openness to an interconnected world, to its risks and to its opportunities, is part of our present: but it is nothing new.*

*But what is most striking about this speech is its resurrection of and
insistence upon liberty in the British political tradition. Most seven-
teenth-, eighteenth- and nineteenth-century commentators took this for
granted. They believed that this polity possessed an 'Ancient Constitution', which was not contained in a single document, but did
manifest itself in significant statements of individual and legal rights,
as well as in institutions. In historical fact, of course, Brown's 'golden*

thread' of British liberties has sometimes unravelled, and was often tied in the past so as to exclude the majority: those who were female, or poor, or non-white, or not Protestant. None the less, bringing words like 'liberty' and 'rights' firmly back into British political vocabulary, and thinking in terms of new documents that will embody both them and civic responsibilities, is very important. One of the things that strikes me as a Briton living abroad is the contrast between the admittedly uneven, but none the less conspicuous prosperity of Britain, and the cynicism, frequent lack of self-confidence, and – occasionally – even outbursts of self-hatred that often characterise its media. A sense of emptiness and frustration often comes over. I am not so naïve as to believe that a new cult of liberty and new constitutional initiatives can be the whole solution. But people need political ideals in order to flourish as well as better incomes, and now that Britain has emerged from its post-imperial blues and its post-war economic malaise, paying attention to the former is overdue.

Countries in drift and in stress – and given the state of the world at present that is all of them – easily succumb to over-authoritarian leaders or to slick, media-friendly figures who seem to offer reassurance and quick fixes. By contrast, Gordon Brown deals in and is not afraid of ideas and debate. He urges us to think constructively about this country, by taking the trouble to think hard and creatively himself.

Linda Colley

The Chancellor has been developing some of the themes which occur in his speeches on Britishness. In these, he introduces a wide-ranging discussion of the way the British people have engaged over time with the principle of liberty, and how, in contrast with other countries, liberty has been linked to respon-sibility and fairness. His case is that it is only in Britain that the links between these three principles (liberty for all, responsibility by all and fairness to all) find wide applicability and acceptance amongst citizens. He argues that a progressive politician who can develop polices which derive from the interaction of these principles can set a new agenda for a modern view of Britishness, and that will lead to a new range of policy initiatives aimed at addressing the major challenges facing our country – our relationships with Europe, America and the rest of the world; how we equip ourselves for globalisation; the future direction of constitutional change; a modern view of citizenship; the future of local government, ideas of localism; our community relations and the balance between diversity and integration; and the shape of our public services.

Starting with the writings of Scottish Enlightenment thinkers, and drawing from a wide range of political philosophical texts, Gordon Brown asks questions about our nation's relationship to liberty: why is it that our passion for liberty did not lead, at least for most of our history, to a cult of self-interested individualism or to a British libertarianism? What prevented the triumph of the idea of the 'isolated individual free from ties or allegiances'? What kept alive the idea of the importance not just of family but also of community? His conclusion is that at the centre of our British heritage, the idea of liberty has always been linked to the equally powerful ideas of responsibility and fairness. People are not just 'individual islands entire of themselves', but citizens where identity, loyalty and a moral sense determine the sense of responsibility and fairness we all feel to each other.

In the first Hugo Young Memorial Lecture, given to an invited audience in Chatham House on 13 December 2005, Gordon Brown used the opportunity to reflect on the life and writings of the distinguished *Guardian* journalist to discuss liberty, responsibility and fairness in the context of internationalism. In particular he argues that at different points in our history, in peace and war, in ascendancy and adversity, we have always emphasised the importance of liberty, responsibility and fairness. But he extends the argument, making the point that, to an extent that has not been fully appreciated, each depends upon the other and all of them are necessary to our nation's future. He suggests that Britain has a choice as we prepare and equip ourselves to address the opportunities and the insecurities of globalisation:

> Britain can either retreat into the old narrow view of liberty as a form of libertarianism, responsibility as little more than paternalism, fairness as just formal rights before the law – leaving people and communities not only ill-equipped for challenges ahead, but with too little liberty, too little responsibility, and too little fairness. Or by meaning what we say about building a Britain of liberty for all, responsibility by all, and fairness to all, we can actively work for a new constitutional settlement, a strong vibrant civic society, and a reformed and renewed public realm delivering security and opportunity for all.

This is clearly an area of interest to the Chancellor, and several of these themes are developed in a companion speech given in January 2006, reproduced in chapter 10 of this book.

Today in tribute to the man who got nearer to the truth than any commentator of his time, I want to talk about the ideas I judge mattered deeply to Hugo Young, and the ideas I judge matter to our future: liberty; responsibility; fairness; and of course internationalism: ideas that are absolutely central to the view of the world in which I too was brought up; ideas that have become central to my view of our country and its future in global society; ideas that I want to discuss not as abstract political theory – and far less as an exercise in hindsight and historical revisionism – but as ideas that should in my view be the foundation for a new agenda of political, economic, social and constitutional reform, a new settlement that will enable us to face up to the scale and size of the global challenges; ideas that are not unique to the British culture – indeed all cultures value liberty, responsibility and fairness – but when taken together, charted through our history, are at the heart of a modern Britishness, central elements of a modern and profoundly practical patriotism: the surest way in which our nation can succeed economically and socially in the twenty-first century will be by building a society in which there is liberty for all, responsibility by all and fairness to all.

Our values do not, of course, float freely without roots; they are rooted in the best of our history. And because they can inspire us we can unite around them: they give us shared purpose. Liberty, responsibility and fairness have each a resonance that echoes from our nation's past. At different points in our history, in peace and war, in ascendancy and adversity, we have emphasised the importance of liberty, responsibility and fairness. But today I want to argue that, to an extent that has not been fully appreciated, each depends upon the other and all of them are necessary to our nation's future. My argument is that it is only by under-standing the critical place of liberty, responsibility and fair-ness together that Britain can meet and master the changing tides of the future. The society which will not only prosper but flourish in these islands in the twenty-first century will be one which draws strength from these values side by side: liberty for all, responsibility by all, fairness to all.

I want to show how a long-term reform agenda for the renewal of our country – the reform and modernisation of institutions and policies – flows from these tested and enduring values. What is my central thesis? It is the view that Britain is defined not by race nor ethnicity – as those who would impose a 'cricket test' would have us do – nor by our ancient institutions, nor just the various national traits for which we are famous across the world, but by our shared values formed and expressed in the best of our history. It is the view that a distinctively British set of ideas about ourselves and our role in the world has emerged from the long tidal flows of our national experience – the 2,000 years of successive waves of invasion, immigration, assimilation and trading partnerships that have both created a uniquely rich and diverse culture and made us an island – stable, outward-looking and open – for whom the Channel was – in David Cannadine's words – 'never a moat but a highway' for commerce and ideas.

The first value I want to highlight is liberty, one I emphasised in a British Council lecture I gave on Britishness last summer – liberty as both the rights of the individual protected against an arbitrary state and, more recently, as empowerment. Ask British people what they think important about our country – and one quality they highlight is our tolerance – ask about a characteristic that makes them ashamed and it is intolerance. Although it took until 1829 for Catholic emancipation, even later for rights for the Jewish community, women and ethnic minorities, John Locke led the way when he said beliefs cannot be compelled and the government existed for the advancement of civil interests. Out of the practice of toleration came the pursuit of liberty. And it was the battle for freedom from the old, from ancient hierarchical obligations – from the arbitrary rule of kings, from the overbearing power of bishops, from a wasteful mercantilism – that inspired seventeenth-, eighteenth- and nineteenth-century philosophers from Locke to Adam Smith and then to John Stuart Mill.

'The civil wars of Rome ended in slavery and those of the English in liberty,' Voltaire wrote. 'The English are the only people upon earth who have been able to prescribe limits to the power of kings by resisting them.' And he added, 'The English are jealous not only of their own liberty but even of that of other nations.'

So powerful did the British idea of liberty become that – perhaps ironically – the American War of Independence was fought by both sides 'in the name of British liberty'. Words- worth wrote of 'the flood of British freedom'. Hazlitt thought an Englishman 'has and can have no privilege or advantage over other nations but liberty'.

I stress how contemporaries here and elsewhere thought of our country as the home of liberty, because I believe that the idea of Britain defined as the home of liberty had as much power at that time as, in our time, the idea of America as land of liberty has for the USA. It was indeed Macaulay's whole theme that under what he called 'the new settlement', 'the authority of law and the security of property were found to be compatible with a liberty of discussion and of individual action never before known'.

There is, of course, the danger of seeing past villains as heroes and I do not wish to do so; for we should not forget the abuses, the discrimination, the injustices done; and it would be wrong to glorify or distort the past, particularly to uphold a particular view of the present. But in British debate after debate, in resolving controversy after controversy, contem- poraries appealed to the British idea of liberty as their judge and jury. In 2007 we will celebrate the two-hundredth anni- versary of Britain leading the world in the abolition of the slave trade. When Charles Darwin challenged Britain on slavery, it was precisely because slavery was an affront to national values which championed liberty. 'He trembled to think that we Englishmen and our American descendants with their boastful cry of liberty have been and are so guilty.' Or as the Scots author of the verses 'Rule Britannia' put it, 'Britons never, never, never shall be slaves.' And nearer our own times, George Orwell summed up the idea of liberty when he wrote that 'The totalitarian idea that there is no such thing as law – there is only power – has never taken root [here]. In England such concepts as justice, liberty and objective truth are still believed in.'

Some, however, would define British liberty as no more than constraining executive power, and – as some on the right argue – that because all the individual craves is to be left alone, the best government is no government. But I believe that across the centuries Britain evolved a far more generous, expansive view of liberty which, even if the concept of citizen did not, in theory, replace that of subject, focused not just on the abuse of power but on the empowerment of the individual – first only men of property and then all the people. While French politics focused on curbing the power of the monarch but not that of the state, the British idea was that rulers should yield power so that parliament and the people could wield it, shaping the decisions that affected their lives.

And British liberty came to mean liberty for all: a democratic view of liberty. So in this century a consensus has evolved that liberty is not just passive, about restricting someone else's powers, but active, people empowered to participate. And I believe that when in our generation Robert F. Kennedy argued for citizen participation and community self-government, and gave us a modern idea of the empowered citizen, he echoed a strong British tradition of civic engagement I would like to recapture.

But ever more so in this century, a consensus is also emerging that our liberties, equal and compatible with the liberties of all, should be tested against the extent to which they enable each individual not just to have protection against arbitrary power or the right to political participation, but to realise their potential. In Britain, this idea of liberty as empowerment is not a new idea. J.A. Hobson asked, 'Is a man free who has not equal opportunity with his fellows of such access to all material and moral means of personal development and work as shall contribute to his own welfare and that of his society?'; and before him T.H. Green stated, 'When we speak of freedom as something to be so highly prized, we mean a positive power or capacity of doing or enjoying something worth doing or enjoying, and that, too, something that we do or enjoy in common with others.'

I have previously talked about our history as both the triumph of the human spirit and yet the story also of the tragic waste of human potential. I was remembering, from a classroom long ago, Gray's 'Elegy Written in a Country Churchyard', and that lying there was – as he put it – some 'mute inglorious Milton': our history the story not just of great creative genius in action, but of men and women of talent or even genius who might have been so much more – poets, philosophers, scientists, doctors, inventors – but were forever denied the freedom to develop their potential.

Perhaps in a pre-industrial or an industrial society we could afford to disregard that loss; but in a post-industrial society where what gives you competitive advantage and wealth is your creative ability, prosperity will depend upon our ability, through investment in education, to tap the potential and bring out the best not just in the few but the many.

In each generation we have found it necessary to renew the settlement between individual, community and state and I cannot see how the long-term credibility of our institutions or our policies can be secured unless our constitutional, social and economic reforms are explicitly founded on these British ideas of liberty. Our long-held commitment to liberty must of course be the starting point for any future discussion of the British constitution and for a new settlement. Because a central feature of our tradition and the protection of our liberties within it is the limits we place on executive power. I am pleased that on my first day in office I took on that challenge, giving up government power over the Bank of England. I made the same point during the general-election campaign when I suggested there was a case for a detailed consideration of the role of parliament in the declarations of peace and war. I would apply this same approach to constitutional questions such as the issue of House of Lords reform, left unfinished by the 1911 Act, which – in the words of its own preamble – was only a temporary step.

Our long-held commitment to liberty demands also that we break up any centralised institutions that are too remote and insensitive, devolving and decentralising power, encouraging structures and initiatives so that the power so devolved brings real self-government to communities. My own view is that new politics cannot be a reality unless we make local accountability work by reinvigorating the democratically elected mechanisms of local areas – local government. And I believe it is in the same spirit that we explore a new pluralism in our politics, searching for not just consensus but for a shared sense of national purpose, seeking new ways of involving people in shaping the decisions that affect them – from citizens' juries to local citizen forums – where the evidence is that participation does not just enthuse those directly involved, but makes the public generally feel more engaged.

But as Hugo Young was first to acknowledge, our passion for liberty which runs though and defines much of recent British history did not lead, at least for most of our history, to a cult of self-interested individualism or to a British libertarianism. And why not? What prevented the triumph of the idea of the isolated or self-interested individual free from ties or allegiances and made us instead praise Edmund Burke for his love of the 'little platoon'? What kept alive the idea of the importance not just of family but also of community even when Hume, separating 'is' from 'ought', appeared to devalue the very idea of duty? When the thrust of eighteenth-century Enlightenment philosophy was its 'relentless focus on the unique and the individual' – appearing to deny the importance of belonging, what kept not just the family but neighbourhood, community and local associations and loyalties right at the forefront of our view of Britishness, and made most of us reject both Mill's extreme view of liberty and, more recently, a crude libertarianism which demanded freedom irrespective of our responsibilities to others? What made us think, in the words of Roosevelt, that 'the man who seeks freedom from responsibility in the name of individual liberty is either fooling himself or trying to cheat his fellow man'.

When we think about it the answer becomes clear. It is because at the heart of our British heritage, alongside the idea of liberty are the equally powerful ideas of responsibility and duty. So that people are not just individual islands entire of themselves, but citizens in whom identity, loyalty and indeed a moral sense determine the sense of responsibility we all feel to each other. 'Liberty means responsibility, that is why most men dread it,' Bernard Shaw wrote. In her recent book *The Roads to Modernity* the historian Gertrude Himmelfarb compares and contrasts the contribution France, America and Britain made to the modern world. She finds that while France and America both had revolutions in the name of freedom, it is Britain and British ideas that led the way into the modern world by focusing on benevolence, improvement, the civic society and the moral sense as necessary for social progress.

And because this comes alive not only in families, but through voluntary associations, churches and faith groups and then on into public service, we, the British people, have consistently regarded a strong civic society as fundamental to our sense of ourselves – that moral space, a public realm in

which duty constrains the pursuit of self-interest. As John Stuart
Mill had to concede, 'there are many positive acts to the benefit
of others which anyone may rightfully be obliged to perform.'
'All for ourselves and nothing for other people' is 'a vile
maxim', wrote Adam Smith. Coming from Kirkcaldy as Adam
Smith did, I have come to understand that his *Wealth of Nations*
was underpinned by his *Theory of Moral Sentiments*, his invisible
hand dependent upon the existence of a helping hand. Of
course Smith wanted people freed from the shackles of obedi-
ence to kings and vested interests, hence the 'wealth of nations'; but while he wanted people freed from the old
constraints he certainly did not envisage people free of civic
bonds and civic duties, hence his theory of moral sentiments.
'Whenever we feel the fate of others is our personal responsibility we are less likely to stand idly by,' he wrote. For Smith the
moral system encompassed the economic system, generating
the responsible virtues of industry, honesty and reliability – and
the stable associations in which we accept our responsibilities
each to one another, habits of cooperation and trust, the moral
sense upon which the market depended. So he always believed
that the centre of a town is far more than a marketplace. And it
is true to say that, even when Enlightenment philosophers –
like Smith – stood under the banner of freedom, they did not
argue that their view of freedom gave men immunity from their
responsibilities to serve their society: the British way always
more than self-interested individualism, at the core of British
history the very ideas of 'active citizen', 'good neighbour', civic
pride and the public realm.

So there is indeed a golden thread which runs through
British history, of the individual standing firm against tyranny
and then of the individual participating in their society. It is a
thread that runs from that long-ago day in Runnymede in
1215 and on to the Bill of Rights in 1689 to not just one but
four great Reform Acts within less than a hundred years.
And the tensile strength of that golden thread comes from

countless strands of common continuing endeavour in our villages, towns and cities, the efforts and achievements of ordinary men and women, united by a strong sense of responsibility, who, long before de Tocqueville found civic associations to be at the heart of America, defined Britain by its proliferation of local clubs, associations, societies and endeavours – a Britain where liberty did not descend into licence and where freedom was exercised with responsibility.

So the two ideologies that have dominated the histories of other countries have never taken root here – neither state power, which chokes individual liberty; nor crude individualism, which has no resonance for the Britain of thousands of voluntary associations, the Britain of mutual societies, craft unions, insurance and friendly societies and cooperatives, the Britain of churches and faith groups, the Britain of municipal provision from libraries to parks and the Britain of public service – mutuality, cooperation, civic associations and social responsibility.

Of course, as Jonathan Sacks explains so eloquently, this popular idea of responsibility and civic engagement was, more often than not, taught in narratives, less the subject of philosophical texts but celebrated in poetry and song, enacted in rituals, embodied in traditions, passed on in families. And we can track the change from a Britain proud of pioneering citizen responsibility through jury service to a Britain today where responsibility by all means corporate social responsibility expected of business, the obligations accepted by the unemployed to seek work, the challenge to residents in poor neighbourhoods to break from a dependency culture, and local initiative and mutual responsibility coming alive in new areas of community life from child care, to drug rehabilitation, to the greatness of our hospices.

So one of the great challenges ahead is the encouragement and renewal for the coming generation of that rich British tradition of voluntary organisations, local democracy and civic life. And it is to make this ideal of responsibility real for a new generation that I announced last week private and public funding for the first British National Youth Community Service that will provide part-time and full-time community service at home and abroad, including the offer of gap years to those who could not otherwise afford them. Just as from America in the 1960s came the Peace Corps which, like the British VSO before it, caught the imagination and harnessed the idealism of that generation, so now from Britain in the first decade of a new century, National Youth Community Service can engage and inspire the coming generation of young people. Our voluntary organisations should neither be captured by the state nor used as a cut-price alternative to necessary public provision – and so we should reject any old left idea of the state assuming the responsibilities of civic society – and reject any new right view of the voluntary sector as a weapon in the battle against any role for government – a view that takes us backwards into an old world of paternalism.

In advance of our Spending Review, I want to energise a new debate on the vital future role of the voluntary, charitable and community sector in our country and how we can do more to encourage the giving of both time and money and to make the necessary decisions to support both. I want this generation to recognise their unique and often irreplaceable qualities – the skill at one-to-one contact, the knowledge of what's happening on the ground, the pioneering of new ways, the encouragement of citizenship. And I believe that any new constitutional settlement should recognise the importance we attach to both their independence and their role as innova- tors in meeting new needs in new areas, in bringing to life in our times the idea of responsibility by all.

Let us recap: in an old world of hierarchy, in feudal and later periods, responsibility was defined narrowly as no more than *noblesse oblige*; in a world of deference in the pre-industrial age, responsibility was little more than a form of paternalism. But we can see the evolution of the idea of responsibility through the great social movements of the last 200 years to today, when it is defined primarily through the concept of fairness. The great Britain we all need cannot be wholly cohesive or successful if built around liberty alone or responsibility alone or even liberty and responsibility together, important as these values are. A modern successful Britain must be built around liberty, responsibility and fairness.

In the 1950s in his last speech to parliament, Churchill spoke of a Britain defined by its sense of fair play. In the 1940s Orwell talked of a Britain known to the world for its 'decency'. A YouGov survey in July 2005 showed that as many as 90 per cent of British people thought that fairness and fair play were very important or fairly important in defining Britishness. Britishness today, as Michael Ignatieff concluded, is parliamentary democracy, rule of law, fairness and decency. Of course the appeal to fairness runs through British history. The call, of course, of the oppressed, the disadvantaged and the left-out, with Raineborough asserting in the 1647 Putney Debates that 'the poorest he that is in England hath a life to live as the greatest he'; but the call throughout the generations of all decent-minded people demanding wrongs be righted in the interests of justice.

The twentieth-century innovation has been to give new expression to fairness as the pursuit of equality of opportunity for all, unfair privileges for no one. And in this century there is an even richer vision of equality of opportunity challenging people to make the most of their potential through education, employment and in our economy, society and culture. Charities can and do achieve great transformative changes, but no matter how benevolent, they cannot, ultimately, guarantee fairness to all. Markets can and do generate great wealth, but no matter how dynamic, they cannot guarantee fairness to all. Individuals can be and are very generous but by its nature personal giving is sporadic and often conditional.

So fairness can be advanced by but cannot, in the end, be guaranteed by charities, however benevolent; by markets, however dynamic; or by individuals, however well meaning, but guaranteed only by enabling government. Take a movement all of us have seen grow from thousands to millions and all of us admire greatly. The organisers of Live Aid 2005 / Live 8 concluded that, however worthy, right and timely Live Aid 1985 was, even these immense efforts were not wholly sufficient. They concluded that while Live Aid 1985 could offer charity through individual donations it needed action by governments to guarantee justice, hence their theme 'From Charity to Justice'. As Bob Geldof said, Live Aid 2005 / Live 8 is not about charity, nor protest, but about making things happen, persuading governments to act. So just as good government is not inimical to civic society, so civic society is not inimical to good government, but complementary to it. For the good society to flourish to the benefit of all, private endeavour must be matched by public endeavour. And while changing needs often require government to withdraw from areas where it should not be – as in the management of interest rates – they can also mean government, aware that as a nation we need to be equipped for a global future, discharging fresh responsibilities too.

Let us recall that in the fifty years after 1945, just about the only services most under-fives and their parents received were basic maternity provision, vaccination and a letter asking you to turn up at school at five. Now we know that the first forty-eight months of a child's life are probably more important than later years to that young child's educational and social development. We also know how just how unfair it was that nursery education was restricted to just the few who could pay for it. Because of that – and because of the changing needs of parents to balance work and family life – a whole new frontier of the Welfare State, a revolution in services, is being opened up with government able to guarantee what no other organisation could ever guarantee – maternity and paternity rights, and Sure Start services for children before three and the right to free nursery education from the age of three.

I am both impressed and excited by the vast range and mixed economy of Sure Start, voluntary, charitable and private-sector providers, and the high level of innovation in this new sector; and we need to do more to encourage new providers. But it is because my underlying philosophy is that every child is special, every child precious and therefore that no child should be left behind – in other words to ensure we empower every child and not just some with opportunity – that we need to recognise the enabling role of government. Parents who want to do best by their children want both the flowering of local initiative in Sure Start, civic society at its best, and the helping hand of public purpose: from the local nursery school, the local Sure Start centre, whoever runs it, to the Child Tax Credit and maternity leave, supportive local and national services that empower from a government on people's side. That a strong civic society needs a good enabling government on people's side to deliver fairness – and that to enlarge the civic space you do not need to eliminate the rest of the public realm – is a lesson we must learn and relearn in every generation.

Take the New Deal for jobs and skills, the modern expression of a big idea, society accepting its responsibility for the goal of full employment and of individuals empowered and equipped to realise their potential, a positive view of liberty for all, the freedom to work. But the modern British way is of responsibility by all: of new opportunities matched by the obligation of the unemployed to work or to learn new skills. In the coming decades – as technological change forces people to make, on average, seven big job changes across their working lives – a New Deal that equips people with the new skills they will need will become more, not less, essential. Of course there are issues of cost and how private, voluntary and community organisations can help deliver the New Deal.

But to oppose the principle of the New Deal is for society to walk away – leaving people on their own, helpless, facing change and insecurity, condemning us to a Britain of liberty for some but not all, responsibility demanded of some but not all, fairness to some but not all.

The same is true of the environment, where private, voluntary and charitable endeavour should not exclude government's responsibilities in this area but complement it. So whether it be enduring responsibilities for full employment, or new frontiers balancing work and family life, or caring for our environment or, more generally, addressing poverty and investing in schools, hospitals, science and infrastructure to equip our country for all the global challenges ahead – if you will the ends, fairness to all, you must be prepared to will the means – enabling, empowering government to make fairness possible.

At the outset I cited Gray's 'Elegy Written in a Country Churchyard', and talked of liberty as empowerment. And does this not come alive today in the idea of individuals challenged to make the most of their potential – challenged to bridge the gap between what they are and what they have it in themselves to become? Let us recall Gray musing in the year 1750 about a 'mute inglorious Milton', a guiltless Cromwell, a village Hampden. Recalling the tragic waste throughout our history of the might-have-been: the great music never composed; the great art never realised; the books never written; the science that never saw past the edge of known truth; the medical breakthrough that never was to save a life; the contributions never made; the potential never realised.

Yet today with China and India turning out 4 million graduates a year and in a race with us not to the bottom but to the top, a small country like ours cannot afford to neglect the potential of any or write off the talents of any young person and if we do so will be left behind by globalisation. So instead of, as in the past, developing only some of the potential of some of the people, our mission for liberty for all and fairness to all summons us to develop all of the potential of all the people. And instead of condoning what Aneurin Bevan called 'a poverty of aspiration' that restricts success to the few, our view of responsibility by all should mean we challenge all young people to make the most of themselves. And we should champion the idea of Britain as a country not diminished by 'a poverty of aspiration' but energised by a wealth of ambition in all areas of our country. That is why education – public investment in it and continuing reform of it – and an assault on the denial of potential, and the abolition of the culture that tolerates a poverty of aspiration, must and will remain at the heart of our mission.

So tonight I have set out an idea of a Britain far better equipped for the global challenge because its future is built upon the most solid foundation of all – enduring values we can readily rediscover and embrace – a passion for liberty for all, anchored in an ethic of responsibility by all, which comes alive for our generation in a commitment to fairness for all. And I have argued that by applying these values of liberty, responsibility and fairness to the modernisation and renewal of British institutions and policies we will best meet the global challenges ahead. Britain does indeed have a choice of two roads as we prepare and equip ourselves to address the opportunities and the insecurities of globalisation. Britain can retreat into the old narrow view of liberty as a form of libertarianism, responsibility as little more than paternalism, fairness as just formal rights before the law – leaving people and communities not only ill-equipped for challenges ahead, but with too little liberty, too little responsibility, and too little fairness. Or by meaning what we say about building a Britain of liberty for all, responsibility by all, and fairness to all, we can actively work for a new constitutional settlement, a strong vibrant civic society, and a reformed and renewed public realm delivering security and opportunity for all.

3

INTERNATIONAL ACTION ON POVERTY

Gordon Brown is one of a small group of political leaders who first embraced the notion that our current generation has the power and the know-how to overcome world poverty. Over the past decade, he has used his influence to place the case for development firmly on the agenda of the developed world. He has been a source of innovation and ideas for new forms of international development cooperation. He has been a driving force in making things happen, showing how the international community can deliver on promises, from debt relief to the genuine scaling-up of development assistance. And he has done this at a make-or-break time for the Millennium Development Goals – and for the world's poor.

It goes without saying, therefore, that the speeches of Gordon Brown are vivid testimony to a rare combination of vision, commitment and action. He was among the first to champion the need for an additional $50 billion a year in overseas development assistance. He has fought tirelessly – and sometimes single-handedly – for debt relief, including on multilateral debt owed to international financial institutions. He was the first finance minister to back the Global Fund to Fight AIDS, Tuberculosis and Malaria. He championed the use of public guarantees to raise market finance for development. And he was instrumental in creating the pilot International Finance Facility (IFF) for immunisation.

A staunch but not uncritical ally of the United Nations, Gordon Brown is playing a leading role in my High-level Panel on UN

System-wide Coherence, charged with exploring ways to make the UN family work more effectively around the world in the areas of development, humanitarian assistance and the environment. And through the UK's $15-billion commitment to ensure universal primary education by 2015, he is yet again demonstrating why it matters to men, women and children in poor countries that finance ministers in rich ones care about development. Because of him, more children are being immunised, more families are escaping poverty and more people have access to safe drinking water. In short, he has been a finance minister who has also spoken and acted like a development minister, and all the world is richer for it.

Kofi Annan

In this chapter is one of a number of fine speeches delivered by the Chancellor in his much-admired campaign to relieve world poverty through pursuit of debt relief; enhanced economic activity through trade; and the establishment of an International Finance Facility. Using his position on the IMF and the World Bank, and working with finance ministers in Europe, the Commonwealth and the G8, with the international agencies and with the UN, the Chancellor and the International Development Secretaries have worked tirelessly to achieve real progress in this area. The impact of the measures so far introduced has been significant, and the approach has been widely praised and supported across the political spectrum. It is also an issue, perhaps more than any other, that has become associated with Gordon Brown personally.

In early January 2005 the Chancellor gave a major speech on international development at the National Gallery of Scotland. It was delivered in the aftermath of the South-Asian tsunami, and he draws attention to the way such natural tragedies link us: they show both our shared vulnerabilities and our linked destinies; an earthquake in one continent has left families devastated in every continent. And, as he says, 'humbled first by the power of nature, we have since been humbled by the power of humanity – the awesome power of nature to destroy; the extraordinary power of human compassion to build anew'. And we have witnessed not only an unprecedented demonstration of sympathy but also 'an unprecedented demonstration of generosity, with more people giving spontaneously than at any time and in any previous appeal'.

At the beginning of this speech, the Chancellor calls for a doubling of effort in 2005 to deliver the Millennium Development Goals; he rehearses the case for a modern 'Marshall Plan'; and then spells out what the benefits would be of a properly funded International Finance Facility: frontloading investment in infrastructure, education and health systems, and economic development so developing countries can benefit from access to markets; providing grants immediately to help ensure a sustainable exit from debt so that poor countries do not need to choose between emergency relief and long-term investment; making primary schooling for all a reality; and cutting infant mortality and maternal mortality through eliminating malaria and TB and treating millions more people who are suffering from HIV/AIDs.

When I delivered the CAFOD lecture a few weeks ago about the economic, social and moral case for us now seeing people we have never met and may never meet in other continents not as strangers but as neighbours, I argued that what impelled us to action where there is need was not just enlightened self-interest that recognises and acts upon our interdependence – our dependence each upon the other for our sustenance and our security – but, even more important, a belief in something bigger than ourselves: our shared moral sense that moves human beings even in the most comfortable places to sympathy and solidarity with fellow human beings even in far-away places in distress.

And the worldwide demonstration in the last few days not just of sympathy but of support shows that even if we are strangers, separated and dispersed by geography, even if diverse because of race, even if differentiated by wealth and income, even if divided by partisan beliefs and ideology – even as we are different, diverse and often divided – we are not and we cannot be moral strangers. We are one moral universe.

And the shared moral sense common to us all makes us recognise our duty to others. And it is this moral sense exhibited in the worldwide response to disaster that shows not only what can be done – in Britain alone, £76 million raised so far by the British public; after Gift Aid, almost £90 million – but also demonstrates what has now to be done – that we address the underlying causes of poverty. So while 2004 was a year which ended in the horror of a natural disaster, 2005 is a year that can start with the hope of human progress. 2005 is a year of challenge but also a year of opportunity when – from the foundation of hope – we can, I believe, see real change. A year which is also the year when the UK has special responsibilities as President of the G7 and European Union, a year in which we can tackle not just the terrible and tragic consequences of the tsunami –

working together to forge a long-term plan for the reconstruction of Asia – but also forge a new 'Marshall Plan' for the entire developing world.

And let me say the urgency and scale of the agenda I am going to propose for debt relief, for new funds for development and for fair trade is now even more pressing given the tragic events of recent days. It is because I want a world that does not have to choose between emergency disaster relief and addressing the underlying causes of poverty and injustice – between advancing first aid and advancing fundamental change – that the proposals I am putting forward today to advance the interests of all the developing world will – the government believes – find support in all parts of the world. In just a few months time, just a few miles from here in Edinburgh, the G8 will meet in Gleneagles to discuss the most important issue of our generation – world poverty. This year is the year when world leaders will first gather here in Scotland and then in September at the United Nation's Millennium Summit to examine just how much we have to do together if we are to seriously address the scale of poverty round the world today. We meet because exactly five years ago in New York and in a historic declaration the world signed up to a shared commitment to right the greatest wrongs of our time, including:

- the promise that by 2015 every child would be at school;
- the promise that by 2015 avoidable infant deaths would be prevented;
- the promise that by 2015 poverty would be halved.

In other words promises that rich countries would work with the poor to right the great wrongs of our time. The Millennium Development Goals were not a casual commitment. Every world leader signed up. Every international body signed up. Almost every single country signed up; the world in unison accepting the challenge and agreeing the changes necessary to fulfil it – rights and responsibilities accepted by rich and poor alike.

But already, so close to the start of our journey to 2015, it is clear that our destination risks becoming out of reach, receding into the distance. The first commitment to be met is that by next year the gap between the chances for girls and boys in primary and secondary education would be closed. But we know already that not only are the vast majority – 60 per cent – of developing countries unlikely to meet the target but most of these are, on present trends, unlikely to achieve this gender equality for girls even by 2015. And we know one stark fact that underlines this failure: not only are 70 million girls and 40 million boys of school age not going to school today but today and every day until we act 30,000 children will suffer and 30,000 children will die from avoidable diseases. At best, on present progress in sub-Saharan Africa:

- primary education for all – the right to education so everyone can help themselves – will be delivered not in 2015 but 2130 – that is 115 years late;
- the halving of poverty – the right to prosper so each and every individual can fulfil their potential – not by 2015 but by 2150 – that is 135 years late; and
- the elimination of avoidable infant deaths – the right to a healthy life so all have the opportunity to make the most of their abilities – not by 2015 but by 2165 – that is 150 years late.

For decades Africa and the developing world have been told to be patient. To those who say Africa should remain patient, the reply now comes from Africa: 150 years is too long to be patient. One hundred and fifty years is too long to wait for justice. One hundred and fifty years is too long to wait when infants are dying while the rest of the world has the medicines to heal them. One hundred and fifty years is too long to wait when a promise should be redeemed, when the bond of trust should be honoured now, in this decade.

In 1948, with much of Europe still in a state of ruins, the American Secretary of State General Marshall proposed, for his generation, the most ambitious plan for social and economic reconstruction. Marshall's starting point was a strategic and military threat but he quickly understood the underlying problems were social and economic. Marshall's initial focus was the devastation wrought in one or two of the poorest countries but he rapidly realised his plan should be an offer to all poor countries in the neighbourhood. Marshall started with a narrow view of aid needed for an emergency but quickly came to the conclusion that his plan had to tackle the underlying causes of poverty and deprivation. Marshall's early thoughts were for small sums of money in emergency aid but very soon his searching analysis brought him to the conclusion that a historic offer of unprecedented sums of money was required. He announced that America would contribute an unparalleled 1 per cent of its national income. He said that his task was nothing less than to fight hunger, poverty, desperation and chaos. His Treasury Secretary argued that prosperity, like peace, was indivisible, that it could not be achieved in one country at the expense of others but had to be spread throughout the world and that prosperity to be sustained had to be shared. And Marshall's plan – and the unparalleled transfer of resources – not only made possible the reconstruction of Europe but the renewal of world trade and the generation of prosperity for both these continents.

And I believe today's profound challenges call, even in a different world, for a similar shared response: comprehensive, inclusive, an assault on the underlying causes of poverty, with unprecedented support on offer from the richest countries. I believe in 2005 we have a once-in-a-generation opportunity to deliver for our times a modern Marshall Plan for the developing world – a new deal between the richest countries and the poorest countries but one in which the developing countries are not supplicants but partners. And as we advance towards the G7 finance ministers' meeting next month and the heads-of-government meeting chaired by Tony Blair in July, our government calls on all countries to join with us in agreeing the three essential elements of a 2005 development plan for a new deal:

- first, that we take the final historic step in delivering full debt relief for the debt-burdened countries;
- second, that we deliver the first world-trade round in history that benefits the poorest countries and ensures they have the capacity to benefit from new trade; and
- third – alongside declaring timetables on increasing development aid to 0.7 per cent of national income – that we implement a new International Finance Facility to offer immediate, predictable, long-term aid for investment and development – building on commitments by individual governments, leveraging in additional funds from the international capital markets, raising an additional $50 billion a year each year for the next ten years, effectively doubling aid to halve poverty.

I make this proposal for a new deal between developed and developing countries because as we meet here today – at the start of 2005 – I am aware not only of the pressures for emergency aid but that the promises we all made five years ago will forever remain unfulfilled unless we act together and act now.

. . .

First, on debt relief, let us in 2005 make a historic offer that finally removes the burden of decades-old debts that today prevent the poorest countries ever escaping poverty and leading their own economic development. Whereas in 1997 just one country was going to receive debt relief, today 27 countries are benefiting with $70 billion of unpayable debt being written off, and 37 countries are now potentially eligible, up to $100 billion of debt relief now possible. And it is because of debt relief in Uganda that 4 million more children now go to primary school; because of debt relief in Tanzania that 31,000 new classrooms have been built, 18,000 new teachers recruited and the goal of primary education for all will be achieved by the end of 2005; because of debt relief in Mozambique that half a million children are now being vaccinated against tetanus, whooping cough and diphtheria. And it is partly because of debt relief that in the past decade in developing countries, primary-school enrolments have increased at twice the rate of the 1980s; the proportion of those aged over fifteen who can read has risen from 67 per cent to 74 per cent; life expectancy has increased from 53 years to 59 years; and the number of people living in extreme poverty has fallen by 10 per cent.

We do not wipe out the debt of the poorest countries simply because these debts are not easily paid. We do so because people weighed down by the burden of debts imposed by the last generation on this cannot even begin to build for the next generation. To insist on the payment of these debts is unjust – it offends human dignity. What is morally wrong cannot be economically right. And when many developing countries are still choosing between servicing their debts and making the investments in health, education and infrastructure that would allow them to achieve the Millennium Development Goals, we know we must do more. That is why this year we must make rapid progress and today I want to set out both the principles to govern the next stage and the measures that can be delivered. While we have achieved bilateral debt write-off, the fact is that up to 80 per cent of the historic debt of some of the poorest countries is owed to international institutions and a solution to the debt tragedy now requires progress on debts owed not just to us but owed to the World Bank, the IMF and the development banks.

So we propose, first, that this year the richest countries match bilateral debt relief of 100 per cent with the bold act of offering 100 per cent multilateral debt relief – relief from the $80 billion of debt owed to the IMF, the World Bank and the African Development Bank; second, that the cancellation of debts owed to the International Monetary Fund should be financed by a detailed plan and timetable we now agree to use IMF gold. Third, we propose that countries make a unique declaration that they will repatriate their share of the World Bank's and the African Development Bank's debts to their own country. I can state that Britain will relieve those countries still under the burden of this debt to these banks by unilaterally paying our share – 10 per cent – of payments to the World Bank and African Development Bank. And we will both deepen and widen our debt relief as we will pay our share on behalf not just of Heavily Indebted Poor Countries but – because their need is just as great – of all low-income countries, as long as they can ensure debt relief is used for poverty reduction. In the G7 finance ministers' meeting next month I will be asking other countries to contribute directly or to a World Bank Trust Fund. And I also ask the European Union, which deserves credit for more than €1.5 billion of debt relief so far, to match that generosity with deeper multilateral debt relief.

Alongside more debt relief, 2005 is the opportunity that may not easily return if missed to agree a progressive approach to trade. Economic development is the key to meeting the Millennium Development Goals and long-term prosperity. And no country has escaped poverty other than by participation in the international economy. Our task is and remains helping developing countries build the capacity – the monetary and fiscal policies, the infrastructure, the support for private investment – essential for their development. But we also know the damage that rich countries' protectionism has done and that the developed world spends as much subsidising agriculture in our own countries as the whole income of all the 689 million people in sub-Saharan Africa taken together. Fair trade is not simply about the financial benefits, it is also about empowerment and dignity – enabling people to stand on their own two feet and use trade as a springboard out of poverty. It is not enough to say, 'You're on your own, simply compete.' We have to say, 'We will help you build the capacity you need to trade'; not just opening the door but helping you gain the strength to cross the threshold.

So in 2005 we need to make urgent progress:

- first, we the richest countries agree to end the hypocrisy of developed-country protectionism by opening our markets, removing trade-distorting subsidies and, in particular, doing more to urgently tackle the scandal and waste of the Common Agricultural Policy – showing we believe in free and fair trade;
- second, while recognising that while bringing down unjust tariffs and barriers is important, agree that developing countries receive the support necessary to carefully design and sequence trade reform into their own poverty-reduction strategies. And
- third, we have to recognise that developing countries will need additional resources to build their economic capacity and the infrastructure they need to take advantage of trading opportunities – and to prevent their most vulnerable people from falling further into poverty as they become integrated into the global economy.

We know that after macro-economic stability, poor infrastructure, lack of transparency, legal problems, poor labour skills and low productivity are key risks and deterrents to both foreign and domestic investment. Nor do many countries have the elasticity of supply to react to international market signals. The World Bank estimates that giving twenty-four of the poorest countries total access to Western markets would have no impact on their economies as they would not have the capacity or infrastructure to make use of the opportunity. Even today, for twelve African countries less than 10 per cent of their roads are paved. Telecommunication costs are such that calls from the poorest countries to the USA are five times the costs of calls from a developed country. While water and sanitation underpin health and development, even today 40 billion working hours in Africa each year are used up to collect water. And while tariff costs are often highlighted, it is actually transport costs that often constitute a bigger burden of the cost of exporting. With freight and insurance costs representing 15 per cent of the total value of African exports it is difficult for them to be competitive. It is also a fact that the informal economy accounts for more than 50 per cent of national income in most poor countries and the International Labour Organisation estimates that in Africa 93 per cent of new jobs are in the informal sector.

So countries need investment in physical infrastructure, institutional capacity – from legal and financial systems to basic property rights and, at root, transparency that avoids corruption – physical infrastructure and, of course, investment in human capital to enable growth, investment, trade and therefore poverty reduction. And to secure investment in development we need funds for development. Two thousand and five can be the year when we free nations from the burden of crippling and unpayable debts and remove unacceptable barriers to trade and private investment, but it is clear that we cannot solve the urgent problems of poverty and development around the world without a third step – a substantial increase in resources for development, for investment in the future. Making better use of existing aid – reordering priorities, untying aid and pooling funds internationally to release additional funds for the poorest countries – is essential to achieve both value for money and the improved outcomes we seek, but we face uncomfortable facts:

- that while ten years ago aid to Africa was $33 per person, today it has not risen but fallen to just $27;
- that when 80 million African children still do not go to school, all the public spending on education in sub-Saharan Africa taken together is still, per pupil, under $50 a year: less than $1 a week for schools, teachers, books and equipment; and
- that when in Africa 25 million people are infected with HIV/AIDS, with, in twenty-four countries, one in every ten children dying before the age of one, sub-Saharan Africa still devotes only $12 per person per year to public health, a fifth of 1 per cent that is spent on the health of each individual in the richest countries – which is why the everyday commonplace tragedy is of mothers struggling to save the life of their infant child and, in doing so, losing their own.

With the AIDS pandemic, average life expectancy in Africa is less than fifty. And today Ethiopia, the focus of Live Aid twenty years ago, has 70 million people but only 2,000 doctors. So it is clear that we are a long way short of the predictable, regular financing necessary to make the difference that is needed.

At the UN Monterrey Financing for Development Conference, donor countries pledged an additional $16 billion a year from 2006. For the UK's part, our level of official development assistance will increase to £6.4 billion – 0.47 per cent of our national income – by 2008. Beyond that we wish to maintain those rates of growth which, on this timetable, would lift the ratio beyond 0.5 per cent after 2008 and to 0.7 per cent by 2013 – and over the next year we plan to ask other countries to join us and nine others in becoming countries which have either already reached 0.7 per cent or have set a timetable towards it. But we know that even if one or two of the G7 could overcome fiscal constraints and go to 0.7 per cent tomorrow, we will still not reach the scale of the resources needed to achieve the Millennium Development Goals – at least $50 billion more a year – not in 2015 but now. And the truth is that the scale of the resources needed immediately to tackle disease, illiteracy and global poverty is far beyond what traditional funding can offer today.

That is why the UK government has put forward its proposal for stable, predictable, long-term funds frontloaded to tackle today's problems of poverty, disease and illiteracy through an International Finance Facility. And let me just explain what the IFF could achieve for the world's poor.

- the IFF is founded upon long-term, binding donor commitments from the richest countries like ourselves;
- it builds upon the additional $16 billion already pledged at Monterrey; and
- on the basis of these commitments and more, it leverages in additional money from the international capital markets to raise the amount of development aid for the years to 2015.

And let me tell you the significance and the scale of what I am proposing. With one bold stroke: to double development aid to halve poverty. Fifty billion dollars more in aid a year each year for the poorest countries. Think of what it could achieve:

- as many as half of all malaria deaths could be prevented if people had access to diagnosis and drugs that cost no more than twelve cents;
- a quarter of all child deaths could be prevented if children slept beneath bed-nets costing only $4 each;

- $3 more for each new mother could save up to 5 million lives over the next ten years;
- for an investment of $9 billion more a year we could build schools so that every child can get primary education;
- $10 – and preferably $20 – billion more a year could tackle TB and malaria, build health systems and address the tragedy of HIV/AIDS.

I believe the International Finance Facility has the following advantages. First, the IFF would urgently create the scale of funding necessary to invest simultaneously across sectors – providing humanitarian assistance as well as investment in education and health, trade capacity and economic development – so that instead of having to choose between first aid and tackling poverty, between health and education, between capacity-building in trade and tackling AIDS, the impact of extra resources in one area reinforces what is being done in others and has a lasting effect. Second, the IFF would provide a predictable flow of aid to developing countries so they no longer have to suffer from an up to 40 per cent variance in the amount of aid they receive from year to year, which prevents them from investing efficiently in health and education systems for the long term and tackling the causes of poverty rather than just the symptoms. Third, the IFF is designed to invest now to prevent problems later – to scale up development aid between now and 2015, enabling us to frontload aid so a critical mass can be deployed as investment now and over the next few years when it will have the most impact in achieving the Millennium Development Goals. Indeed, the fact is that unless we adopt the IFF or a similar mechanism immediately there is simply no other way of meeting the Millennium Development Goals in time.

The IFF is not only complementary to existing commitments to the 0.7 per cent target – allowing participating countries to take faster steps towards 0.7 per cent by increasing the resources available now – but can be implemented alongside continuing consideration of other proposals to provide financing in the longer term – including international taxes, special drawing rights and other forms of revenue-raising on a worldwide basis. I believe that the advantage of the International Finance Facility I have described is not just that it is a means of providing the necessary resources immediately and thus far faster than other initiatives, but also that we can move quickly with a committed group of countries – not moving at the pace of the slowest but tackling the problem head-on now with those that are prepared to sign up.

And so the practical benefits of the IFF are:

- we provide the support poor countries need straightaway – frontloading investment in infrastructure, education and health systems, and economic development so they can benefit from access to our markets;
- we provide grants immediately to help ensure a sustainable exit from debt so poor countries do not need to choose between emergency relief and long-term investment;
- we make primary schooling for all not just a distant dream but a practical reality – meeting these needs and rights now and not deferring them to an uncertain future; and
- we advance towards our global goals of cutting infant mortality and maternal mortality on schedule, eliminating malaria and TB and treating millions more people who are suffering from HIV/AIDS.

Let me give an illustration of what – because of the IFF model – could already be possible. The Global Alliance for Vaccines and Immunisation (GAVI) – who have immunised over the

last five years not a few children but a total of 50 million
children round the world – is interested in applying the
principles of the IFF to the immunisation sector, with donors
making long-term commitments that can be leveraged up via
the international capital markets in order to frontload the
funding available to tackle disease. If, by these means, GAVI
could increase the funding for its immunisation programme
by an additional $4 billion over the next ten years, then it
would be possible that their work could save the lives of an
additional 5 million people between now and 2015 and a
further 5 million lives after 2015. And I praise Bill Gates and
Bono for their far-sightedness – coming together to urge this
week a financing proposal for making immunisation available
to millions more.

So in one fund, with one initiative, we can glimpse the
possibilities open to us if we act together. And there are other
possibilities that could change the world. Let me say that with
proper funds the medical breakthroughs now being achieved
in developing a preventive vaccine for malaria could be
matched by the far-sightedness of an advance-purchase
scheme that could prevent the loss of more than 1 million
lives a year because of this dread disease. Only £400 million a
year is spent on research for a preventive vaccine for HIV/
AIDS, despite the fact that 75 million are affected and 25
million have died. And as we examine what can be done to
prevent as well as treat HIV/AIDS it is obvious that with
proper funds there could be a similar bold initiative on
research and development – to internationalise and advance
the research and then to provide support for the development of preventive vaccines . . . once again showing the
possibilities for the global fund for health and for building
health capacity that the International Finance Facility we
propose opens up for the world. And if what we achieve
for health we could also achieve for schools, for debt relief,
for the capacity to trade, for anti-poverty programmes, for

economic development, think of the better world we can achieve.

So the aim of the International Finance Facility is to bridge the gap between promises and reality. Between hopes raised and hopes dashed. Between an opportunity seized and an opportunity squandered. And in the forthcoming G8 discussions we will ask all countries to join dozens of countries who have already given their backing to support and sign up to the IFF and we will be setting out a framework within which we can implement it.

2005 is therefore a once-in-a-generation opportunity. And when people ask whether it is possible to make a breakthrough, and say our proposals are too difficult, I say:

- people thought the original plans for the World Bank were the work of dreamers;
- people thought the Marshall Plan unattainable;
- even in 1997 when we came to power people thought debt relief was an impossible aspiration and yet we are wiping out $100 billion of debt; and
- people thought no more countries would sign up to a timetable for 0.7 per cent in overseas development aid and yet, this year alone, five countries have done so.

Each of us of course has our respective responsibilities, our very different duties, as politicians, aid organisations, individuals. But for all of us an even greater measure of the potential is that in 2000 first hundreds, then thousands, then millions of people first in one country then in one continent, then in all countries and in all continents, came together to demand debt relief and in doing so changed the world. And we can do this again. Even today that coalition is not just being reformed but growing in strength. And I pay tribute to all of you here today – aid workers, supporters, contributors, campaigners – who are fighting for great causes, standing for the highest ideals, often bearing huge burdens and bringing the greatest of hope to those in the greatest of needs.

A few months ago I quoted a century-old phrase, saying 'The arc of the moral universe is long but it does bend towards justice'. This was not an appeal to some iron law of history but to remind people in the words of a US president that 'The history of free peoples is never written by chance but by choice – that it is by our own actions that people of compassion and goodwill can and do change the world for good'.

Of course it is difficult – as we are witnessing in South-East Asia – and there are disappointments and set-backs in international development when progress is slow, but when we are stalled or set back in our development aims I am reminded of the words of the former head of the UN, Dag Hammarskjöld, who said:

> When the morning's freshness had been replaced by the
>   weariness of midday . . .
> When the leg muscles quiver under the strain . . .
> When the climb seems endless . . .
> And suddenly nothing will go quite as you wish . . .
> It is then that you must not hesitate.

And if we do not hesitate but press on, if we do not allow setbacks to discourage us but let them challenge us to do even more on aid and trade and as a result are inspired to work and strive even harder – our determination not diminished but intensified – I believe that:

- with the scale of the challenge revealed in its starkest form this week and this month, summoning us to action;
- with the tsunami showing the capacity of people everywhere to unite in response;

- and with the growth, organisation and now clamour of public opinion calling for action now – 'the passion of compassion' – resonating here in Britain and reverberating across all countries; and
- with a determination among world leaders to be bold – shown by united global action over the Asian crisis

the arc of the moral universe, while indeed long, will bend towards justice in the months and years to come.

4

PROTECTING AND
IMPROVING THE ENVIRONMENT

*I want to say before I begin my substantive comments that it is a deep
honour for me to be introduced by Gordon Brown. I am an unabashed
and enthusiastic admirer of Gordon, and have been for a long time. . . .*

*Gordon and I share a Calvinist heritage and a Scottish gene pool,
though my forebears were not Presbyterian. He is a global leader and I
say in all sincerity that his vision and scope and breadth, as well as
depth, of thought is truly extraordinary and unique . . . You know,
when the Labour Party tackled the difficult social issues of old-age
pensions, health care for working families and so many other policies
now taken for granted that were difficult at the time, it was because the
Labour Party saw the need for social justice in a larger context, and
dealing with social justice one year at a time, one Budget at a time, is
insufficient if you really want to reach the goal. They thought freshly
and now we are in a new era when we have to think freshly about the
relationship between the global environment and social justice.*

Al Gore
John Smith Memorial lecture, London
November 2005

*When I received the Nobel Peace Prize in December 2004, I called on
industry and global institutions to appreciate the value of economic*

justice, equity and ecological integrity. I also urged them to recognise that extreme global inequities and prevailing consumption patterns at the expense of the environment and peaceful coexistence cannot be sustained for long.

Gordon Brown is one who understands these linkages. As his speeches on the environment, development and security show, he is one of the few world leaders who understand that environmental concerns cannot be placed in a category separate from the economy and from economic policy. Through this understanding, he is saying that a threatened environment threatens future economic activity and growth. Soil erosion, the depletion of marine stocks, water scarcity, air pollution – all these problems endanger all of us.

As the Green Belt Movement has been arguing, he goes further and acknowledges that the poorest members of the community – those most dependent on the natural world for their survival, and those with the fewest resources to buy their way out of unhealthy environments – suffer the most. And he knows that such suffering can lead to further suffering – to violence and war. As do I, Gordon Brown believes that we can overcome the many kinds of injustice. And, as so many others and I do, he has the courage to hope.

Like the Green Belt Movement, Gordon Brown, through his words and actions, is planting seeds for peace. I hope that you will read his words and honour his actions.

Wangaari Maathai

In March 2005, the Treasury made protecting and improving the environment an explicit part of its objectives and performance targets. Objective 8 now reads: 'to protect and improve the environment by using instruments that will deliver efficient and sustainable outcomes through evidence-based policies'. The implications of this decision are substantial, and accounted for major initiatives in the 2006 Budget.

On 20 April 2006, the Chancellor addressed the United Nations Ambassadors in New York. He opened the speech by suggesting that how we protect our environment, secure our planet and safeguard our future for our generation and for generations to come is one of the greatest international challenges of our time.

This speech stresses the need for environmental priorities – including climate change – to be considered in future alongside economic priorities. The Chancellor argues that they are not mutually exclusive: we simply cannot have a situation in the future where economic growth is prioritised at the expense of the environment, or environmental care at the expense of growth and prosperity. But he takes the arguments about the interrelation of economic objectives and our environmental objectives a step further, arguing not only that jobs, economic growth and prosperity now increasingly reinforce each other, but that this is the way to develop social justice as well.

He also argues that since climate change is a global problem, it requires a global solution, and he suggests that it will be necessary to build a global consensus for tackling environmental change. Appropriately enough, given the location of the speech and the audience, he concludes by suggesting that just as the post-1945 international institutions were founded for the world problems of that generation and their times, we need to find ways for our global institutions – primarily the UN and the World Bank – to meet and master the challenges of our generation and our times.

The Chancellor uses his substantial experience of successful policy-making within the UK to set out in this speech some concrete steps which can be taken at country and at global level to make an impact on climate change. As he says, 'I know from experience of the long but ultimately successful journey to debt relief for the poorest countries that to build a consensus for environmental action founded on detailed practical policies for change will take time but is an essential element for success.'

Building on his experience as one of the longest-serving and most experienced finance ministers in the world, his chairmanship of key World Bank committees, and his membership of the UN Review Committee, the Chancellor is in an extremely powerful position to make progress on what he calls 'a new framework for environmental progress at a global level'. As he concludes, great challenges require great acts of statesmanship. We are indeed lucky to have him in the right place at the right time to move us all from words to a commitment to deliver practical policies that can unite world opinion in a new and broad-based consensus that could bring about change: 'so that we can make the world anew'.

Environmental sustainability is not an option – it is a necessity. For economies to flourish, for global poverty to be banished, for the well-being of the world's people to be enhanced – not just in this generation but in succeeding generations – we have a compelling and ever more urgent duty of stewardship to take care of the natural environment and resources on which our economic activity and social fabric depends.

So the new synthesis we need is that economic growth, social justice and environmental care advance best when they all advance together. This imperative applies most strongly of all to the greatest of the environmental challenges we face, that of climate change.

It is now clear that, if current trends are left unchecked, the economic costs of climate change will be far greater than previously thought. And yet at the same time it is becoming evident that the means of tackling it are increasingly available and the costs could become affordable – and that tackling it offers real economic benefits and opportunities to developed and developing countries alike. So I want to argue today that it is through the new economics of climate change that a new global consensus for tackling environmental change can be built. Whether we agree with *Time* magazine, which observed last week that 'the serious debate has quietly ended' or not, the real question now is not whether climate change is happening or indeed what are its causes: the question is how fast it is happening and how we address these causes.

Since the start of the Industrial Revolution global greenhouse gases have risen by 30 per cent. In the last century alone, global temperatures have risen by almost one degree Celsius – probably the fastest rate of increase for a thousand years. And the rate of change has been speeding up. The ten hottest years since records began over 150 years ago have all occurred in the past twelve.

The consequences of this warming are now evident right across the world. In the past century, almost all the major ice caps have started melting – adding 20 billion tonnes of water each year to the oceans. Since 1900, global sea levels have risen by 10–20 centimetres. And the Intergovernmental Panel on Climate Change suggests that, by the end of this century, sea levels could rise by up to a further 90 centimetres and temperatures could rise by a further five to six degrees. And with rising sea levels and temperatures on this scale, we must assess the consequences for agricultural productivity, for water stress, for ecosystems, for flood defences and for human health. Studies for the UK Environment Department suggest that by 2050 African cereal production could fall by 10–30 per cent, up to 3 billion people could live in areas of increased water stress and millions could be at increased risk of malaria and dengue fever. Already we are seeing changing rainfall patterns and increased weather extremes. And the Inter-governmental Panel estimates that the global economic costs of a temperature rise of just 2.5 degrees could be up to 2.5 per cent of global GDP.

So climate change is not just an environmental issue, but most definitely an economic issue. And the time lags between greenhouse-gas emissions and climatic impacts mean that, to affect climate in twenty years' time, we have to act now. This is why, last year, I asked Sir Nicholas Stern – former Chief Economist at the World Bank and Head of the British Government Economic Service – to report on the economics of climate change. And what his initial findings suggest is that the risks of climate change will not be evenly spread, but will hit poorest countries most. This makes the issue of climate change one of justice as much as of economic development: a problem whose causes are led by industrialised countries but whose effects will disproportionately fall on developing countries – most recently drought in the Sahel and the Horn of Africa. And because we are now spending $6 billion in aid simply to respond to this humanitarian crisis, resources are being diverted to tackling the short-term consequences of environmental change and away from dealing with the causes of underdevelopment and environmental neglect. So it is not surprising and indeed it is right that anti-poverty campaigners have taken up the environmental as well as the poverty challenge. Round the world, as they know, it is the poorest – those who depend most upon the natural world for their survival, and those with the fewest resources to buy their way out of unhealthy environments – that suffer the most.

'Today, we understand that respect for the environment,' Kofi Annan rightly said, 'is one of the main pillars of our fight against poverty,' and thus essential for achieving the Millennium Development Goals. Indeed an unstable climate can lead to economic instability, thus threatening investment and economic development and growth.

So we must start from the profound truths: that economic development in poor countries is going to take place in the context of a changing climate, that underdevelopment and environmental neglect go hand in hand, that future development strategies are going to have to adapt to meet this new twin challenge. This is not a question of making climate change a priority over poverty reduction, it is ensuring that policies for growth offer the technological advance and necessary resources to overcome both poverty and underdevelopment and environmental degradation.

Climate change is therefore a global problem. And it requires a global solution. This is not to say that countries do not individually have a responsibility to act. We do. And we will. But it is to acknowledge the reality that no country can solve this problem on its own. Britain produces only 2 per cent of the world's greenhouse gases; even America – the single largest source – produces less than one quarter. The message that global problems require global solutions underpinned the United Nations Framework Convention on

Climate Change agreed at the Earth Summit in Rio nearly fifteen years ago. And, whatever its shortcomings, this also underpins the Kyoto Protocol – now ratified by over 160 countries, representing over 60 per cent of the world's emissions. And now I believe it is not just more urgent than ever before but also more possible than before to build a global consensus for tackling environmental change.

Such a consensus is not easy. It must be founded first on a shared understanding of the challenge ahead. But under Tony Blair's chairmanship, the G8 began a process of dialogue with other major energy-consuming nations on climate change and clean energy. Agreement at the UN Convention in Montreal shows that the will is potentially there. And I believe that this global consensus, which over recent years has often seemed impossible, is now within our grasp – because the policies we need to meet economic and environmental needs are now converging.

First, as Kofi Annan said last month: 'Today's high oil prices make the economic and environmental arguments even more mutually supportive.' And with the trebling of oil prices over three years, the demand for a supply of energy that is secure, stable and sustainable is more broadly based than ever. Indeed, a more sustainable and efficient use of energy resources was the focus of discussions among both consuming and producing nations' discussions at the opening of the new headquarters of the International Energy Forum in Saudi Arabia which I attended last November. President Bush's State of the Union Address in January highlights both America's dependence on oil and the need for change. But the concern goes far beyond America. Previous shocks have been triggered by supply shortages. And indeed today's high prices can be attributed in part to uncertainty of supply from political instability in major producers to the impact of hurricanes. But few doubt that the underlying issue is one of demand – with a rising Asia now consuming one-third of the world's oil. Higher prices are now requiring countries and businesses to examine their energy costs, in particular greater efficiency of use and diversification of supply.

Of course major advances in the efficiency of the use of oil have been made since the last oil-price spike in the 1970s. New technology has made drilling more successful and increased the yield from fields. In addition to this continued advance, new finds in oil and gas will almost certainly give us greater supply than previously documented. But even with this progress, we cannot escape the conclusion that more environmentally sensitive uses of energy must become an essential element of delivering future economic growth rather than being seen as at odds with it. And in Washington tomorrow – with global oil prices now again above $70 a barrel – based on the plan Britain set out last year, I will ask the G7 to discuss not only how we ensure greater security of energy supply but support alternative sources of energy and greater efficiency of energy use. So, reducing carbon emissions is an energy, and thus an economic, imperative as much as it is an environmental imperative.

But, second, the economic agenda and the environmental agenda are not only now converging: the one now reinforces the other more than ever before. So while, of course, there will be costs to reducing greenhouse-gas emissions, preventing climate change can contribute to the next stage of economic growth. It is a lesson we are learning from Britain's recent experience. We are on course not just to achieve but to go beyond – indeed nearly double – our Kyoto target for greenhouse-gas emissions. But these numbers do not tell the whole story. For in the last decade our economy has grown much faster than in previous decades and faster than the rest of Europe. Yet in Britain in this period of high growth, greenhouse-gas emissions have not risen. So without being complacent about what more we have to do, which we are not, it is correct that the carbon intensity of the British economy – carbon emissions per unit of GDP – has fallen by a third.

If in the future all countries are to both change and grow, we must set the common framework that allows this to happen:

- by acting multilaterally, we can ensure in the new global economy that there is no race to the bottom in business competitiveness;
- by developing long-term incentives, we provide the certainty that business requires to invest; and
- by working with the grain of the market, we free innovation, flexibility and entrepreneurship that promotes growth rather than holding it back.

This is why we strongly support the innovation of carbon-trading. It offers us a way to reinforce economic and environmental objectives. It gives carbon an international price. It means carbon-saving can be a way of making money and increasing returns on investment. And it makes the economic opportunities of a climate-friendly energy policy real and tangible.

We first saw the potential of trading in America with sulphur and nitrous-oxide trading in the 1990s – reducing acid-rain emissions by one million tonnes. In Britain our voluntary carbon scheme, with more than thirty companies, helped reduce carbon emissions by more than 1.6 million tonnes. And the City of London is now a global centre for carbon-trading. And now in Europe, we have adopted a scheme that will cut emissions across all twenty-five Member States. And Britain is now proposing to extend and strengthen the European scheme beyond 2012. By matching it with an extension of the Clean Development Mechanism beyond 2012 – our aim is for it to support investment not just in Europe, but in developing countries. So we will examine how we can guarantee a continued market for carbon credits up to and beyond 2012. And by linking it with other initiatives now being developed across the world from states in America and Australia to countries such as Canada and South Korea, our aim is for it to become the driver for a deep, liquid and long-term global carbon-trading system. Our ultimate goal must be a global carbon market.

And with a global framework in the making, the environment can itself become a driver of future economic growth. Economic competitiveness can actually increase by improving environmental efficiency as we secure more wealth from less energy and fewer resources. Increasing labour productivity has always been a core goal of all successful businesses. Now, as energy costs rise and materials become more scarce, we need to pay the same attention to resource productivity.

Perhaps the most promising development is that new jobs, new industries and new exports come from rising investment in new, low-carbon technologies. In Britain alone, the environment market has increased from £16 billion, 170,000 jobs and 7,000 companies in 2001; to £25 billion, 400,000 jobs and 17,000 companies in 2004. Over the next ten years it is estimated that a further 130,000 jobs could be created. In Europe, the environment sector already accounts for 1.3 per cent of employment – 2 million jobs. And in 2010 the global environmental market – clean energy, waste and water – could be worth almost $700 billion – a sector as big as the successful aerospace or pharmaceuticals sectors.

In this field the role of governments – in partnership with business and science – is to harness market power and dynamism by stimulating the discovery and development of these technologies. Because while the technologies that will set us on the path to the low-carbon economy of the next twenty years exist now, those of the following twenty do not. America is the world's largest investor in environmental R&D. And is now joining in a new Asia-Pacific technology initiative with Australia, India, Japan, China and South Korea. Europe's environmental research funding is the basis for a new partnership with China on a virtually zero emissions coal power plant. For our own part, Britain already spends over £800 million a year on environmental research, backed up with tax breaks and capital allowances to encourage innovation. And Britain is jointly working with Norway on developing the potential of carbon capture and storage in the North Sea.

In my Budget last month, I announced proposals for a new National Institute of Energy Technologies, a public-private partnership – with the aim of raising finance of £1 billion – to create a new facility at the cutting edge of research and innovation. Its mission is to bring together the best engineers, scientists and companies from around the world – our investment in science and technology going hand in hand with the new market incentives.

And thus with a developing global environment market, the new global consensus I believe to be possible grows into more than a shared understanding of a shared problem, and becomes a set of shared solutions in the shared interest of us all. And it is this that underpins the next driver for consensus: all of us – countries, consumers and companies – are increasingly realising our responsibilities for environmental care. So just as a growing sense of personal and social responsibility which is more than just enlightened self-interest paved the way in the past to socially responsible growth, so today in the twenty-first century such personal and social responsibility can be the basis for mutually beneficial environmental and economic progress.

With the scientific evidence now clear, we are as individuals increasingly aware of what we can do. Encouraged by market solutions, companies are also increasingly aware of their corporate responsibilities. And with internal carbon markets, commitments to become carbon neutral and energy efficiency initiatives, the world's leading firms are already showing that the flexible will invariably defeat the inflexible. And with many new and smaller far-sighted firms emerging into these markets the companies that look like leading tomorrow are those that are already investing in a low-carbon economy today. And as the market increasingly pioneers answers to climate change – governments also need to act with imagination and initiative, recognising our responsibilities – by putting in place the right long-term policy framework with clear, credible and forward-looking signals.

Of course even within a multilateral framework, no two countries will have the same policies for their own specific needs. But the principles are common: ranging from the most basic – that consumers have the information they need to make informed choices about their environmental impact; to introducing fiscal and other incentives for environmentally friendly behaviour; and then to setting, where it is right to do so, standards for environmental protection, including our proposed annual carbon report. In this way not just the Department of Environment but every department of government from transport to foreign affairs, from education to overseas development, becomes a department of the environment.

In Britain our new Climate Change Programme, published last month, sets out the details of our approach. And our Energy Review, concluding this summer, is examining our future energy options – including renewables and nuclear – and will set our future strategy.

Central to our approach has been our willingness to take the difficult decision to introduce a Climate Change Levy. By incentivising better energy use, the levy has increased the energy efficiency of British business by over 2 per cent each year. Alongside the levy there are now 5,000 Climate Change Agreements to increase business energy efficiency, and we have created the Carbon Trust, which has already provided advice and support to over 3,000 businesses. At the same time we have recycled the revenues from the levy into reductions in businesses' National Insurance contributions. So by targeting the marginal use of energy, the Climate Change Levy has provided real market incentives to energy efficiency, while showing how by taxing 'bads' (emissions) we can reduce taxes on 'goods' (jobs). Together, in each of the next five years, these climate change measures will cut emissions by more than 6 million tonnes, accounting by 2010 for a third of our total carbon reductions.

Nearly a quarter of carbon emissions come from vehicles. So we are incentivising fuel-efficient cars with measures that range from variable rates of vehicle duty (starting with no duty at all for the cleanest cars) to support for bio-fuels. Our new obligation in electricity supply – now underpinned by new support for micro-generation technologies – is increasing the share of renewables to 10 per cent.

The energy used by buildings and the products in them account for half of our emissions. So far bolder new regulations introduced this month will make new buildings 40 per cent more energy efficient than they were just ten years ago – showing that, alongside exhortation, information and incentives, targeted standards can make a difference, in the same way that new regulations for fridges cut CFCs and ozone damage twenty years ago; and the Clean Air Acts did away with London's infamous smog fifty years ago.

But our new approach also offers a way out of the trap that so often governments round the world have fallen into: we are pioneering risk-based regulation which means increasingly that only on the basis of risk will we demand information, form-filling and inspection. We are recognising too that even the most basic addition of information can play a powerful role in making self-driven change happen: providing people with their right to information can play a powerful role in making self-driven change happen. In Britain, for example, we are now piloting better labelling on electronic goods and smart meters in homes. But here too with a global goods market – with more products than ever made in one country but bought in another – we also need global action. Today consumer goods left on standby worldwide are responsible for 1 per cent of global emissions. So Britain will propose that the EU and the International Energy Agency bring together leading manufacturers and countries to speed up the international implementation of the one-Watt standard for energy efficiency.

Finally, I believe that a global consensus for action on climate change is possible because we can see how all countries can share in the benefits from it. For this to happen, developed countries must be prepared to support, with public investment, through grants or loans, the efforts of developing countries. And we have a special responsibility to help the poorest countries both to adapt to climate change and to invest in climate-friendly energy production and energy efficiency. Only in this way can we ensure that all the Millennium Development Goals are met – not at the cost of economic growth, but to achieve it. Indeed new alternative-energy technologies offer not only the possibility of meeting Africa's growing needs, but also the potential of new exports to the rest of the world. And when I was in Africa last week, Britain began discussions with Mozambique and South Africa on a new partnership with Brazil – today the world's largest producer of renewable bio-fuels – on how southern Africa could become a leader in bio-fuels production as well.

Yet globally there is an estimated $60 billion annual shortfall in energy investment in developing countries. So at the G8 meeting in Gleneagles in Scotland last year, Britain proposed a new global energy investment framework. The aim of the framework is to remove the barriers that prevent investment, by developing new financing mechanisms which leverage private and public finance from both within and outside developing countries. And in Washington tomorrow,

I will propose a new public-private partnership, a World Bank led facility, a $20 billion fund for developing economies to invest in alternative sources of energy and greater energy efficiency. I believe it is by providing in these ways for a flow of public and private investment funds for developing countries that we will be able to bring these countries into the global consensus on climate change that I am calling for today.

But globally we can do more. For just as the post-1945 international institutions were founded for new world problems of their time, we need to find ways for our institutions to meet and master the challenges of our generation. Our international institutions are essential to global action on the environment because, as I have said, the impact is global and felt disproportionately by the poor and there can be no development without environmental care. In the review Kofi Annan has constituted, chaired by three prime ministers – of Mozambique, Norway and Pakistan – and of which I am privileged to be a member, the United Nations is testing its global remit against the challenges ahead and it is clear that if we were starting afresh, environmental stewardship would play a more dominant and central part. The UN Environment Programme based in Nairobi plays a key global role in setting global standards and ensuring that the environment is properly integrated into the UN's development and humanitarian work. And next month the Commission for Sustainable Development will launch its next two-year energy strategy. Increasingly, as a sister international organisation, the World Bank has become the key financier of environmental standards and programmes in the developing world.

If we are to encourage lower-carbon energy supply, energy efficiency and adaptation to climate change, we must do more at a global level. Take one example – while we are in the process of forming national institutes for environment and energy, research into the environment remains under-developed in contrast to medical and IT research work and we lack a global network. The UN's uniqueness lies in its representativeness, and thus accountability and legitimacy. The World Bank has financial power and experience of long-term project investment to make the right connections between tackling environmental neglect and addressing poverty and underdevelopment. Both can be both voices for the poor and vehicles for action against poverty. So I believe that to meet and master the scale of the challenges ahead together the UN and the World Bank must work to create a global environmental presence that exhorts, incentivises, researches and monitors change and most of all is in a position – alongside the private sector – to invest in change. So I hope that the UN review, which will report later this year, will make concrete recommendations on this new framework for environmental progress at a global level.

Great challenges require great acts of statesmanship. And this is the right time to move from words to a commitment to deliver practical policies that can unite world opinion in a new and broad-based consensus that could bring about change. In facing up to the challenges of their times, the world leaders of sixty years ago created new international institutions – the United Nations, the IMF, the World Bank – and demonstrated by their actions that international cooperation was the best way to solve the economic challenges of the post-war world. But such path-breaking statesmanship and leadership also brought the Marshall Plan of the 1940s. Starting from Communist threats in Greece, Turkey and the Balkans, the statesmen of the day quickly realised that there was an even bigger challenge: the political economic and social reconstruction of Europe. For four years America contributed 1 per cent of its GDP to the rebuilding of Europe. But the greatest contribution was in the transatlantic trade and commerce and flows of people and ideas between both continents. I believe that today – in the first decade of a new century – international cooperation built on bold innovative statesmanship is again the best way forward. And by our actions we could in reality realise the ideal of an international community acting for the public good – for the present generation, and for generations to come.

But this is an endeavour that, because it has not yet been met, challenges us to reach out in dialogue and debate. The visionaries of the 1940s understood also that the global challenges they faced required them not just to have the right policies but that they should seek to build a consensus for stability and change across the world. And I know from experience of the long but ultimately successful journey to debt relief for the poorest countries that to build a consensus for environmental action founded on detailed practical policies for change will take time but is an essential element for success. I have suggested today how a progressive consensus can be built for sustainable, stable and equitable growth for both developed and developing countries; how a new paradigm that sees economic growth, social justice and environmental care advancing together can become the common sense of our age. The scale of environmental challenge we now face brings home to us that working apart we will fail but working together we can make progress. And by acting boldly together, it is in our power to achieve for our times what the post-1945 pioneers achieved for theirs. In our generation we can indeed make the world anew.

5

TOWARDS A MODERN ECONOMY

Kirkcaldy – the birthplace, in 1723, of Adam Smith and, by extension, of modern economics – is also, of course, where your Chancellor of the Exchequer was reared. I am led to ponder to what extent the Chancellor's renowned economic and financial skills are the result of exposure to the subliminal intellect-enhancing emanations of this area.

Alan Greenspan
Adam Smith Memorial Lecture, Kirkcaldy, Scotland
6 February 2005

The Chancellor, as you heard a short while ago, has achieved an exemplary record as steward of the economy of the United Kingdom and, indeed, is without peer among the world's economic-policy makers. Gordon, I would like to thank you in particular for your leadership of the Group of Seven this past year. It has been a challenging year, and your voice and vision have been indispensable to the G7's efforts to maintain global stability and growth in the face of terrorism, further rises in global oil prices, and protectionist pressures.

Alan Greenspan
Acceptance of honorary degree,
along with Gordon Brown MP
New York University
14 December 2005

It has become a commonplace to assert that the defining characteristic of the new Labour government was the decision to make the Bank of England independent, within a few days of taking office in May 1997. Indeed, looking back, it sometimes seems that that decision was the only one taken in the economic field.

Most commentators now agree that the decision to make monetary decisions independent of political influence (within a long-term framework where the objective, set by government, is to promote high and stable levels of growth and employment) has been a major plank in the creation of a stable macro-economic climate in the UK, leading to huge economic, social and political benefits. But what is not always picked up is that the decision to make the Bank of England independent was only one of a raft of carefully planned and executed macro-economic policy decisions which also led into a range of micro-economic decisions aimed at equipping all nations and regions of the UK for the challenges of the future, including higher levels of investment, improved competitiveness and improving employment opportunity through the modernisation of the Welfare State.

This chapter contains extracts from three key speeches which, taken together, set out the steps taken by the Chancellor towards creating a modern economy for the UK. In both style and content, the announcement of Bank of England independence, only five days after the 1997 General Election, was a tangible sign of the new energy and commitment of the Chancellor and of his determination to make stability the cornerstone of the government's economic policy. The Mais Lecture deals with the link between the macro- and micro-economic policies, and in refuting the efforts of the previous administration (and in particular Nigel Lawson) the Chancellor restates the government's economic policy as being to ensure a long-term and stable framework; economic fundamentals that are sound; objectives for policy that are clearly understood; and public decisions that are made in an orderly and transparent way. The final speech in this chapter gives a summary of the decisions taken which, in the words of the Chancellor, make Britain fit for glabalisation.

The first speech is an extract from the announcement about making the Bank of England independent, delivered on 6 May 1997, a few days after the General Election.

The central economic objectives of the new government are high and stable levels of growth and employment. Our aim therefore is to rebuild British economic strength with a modern industrial base, high levels of investment and a culture of entrepreneurship that, through economic opportunity for all, unlocks British economic potential.

This can only happen if we build from solid foundations of prudent economic management and sound finance. The enemy of growth, and the investment necessary for it, is the instability of short periodic bursts of high growth followed by recession. So we must break from the short-termism of the past – the economic instability that has characterised the British economy not just in recent years but for most of the century. That is why I want British economic success to be built on the solid rock of prudent and consistent economic management, not the shifting sands of boom and bust.

Now is the time for long-termism. This is the time to set the British economy on a new long-term course that will deliver high levels of growth and employment through lasting stability.

. . .

Price stability is, as I have said, an essential precondition for the government's objectives of high and sustainable levels of growth and employment. The question is how to achieve the long-term stability that we seek?

As the Prime Minister and I have always made clear, this is a new government that is going to move beyond the old dogmas of the past, and provide a modern and lasting framework for economic prosperity. I have said on repeated occasions that we must tackle the underlying weakness of the British economy – low investment, skill shortages and inadequate infrastructure – all of which have beset the British economy in recent years. These problems are themselves some of the underlying causes of inflation. I have also made clear that reform is required to put monetary policy on a stable, long-term footing. In a speech in May 1995 and subsequently in our 1995 policy document, 'A New Economic Future for Britain', I set out my view of the proper roles of the government and the Bank of England in economic policy.

Government has a responsibility to the public in setting the objectives of economic policy and that means that the government rather than the Bank of England must set the targets for monetary policy. However, as I have repeatedly made clear since 1995, we will only build a fully credible framework for monetary policy if the long-term needs of the economy, not short-term political considerations, guide monetary decision-making. We must remove the suspicion that short-term party-political considerations are influencing the setting of interest rates.

As our election manifesto said: 'We will reform the Bank of England to ensure that decision-making on monetary policy is more effective, open, accountable and free from short-term political manipulation.'

It has become increasingly clear that the present arrangements for policy-making are not generating the confidence that is necessary. That is one reason why Britain has higher long-term interest rates than most of our major competitors. And the perception that monetary policy decisions have been dominated by short-term political considerations has grown.

I am now satisfied that we can put in place, with immediate effect, reforms of the Bank of England to ensure that it can discharge responsibilities for setting interest rates in an effective, open and accountable way. This is the time to take the tough decisions we need for the long-term interests and prosperity of the country. I will not shrink from the tough decisions needed to deliver stability for long-term growth.

I have therefore decided to give the Bank of England operational responsibility for setting interest rates, with immediate effect. The government will continue to set the inflation target and the Bank will have responsibility for setting interest rates to meet the target. The government's policy is set out in a letter I sent to the Governor yesterday, the text of which I am releasing now. It is the government's intention to legislate for these proposals as soon as possible. In the interim, the Governor has agreed to put in place the arrangements that will apply once the legislation has been enacted.

The main elements of the reforms are as follows. In place of the current personalised system of decision-making, decisions will be made by a new nine-member Monetary Policy Committee, on the basis of a majority vote. This is similar to arrangements in other countries, including the USA and other G7 members. In addition to the Governor and two Deputy Governors, nominated by the government, who will sit on the committee, the government will also appoint four members of the Monetary Policy Committee from outside the Bank of England. Openness of decision-making will be ensured by the publication of minutes of proceedings and votes of the Monetary Policy Committee. There will be enhanced requirements for the Bank of England to report to the Treasury Select Committee of the House of Commons to explain and be questioned on their decisions.

The Court of the Bank of England will review the performance of the Bank of England, including that of the Monetary Policy Committee. The Court will be substantially reformed to make it representative of the whole of the United Kingdom and to take account of the full range of Britain's industrial and business sectors.

These changes in accountability and the new breadth of representation on the Court amount to the most radical internal reform to the Bank of England since it was established in 1694 – over 300 years ago.

Britain is, in fact, one of the few major industrial nations in which the central bank does not have operational responsibility for decisions on interest rates. And our record on inflation and interest rates over recent years is poor, while other countries with independent central banks have performed better.

Taken as a whole, these proposals will ensure that decisions are taken for the long-term interests of the economy and not on the basis of short-term political pressures. This is the way to create the stability we need for higher investment and high levels of growth and employment. The changes I have proposed are the right decisions: the right decisions for business which wants to plan ahead with confidence, the right decisions for families who have suffered enough from the uncertainties of short-term economic instability, and the right decisions for Britain.

The specific reforms I am proposing are British solutions, designed to meet British domestic needs for long-term stability. Our monetary reforms provide the platform for stability and are the building block for a new economic policy that will equip us for the challenges of the future: one that takes steps to ensure higher levels of investment, for which I will announce new measures in due course, and improving employment opportunity by the modernisation of the Welfare State. These measures will be addressed in the coming Budget and future Budgets.

But there is, as I have suggested today, a more long-term context. In the last century, Britain was industrially pre-eminent. The history of this century has been one of economic decline, not least because of short-termism and the pursuit of stop–go economics. I am determined that we make the right preparations for long-term national economic success, as we look to the century that lies ahead, so that we can move forward again economically. I am therefore setting in place a long-term policy for long-term prosperity. The ultimate judgement of the success of this measure will not come next week, or indeed in the next year but in the long term. I am convinced that this radical reform, together with

measures we will announce to equip our economy for the
challenges ahead, creates the platform of stability upon which
Britain can build.

The Chancellor gave the Mais lecture on 19 October 1999. The
speech began with a reminder that the first act of the incoming
new Labour government was not in fact Bank of England independence, but setting the Treasury the objective of achieving high
and stable levels of growth and employment for the nation. This
was a direct reference to the 1944 White Paper which first set out
these objectives. And as the Chancellor points out, the government of that time was clear that if full employment was to be
sustained there were other conditions which had to be in place as
well: stability, employability, productivity and individual responsibility. In other words this was a task for the whole of government,
not just the Treasury. Contrary to Nigel Lawson's distinction
between the roles of macro-economic and micro-economic policy
as set out in his 1984 Mais Lecture, Gordon Brown argues that the
role of a macro-economic policy is not simply to bear down on
inflation but rather, by creating a platform of stability, to promote
growth and employment; and that an active supply-side policy is
necessary not only to improve productivity and employment, but
to make it possible to sustain low inflation alongside high and
stable levels of growth and employment. He concludes that while
the shared economic purpose of 1944 broke down in fifty years of
endless and sterile divisions between capital and labour, between
state and market and between public and private sectors, denying
Britain the national direction it needed, these issues are now at the
heart of government policy.

In this Mais Lecture – which has been, from time to time, a
platform for politicians of all parties to reflect, to analyse and
– as is the case with us politicians – often to get things wrong, I

will seek to detail the conditions in our times under which the high ideals and public purpose contained in this economic goal of 1944 can be achieved.

Full employment – defined in 1944 as 'high and stable levels of employment' – was a reality for the twenty years after the Second World War. But rising unemployment in the 1970s was followed in the 1980s by unemployment rising to above 3 million, beyond its peak in the 1930s. As recently as 1997, 20 per cent of working-age households – one in five – had no one in work.

Some believe that full employment can be restored only by a return to macro-economic fine-tuning. Others believe that in the new more open economy governments cannot hope to meet the 1944 objectives. I reject both the dogma of insisting on old ways and the defeatism of abandoning the objectives.

So since 1997 the new government has been putting in place a new framework to deliver the objectives of high and stable levels of growth and employment. And as I said in New York last month there are four conditions which must all be met – and met together – if we are to deliver in our generation those objectives of 1944:

- first: stability – a pro-active monetary policy and prudent fiscal policy to deliver the necessary platform of stability;
- second: employability – a strengthening of the programme to move the unemployed from welfare to work;
- third: productivity – a commitment to high-quality long-term investment in science and innovation, new technology and skills;
- fourth: responsibility – avoiding short-termism in pay and wage-bargaining across the private and public sectors, and building a shared sense of national purpose.

I will show that these conditions – requirements for stability, employability, productivity and responsibility – are and have always been the necessary conditions for full employment. The first condition, stability, is needed to ensure a sustainable high demand for labour. The second, employability, promotes a sustainable high supply of labour. The third, raising productivity, provides a sustainable basis for rising living standards. And the fourth, responsibility in bargaining, ensures a sustainable basis for combining full employment with low inflation.

I will show that the failure to meet these conditions led to persistently high unemployment in Britain in recent decades. And I will demonstrate how, by putting these conditions in place, we are restoring the goal of full employment for the next century.

If we start with that famous 1944 White Paper, we see that the government of the time was clear that if full employment was to be sustained all these conditions – stability, employability, productivity and responsibility – had to be in place. While the 1944 White Paper asserted the need for active macro-economic policy – to balance supply and demand – it also recognised there was no long-run gain by trading lower unemployment for higher inflation. Indeed, the 1944 White Paper included an explicit requirement for stability. And I quote: 'action taken by the government to maintain expenditure will be fruitless unless wages and prices are kept reasonably stable. This is of vital importance to any employment policy.'

As important for future generations was the White Paper's recognition that macro-economic action was a necessary but not sufficient condition for full employment and that policies for stability had to be accompanied by policies for employability, productivity and responsibility, not least in pay.

The 1944 White Paper stated that 'it would be a disaster if the intention of the government to maintain total expenditure were interpreted as exonerating the citizen from the duty of fending for himself and resulted in a weakening of personal enterprise'. It required that 'every individual must exercise to the full his own initiative in adapting himself to changing circumstances . . . [the government] will also seek to prevent mobility of labour being impeded . . . Workers must be ready and able to move freely between one occupation and another.'

And the 1944 vision was explicit about responsibility in pay, saying: 'if we are to operate with success a policy for maintaining a high and stable level of employment, it will be essential that employers and workers should exercise moderation in wages matters'.

So while that White Paper is remembered for its commitment to pro-active monetary and fiscal policy, it should also be remembered for its emphasis on employability, productivity and responsibility, not least in pay. And the evidence suggests that it was the accumulating failure – cycle by cycle – to meet not just one but all four of these conditions together that led to the rise of unemployment from the late 1960s onwards.

The 1945 government was resolved that Britain never would return to the unemployment of the 1930s. Indeed over the first two decades it seemed that it was possible to sustain both low inflation and low unemployment, a period many have called a golden age for the British economy. But we all now accept that a more detailed historical examination reveals that successive governments left unaddressed underlying long-term weaknesses. Once price and capital controls were dismantled, these weaknesses began to be revealed in low productivity and recurrent balance-of-payments difficulties. Governments repeatedly attempted to address these problems – through policies to enhance employability, productivity and responsibility. Indeed, the theme of the 1960s was a productivity revolution to be achieved through national planning; of the seventies, a social contract which would responsibly resolve distributional conflicts; of the eighties, deregulation which would 'set the economy free'.

Supply-side action to improve productivity included the NEDC, the national plan, regional plans, the IRC, and later the NEB – all attempts to harness new technology to the productivity challenge and secure high growth. Supply-side action to enhance employability in the labour market ranged from selective employment taxes to trade-union reforms. But the swift succession of improvisations to control pay – which ranged from guiding lights and pay pauses, to latterly 'severe restraint' and the social contract – showed just how elusive was the shared purpose necessary for pay responsibility to work. In their desire to maintain the 1944 objectives, even as supply-side action failed, governments resorted to attempting to control the economic cycle through doses of reflation.

And every time the economy grew, from the fifties onwards, a familiar pattern of events unfolded – a pattern we characterise as the British disease of stop–go – rising consumption unsupported by sufficient investment, growing bottlenecks and balance-of-payments problems as the sterling fixed exchange-rate link came under pressure – and then monetary and fiscal retrenchment as growth in the economy had to be reined back. Unemployment around 300,000 in the mid-fifties rose to over half a million in the late sixties and 1 million by the late seventies, and with hindsight we can conclude that at no time in this period was Britain meeting all the conditions judged in 1944 to be necessary for full employment.

- Despite the promise of stability, no credible institutional arrangements were put in place to deliver that stability.
- Despite talk of rights and responsibilities in the labour market, no serious reform of the Welfare State was instituted, even though – from the late 1960s onwards – growing global competition and new technologies were transforming our labour markets.

- Despite repeated expressions of concern about our productivity gap, no long-term strategy for tackling it ever succeeded.
- While pay restraint was a central issue for most of the period, the initiatives that were introduced to ensure pay responsibility were invariably short-term and were not underpinned by a broadly based consensus that resolved the difficult issues.

Each time governments sought to restore the shared, long-term purpose of 1945, they found it more – not less – difficult and attempts to do so descended into a mixture of exhortation – like the 'I'm backing Britain' campaign – and a British version of corporatism – vested interests cooking up compromises in smoke-filled rooms in London, far removed from the workplaces where such agreements would have to be sustained. The national consensus – which Mr Wilson sought around his national plan, Mr Heath sought around low inflation, Mr Callaghan sought around the social contract – broke down in a series of divisive conflicts – state versus market, capital versus labour, public versus private.

And the more governments failed on pay, productivity and industrial relations, the more they fell back on short-term fine-tuning in a doomed attempt to square the circle and deliver higher living standards and jobs despite sluggish productivity growth: problems massively compounded by the collapse of the Bretton Woods system of fixed exchange rates and the 1973 oil shock. So the golden age gave way to the era of boom and bust. With each successive cycle, a clear pattern developed. Unsustainable growth, leading to stagnation, and cycle by cycle to ever higher levels of inflation and unemployment. Inflation rising from 3 per cent in the late fifties to 9 per cent in the early seventies and more than 20 per cent by 1975; unemployment ratcheted up every cycle and doubling over the period.

What began in 1944 as a comprehensive long-term strategy for growth and employment built on a commitment to stability, employability, productivity and responsibility had by the seventies descended into short-termism and rising unemployment. Quite simply governments could not deliver growth and employment through a macro-policy designed to exploit a supposed short-term trade-off between higher inflation and lower unemployment. A crude version of the 1944 policy – using macro policy to expand demand and micro policy to control inflation – simply could not work. And it was this insight that the 1979 Conservative government seized upon with what they termed a medium-term financial strategy to return Britain to economic stability.

But the Conservatives went further than simply arguing that fine-tuning was the problem. For them the very idea that dynamic economies required active governments was the problem. As they stated, their policies reflected a neo-liberal view of the state:

- first, the application of rigid monetary targets to control inflation – choosing in succession £M3, £M1, then £M0; then, when they failed, shadowing the Deutschmark; then the Exchange Rate Mechanism as the chosen instrument for monetary control;
- second, a belief in deregulation as the key to employability – in the absence of an active labour-market policy or an active, reformed Welfare State;
- third, as the route to higher productivity, again deregulation alone in capital and product markets – a philosophy of 'the best government as the least government';
- fourth, an explicit rejection of consensus.

The clearest intellectual statement of the new position was Nigel Lawson's Mais Lecture in 1984. Its central thesis was that the proper role of macro-economic and micro-economic policy 'is precisely the opposite of that assigned to it by the conventional post-war wisdom'. The conquest of inflation, not the pursuit of unemployment, should be the objective of macro-economic policy. The creation of conditions conducive to growth and employment, not the suppression of price rises, should be the objective of micro-economic policy. On one point, arguing against a crude version of the 1944 policy of using macro policy to expand demand and micro policy to control inflation, he drew the right lesson from the failures of previous decades. But far from tackling the boom–bust cycle endemic to the British economy, the early 1980s and nineties saw two of the deepest recessions since 1945. And even at the peak of growth in 1988, unemployment was still over 2 million, before it rose again to 3 million in 1993. As the late-eighties boom showed, the government of the day eventually relapsed into the very short-termism they had come into government to reverse. Just as the fine-tuners had in the 1970s given way to the monetarists, so now monetarism lapsed into fine-tuning.

By 1997 there were strong inflationary pressures in the system. Consumer spending was growing at an unsustainable rate and inflation was set to rise sharply above target; there was a large structural deficit in the public finances. Public-sector net borrowing stood at £28 billion. By the mid-1990s, the British economy was set to repeat the familiar cycle of stop–go that had been seen over the past twenty years. So against a background of mounting uncertainty and then instability in the global economy, the new government set about establishing a new economic framework to achieve the four conditions for high and stable levels of growth and employment – to promote new policies for stability, employability, productivity and responsibility. We started by recognising we had to achieve these 1944 objectives in a radically different context – integrated global capital markets, greater international competition, and a premium on skills and innovation as the key to competitive advantage.

The first condition is a platform of economic stability built around explicit objectives for low and stable inflation and sound public finances – in our case an inflation target and a golden rule – along with a commitment to openness and transparency.

The new post-monetarist economics is built upon four propositions:

- because there is no long-term trade-off between inflation and unemployment, demand management alone cannot deliver high and stable levels of employment;
- in an open economy rigid monetary rules that assume a fixed relationship between money and inflation do not produce reliable targets for policy;
- the discretion necessary for effective economic policy is possible only within an institutional framework that commands market credibility and public trust;
- that credibility depends upon clearly defined long-term policy objectives, maximum openness and transparency, and clear and accountable divisions of responsibility.

Let me review each proposition one by one. A few decades ago many economists believed that tolerating higher inflation would allow higher long-term growth and employment. Indeed, for a time after 1945, it did – as I have said – appear possible to fine-tune in this way – to trade a little more inflation for a little less unemployment – exploiting what economists call the Phillips curve. But the immediate post-war period presented a very special case – an economy recovering from war that was experiencing rapid growth within a rigid system of price and capital controls. We now know that even at this time fine-tuning merely suppressed inflationary pressures by causing balance-of-payments deficits. And by the 1960s and 1970s, when governments tried to lower unemployment by stimulating demand, they faced not only balance-of-

payments crises but stagflation as both inflation and unemployment rose together.

Milton Friedman argued in his 1968 American Economic
Association Presidential Lecture that the long-term effect of
trying to buy less unemployment with more inflation is simply
to ratchet up both. And here in Britain conclusive evidence
for this proposition came in the 1980s experience of high
inflation and high unemployment occurring together. So,
because there is no long-term trade-off between inflation and
unemployment, demand management alone cannot deliver
high and stable levels of employment. Friedman was right in
this part of his diagnosis: we have to reject short-termist
dashes for growth. But the experience of these years also
points to the solution. Because there is no long-term trade-off
between inflation and unemployment, delivering full employment requires a focus on not just one but on all the levers of
economic policy.

The second proposition in the new post-monetarist economics is that applying rigid monetary targets in a world of open
and liberalised financial markets cannot secure stability. Here
experience shows that while Friedman's diagnosis was right his
prescription was wrong. Fixed intermediate monetary targets
assume a stable demand for money and therefore a predictable relationship between money and inflation. But since the
1970s, global capital flows, financial deregulation and changing technology have brought such volatility in the demand for
money that across the world fixed monetary regimes have
proved unworkable. So why, even as monetary targets failed,
did the British government persist in pursuing them? Why
even as they failed was their answer more of the same? The
answer is that they felt the only way to be credible was by tying
themselves to fixed monetary rules. And when one target failed
they chose not to question the idea of intermediate targeting
but to find a new variable to target, hence the bewildering
succession of monetary targets from £M3 to £M0; then sha-

dowing the Deutschmark; then the Exchange Rate Mechanism as the chosen instrument for monetary control. As with fine-tuning, the rigid application of fixed monetary targets was based on the experience of sheltered national economies and on apparently stable and predictable relationships which have broken down in modern liberalised global markets. And yet the more they failed, the more policy-makers felt they had to tie their hands, first by adding even more monetary targets and then by switching to exchange-rate targets. But having staked their anti-inflationary credentials on following these rules, the government – and the economy – paid a heavy price. The price was recession, unemployment – and increasing public mistrust in the capacity of British institutions to deliver the goals they set.

What conclusion can be drawn from all this? Governments are in theory free to run the economy as they see fit. They have, in theory, unfettered discretion. And it is not only the fact that they have this unfettered discretion but the suspicion they might abuse it that leads to market distrust and thus to higher long-term interest rates. That is why governments have sought to limit their discretion through rules. The monetarist error was to tie policy to flawed intermediate policy rules governing the relationship between money demand and inflation. But the alternative should not be a return to discretion without rules, to a crude version of fine-tuning. The answer is not no rules, but the right rules. The post-monetarist path to stability requires the discipline of a long-term institutional framework.

So my second proposition – that in a world of open capital markets fixed monetary targets buy neither credibility nor stability – leads directly to my third. The third proposition is that in this open economy the discretion necessary for effective economic policy is possible only within a framework that commands market credibility and public trust.

Let me explain what I mean when I talk of the new

monetary discipline: in the new open economy subject to instantaneous and massive flows of capital, the penalties for failure are ever more heavy and the rewards for success are even greater. Governments which lack credibility – which are pursuing policies which are not seen to be sustainable – are punished not only more swiftly than in the past but more severely and at a greater cost to their future credibility. The British experience of the 1990s is a case in point. It shows that once targets are breached it is hard to rebuild credibility by setting new targets. Credibility, once lost, is hard to regain. The economy then pays the price in higher long-term interest rates and slower growth.

On the other hand governments which pursue, and are judged by the markets to be pursuing, sound monetary and fiscal policies, can attract inflows of investment capital more quickly, in greater volume and at a lower cost than even ten years ago. The gain is even greater than that. If governments are judged to be pursuing sound long-term policies, then they will also be trusted to do what is essential – to respond flexibly to the unexpected economic events that inevitably arise in an increasingly integrated but more volatile global economy. So in the era of global capital markets, it is only within a credible framework that governments will command the trust they need to exercise the flexibility they require.

This leads to my fourth proposition – a credible framework means working within clearly defined long-term policy objectives, maximum openness and transparency, and clear and accountable divisions of responsibility. It is essential that governments set objectives that are clearly defined and against which their performance can be judged. That is why we have introduced clear fiscal rules, defined explicitly for the economic cycle. That is why, also, we have a clearly defined inflation target.

Let me say why it is so important that our inflation target is a symmetrical target. Just as there is no gain in attempting to trade higher inflation for higher employment, so there is no advantage in aiming for ever lower inflation if it is at the expense of growth and jobs. If the target was not symmetric – for example, if in the UK case it was 2.5 per cent or less, rather than 2.5 per cent – policy-makers might have an incentive to reduce inflation well below target at the cost of output and jobs. Instead a symmetrical target means that deviations below target are treated in the same way as deviations above the target.

But, to be credible, the monetary and fiscal framework must also be open, transparent and accountable. The greater the degree of secrecy the greater the suspicion that the truth is being obscured and the books cooked. But the greater the degree of transparency – the more information that is published on why decisions are made and the more the safeguards against the manipulation of information – the less likely is it that investors will be suspicious of the government's intentions.

That openness needs to be underpinned by accountability and responsibility. So public trust can be built only on a foundation of credible institutions, clear objectives, and a proper institutional framework. The flaw in Conservative economic policy was not just the failure of monetary targets. It was that the 'medium-term financial strategy' had no credible foundation – it was neither consistent in objectives, nor transparent in its operation, nor underpinned by credible institutional reforms. Failure led, after 1992, to some reform. The inflation target was an important step forward. But it was ambiguously defined and it was not underpinned by anything other than an improvised and still highly personalised institutional framework. Minutes of meetings between the Bank of England and the Chancellor were published, but they could not allay the suspicion that policy was being manipulated for political ends. In fact despite the then government's commitment to an inflation target of 2.5 per cent or less,

financial market expectations of inflation ten years ahead
were not 2.5 per cent or less but 4.3 per cent in April 1997,
and never below 4 per cent for the whole period. Long-term
interest rates remained 1.7 per cent higher in Britain than in
Germany.

This has changed significantly in the last two years: long-
term inflation expectations have fallen from 4.3 per cent to
2.4 per cent, a figure consistent with the government's inflation target; the differential between British and German long-
term interest rates has fallen from 1.7 per cent, to just 0.2
percentage points. I believe the explanation for this improvement lies in the immediate and decisive steps that our new
government took in May 1997 – to set clear monetary and
fiscal objectives; to put in place orderly procedures, including
a new division of responsibility between the Treasury and an
independent central bank; and to insist on the maximum
openness and transparency.

Contrary to Nigel Lawson's distinction between the roles of
macro-economic and micro-economic policy as set out in his
1984 lecture, we recognise that the role of a macro-economic
policy is not simply to bear down on inflation but, by creating
a platform of stability, to promote growth and employment;
and that an active supply-side policy is necessary not only to
improve productivity and employment, but to make it possible to sustain low inflation alongside high and stable levels of
growth and employment. In other words, macro-economic
and micro-economic policy are both essential – working
together – to growth and employment.

In short we have sought to learn the lessons of the post-
war years and build a new platform of stability. Making the
Bank of England independent was and is only one of the
institutional reforms that form our new post-monetarist
approach to economic policy. First, clear long-term policy
objectives:

- a pre-announced and symmetrical inflation target; and
- strict fiscal rules to ensure sustainable public finances.

Second, well-understood procedural rules:

- a clear remit for the Monetary Policy Committee of the Bank of England to meet the inflation target set by government supported by the open-letter system and the code for fiscal stability; and
- effective coordination between fiscal and monetary policy – including the presence of the Treasury representative at the Monetary Policy Committee meetings.

Third, openness and transparency to keep markets properly informed, ensuring that institutions, objectives and the means of achieving the objectives are seen to be credible:

- publication of the minutes and votes of Monetary Policy Committee meetings; and
- transparency in fiscal policy, including the independent auditing of key fiscal assumptions.

It is the same search for stability in an open economy that has led to European Monetary Union. And at the global level, the same lessons are being learnt. In Washington last month, the IMF agreed a new framework of codes and standards, new economic disciplines for openness and transparency to be accepted and implemented by all countries which participate in the international financial system. These codes and standards – including fiscal, financial and monetary policy – will require that countries set out clear long-term objectives, put in place proper procedures, and promote the openness and transparency necessary to keep markets informed.

With the reforms we have already made in Britain, I believe that we have now – for the first time in this generation – a sound and credible platform for long-term stability for the British economy. We will not make the old mistake of relaxing our fiscal discipline the moment the economy starts to grow. The same tough grip will continue. The Monetary Policy Committee will be, and must continue to be, vigilant and forward-looking in its decisions, as we build a culture of low inflation that delivers stability and steady growth. We will not repeat the mistake of the late eighties. Those who today are arguing that economic stability comes by opposing necessary changes in interest rates and by avoiding the tough decisions necessary to meet the inflation target would risk returning to the boom and bust of the past. We can achieve high and stable levels of employment and meet our inflation target. Indeed we will not achieve and sustain full employment for the long term by failing to meet our inflation target.

This credible platform of stability, built from the solid foundations I have just described, allows people to plan and invest for the long term. This is our first condition for full employment.

The second condition for full employment is an active labour-market policy matching rights and responsibilities. The idea of a fixed natural rate of unemployment consistent with stable inflation was discredited by the evidence of the 1980s. For even when the economy was growing at an un-sustainable pace – above 5 per cent in 1988 – in all regions of the country there were high levels of vacancies, including vacancies for the unskilled, alongside high unemployment. How did this happen? Part of the explanation was the 'scarring' effect on skills and employability inflicted by the deep and long recession of the eighties; partly also the mismatch between the skills and expectations of redundant manufacturing workers – and the new jobs in service indus-tries; partly the failure to reform the Welfare State, especially its unemployment and poverty traps which, for many, meant work did not pay.

So there was a rise in what, in the 1980s, economists termed 'the non-accelerating inflation rate of unemployment' or the NAIRU. Whether measured by the relationship between wage inflation and unemployment – as Phillips stressed in the 1950s – or vacancies and unemployment as Beveridge had highlighted in the 1940s – Britain had clearly seen a dramatic structural deterioration in the UK labour market. The same level of wage pressure or vacancies existed alongside much higher levels of unemployment than in the past.

So the new government has taken a decisively different approach to employment policy over the past two years, aimed at reducing the NAIRU. All our reforms are designed for the modern dynamic labour market, now being transformed by the new information technologies. We recognise that people will have to change jobs more often, that skills are at a premium and that reform was needed in the 1980s to create more flexibility. The New Deal which offers opportunities to work but demands obligations to do so is the first comprehensive approach to long-term unemployment. Designed to re-engage the unemployed with the labour market, it addresses both the scarring effect of unemployment and the mismatch between jobs and skills. The Working Families Tax Credit and associated reforms that integrate tax and benefit are, for the first time, making work pay more than benefits; and our educational reforms including lifelong learning, the University for Industry, Individual Learning Accounts and our Computers for All initiative will tackle skill deficiencies.

The last two years have brought record levels of employment and sharp falls in youth and long-term unemployment – early signs that our policies are having an impact. But with still 1.2 million claimant unemployed and others excluded from the labour market – even at a time when there are around 1 million vacancies spread throughout all areas of the country – there is much more to do. The Working Families Tax Credit is now being extended to new Employment Credits for the disabled and for those over fifty. And as the New Deal extends its scope from the under-25s to the long-term unemployed, opportunities to work and obligations to work will be extended together. The more our welfare-to-work reforms allow the long-term unemployed to re-enter the active labour market, the more it will be possible to reduce unemployment without increasing inflationary pressures. And the more our tax and benefit reforms remove unnecessary barriers to work, and the more our structural reforms promote the skills for work, the more it is possible to envisage long-term increases in employment, without the fuelling of inflationary pressures.

Next our third condition: only with rising productivity can we meet people's long-term expectations for rising standards of living without causing inflation or unemployment. It is important to be clear about the relationship between productivity, employment and living standards. Low productivity can exist side by side with low unemployment if people accept that living standards are not going to rise – as happened to the United States in the 1980s. But rising productivity can exist side by side with high unemployment if we pay ourselves more than the economy can afford. If people demand short-term rewards which cannot be justified by economy-wide productivity growth, the result is first inflation and then the loss of jobs. That has been the historic British problem – repeated bouts of wage inflation unmatched by productivity growth, leading in the end to higher unemployment. Indeed between 1950 and 1996 productivity growth in Britain was only 2.6 per cent a year compared to 3.7 per cent and 3.9 per cent in France and Germany.

But if we can now achieve rising productivity, bridging the gap with our competitors, high levels of employment and rising living standards can go together. Britain cannot assume that the new information technologies will automatically bring the higher productivity growth now seen in the United

States. So we must work through a new agenda that involves a shared national effort to raise our game. Policies to encourage higher productivity will be the theme of the government's Pre-Budget Report on 9th of November. While thirty years ago governments responded to the productivity challenge with top-down plans, and grant aid primarily for physical investment, today the productivity agenda is more complex and more challenging. So we are developing new and radical policies for the modernisation of capital and product markets, the encouragement of innovation and an enterprise culture open to all, as well as the building of a modern skills base.

I come now to our fourth and final condition for full employment – responsibility, not least in pay, and by responsibility I mean, as I have stressed throughout this lecture, a willingness to put the long term above the short term, a willingness to build a shared common purpose. To succeed we must all be long-termists now.

The reality of the more complex and flexible labour markets of Britain today is that pay decisions are dictated not by the few in smoke-filled rooms but made by millions of employees and employers across the country. And the more that we are all persuaded to take a long-term view of what the economy can afford, the more jobs we will create, the more we can keep inflation under control so interest rates can be as low as possible. The Bank of England has to meet an inflation target of 2.5 per cent. The target has to be met. Unacceptably high wage rises will not therefore lead to higher inflation but higher interest rates. It is in no one's interest if today's pay rise threatens to become tomorrow's mortgage rise. The worst form of short-termism would be to pay ourselves more today at the cost of higher interest rates tomorrow, fewer jobs the next year and lower living standards in the years to come. So wage responsibility – to rescue a useful phrase from its old woeful context – is a price worth paying to achieve jobs now and prosperity in the long term. It is moderation for a purpose. But responsibility means not just responsibility in pay but building a shared commitment to achieve all the conditions necessary for full employment – in other words, to work together as a country to promote stability, employability and higher productivity too.

It is undeniable that the shared economic purpose of 1945 broke down in fifty years of endless and sterile divisions between capital and labour, between state and market and between public and private sectors, denying Britain the national direction it needed. Britain and the British people can now move beyond these outdated conflicts. Building a consensus around the need for stability, employability, productivity and responsibility we can define anew a shared economic purpose for our country. The conditions for full employment can all be met. And the surest way is that the whole country is determined to meet them.

Rightly proud of the success of the UK economy, the Chancellor has been anxious to draw this experience to the attention of European neighbours, and to reform the approach and processes in the European Union. An exposition of this approach is given in the speech made by the Chancellor to the Centre for European Reform at Church House, London, on 10 March 2003. Entitled 'The Road to Full Employment: Economic Reforms for a More Flexible and Dynamic Britain and Europe', the speech took place just before the Iraq conflict, and in the wake of 9/11, and is influenced by this timing. None the less the speech focuses on changes required to the economies of countries in the EU so as to bring about modern ways of achieving high and stable levels of growth and employment. In particular the Chancellor focuses on the role of governments in the modern world, setting out three areas of concern: the need for stability, because investment will flow most to those countries that are the most stable, and ever more rapidly away from those that risk stability; the need to create the best environment for high-quality investment – through policies for education, research and development, and infrastructure; and how enhancing productivity and competitiveness in a more open economy demands a new flexibility in labour, capital and product markets, and a commitment to root out inflexibilities, at both a national and increasingly a regional level.

This is an important speech, not just because of the message it sends to Europe, but because it encapsulates many of the macro-economic and micro-economic policies which have been employed by the Treasury under the Chancellor. However, it goes further than this, giving a social-inclusion context for much of the economic thinking. The Chancellor is fond of quoting a maxim coined by John Smith QC MP, the leader of the Labour Party 1992–4, that 'economic efficiency and social justice are two sides of the same coin'. This speech is a good exposition of how this maxim (and his own related 'prudence with a purpose' maxim) have been implemented under the Labour government since 1997. As he concludes: 'Britain has a unique opportunity to be, once again, a beacon to the world advancing enterprise and fairness together – a dynamic, vibrant economy that is the first economy in the new era of globalisation to match flexibility with fairness and, in doing so, to attain the high levels of growth and employment that are the best route to prosperity for all.'

If the last decade of the twentieth century will go down as the decade that ended the Cold War, the first decade of the twenty-first century will be remembered as the time when nations had to adjust to both the opportunities and insecurities of globalisation. A generation that has grown up free of the horror and pain of world wars, survived the uneasy truce of the Cold War, dared to hope that the fall of the Berlin Wall would mean a halt to the proliferation of weapons of mass destruction, is now having to confront the proliferation of chemical, biological and, often, nuclear weapons in the hands of terrorists and failed states.

. . .

This new era of globalisation brings insecurities as well as opportunities, so too in economic policy insecurities and opportunities arise together and challenge us to devise modern ways of achieving our traditional economic objective: high and stable levels of growth and employment.

Globalisation means that there is hardly a good we produce here in Britain that is not subject to intense competition from at home and abroad, not just competition from traditional competitors in the advanced industrial economies but competition from emerging market economies, not least in Asia and the east of Europe – competition which is itself a spur to growth and prosperity.

Twenty years ago, even ten years ago, it was just about possible – if costly and wrong – for countries to shelter their industries and sectors, protecting them from global competition. But today there is no safe haven, no easy escape from global competition without putting at risk long-term stability, growth and employment.

Some say governments are powerless facing these new global forces, that they cannot any longer play their part in achieving the old objectives: high and stable levels of growth and employment. I believe the opposite to be true. Globalisation has rightly limited the scope of government and in the modern, open, more fiercely competitive global economy governments cannot use the old levers to achieve their objectives. They cannot easily impose exchange controls, trade off inflation for growth, resort to old-style protectionism, competitive devaluations or costly state aids – the policy of subsidies in one country – without undermining their long-term goal of high and stable levels of growth and employment. But it is because in a more open global economy countries pay such a heavy price, not least in long-term investment, for getting the big decisions wrong that I believe governments are even more important today to the attainment of high levels of growth and employment.

Because investment will flow most to those countries that are the most stable, and ever more rapidly away from those that risk stability, there is an even greater premium than before on governments running a stable and successful monetary and fiscal regime to achieve high and stable levels of growth and employment. That is why we attached so much importance to the first decision our government made – to make the Bank of England independent – and why, with low inflation, low interest rates and low debt, our stability makes us a far stronger economy today.

Globalisation also describes a world whose very mobility of capital and openness to competition is ushering in a restructuring of industry and services across continents. And while emerging-market countries are ready to attract low-value-added, low-investment and low-skilled work, we have to compete on ever higher levels of skill and technology rather than ever lower levels of poverty pay. So countries that make the right forward-looking decisions to create the best environment for high-quality investment – through policies for education, research and development, and infrastructure – will be better placed to achieve high and stable levels of growth and employment. It is for this reason that in our recent Spending Review we decided to match new resources to major reforms in education, science and innovation.

But because high levels of productivity growth are essential to high levels of growth and employment, there is a third essential element that distinguishes the successful high-employment, high-growth economies from the least successful – and it is also one where governments can also make a difference. And it is this I want to talk about today both for Britain and for the Euro area: how enhancing productivity and competitiveness in a more open economy demands a new flexibility in labour, capital and product markets.

A few weeks ago I urged Labour to reverse traditional, often hostile attitudes to markets and recognise the need to strengthen markets in important areas. And today I want to set out how Britain proposes to lead the way in labour-, product- and capital-market reform and how in this process of market liberalisation we can make progress with European economic reform. Some still argue that when global competition is challenging every industry and almost every service, the state should replace markets or, as difficult, seek to second-guess them through a corporatist policy of supporting national champions. But competition at home is not only essential for competitiveness at home and abroad, but if we are to make the most of the potential of open trade and the European single market, we will need greater flexibility as we respond to new technologies, and adjust to changes in consumer demand. Indeed in a single-currency area where the old flexibilities to adjust exchange rates and interest rates are no longer available at a national level, labour-, product- and capital-market flexibilities are even more essential. Adjusting to shocks without putting at risk high and stable levels of growth and employment demands even greater market flexibility.

America's experience as a large and mature monetary union demonstrates the importance of sufficient flexibility to ensure that monetary union works well. In monetary unions, whatever their size, local economies need to respond to shocks and there is a premium on effective internal market-adjustment mechanisms. In the USA competitive pressures are strong, ensuring that prices respond quickly and efficiently. With risk-sharing diversified across a broad and deep capital market they can limit the impact of shocks. And a high level of product- and capital-market flexibility complemented by a high level of labour flexibility has helped sustain high levels of employment and growth.

In the past, supporters of full employment have not been in the habit of thinking of flexibility as a route to full employment. And supporters of greater flexibility in our economy have seldom described its benefits as the attainment of full employment. Yet today flexible economies are also the economies with higher employment. And I want to demonstrate how in the new world of global competition it is by creating a more flexible and dynamic economy in which firms and individuals respond to the challenges of change that we will best achieve our historic goals for full employment.

Britain and Europe have, of course, long since moved from the old assumption that there is a long-term trade-off between inflation and growth and employment. But, in a world where business must respond quickly and people must adapt to change, Europe has too often been unwilling to go beyond old assumptions that the labour-, capital- and product-market flexibility necessary for productivity is the enemy of social justice.

Yet the road to full employment starts with monetary and fiscal stability, is built on investing in skills and responsibility in the workplace, and demands attention to enterprise, competition and employability as necessary means of achieving high productivity. And this road to full employment in Britain depends on achieving economic reform not just in Britain but in Europe too. In the past the Labour Party – like the rest of Europe – has not been very good at facing up to issues relating to flexibility. Indeed flexibility has often been a term of abuse, derided as the antithesis of fairness, as the race to the bottom, as poverty pay – and it is often suggested that flexibility is a synonym for exploitation. Yet flexibility is, in reality, the ability to respond to change with speed. Changes in a marketplace include the impact of innovation and changing technology, changing consumer preferences and the changing need for particular skills.

Failure to respond to these changes by companies and by

individuals leads to an unproductive use and wasteful allocation of resources in the economy and thus huge costs in lost
output, jobs and prosperity. So in an open and far more
rapidly changing global trading economy, flexibility – the
ability to respond quickly – is not an option. It is a necessary
precondition of success. Without firms prepared to innovate
and adjust, economies become sclerotic. Without the capacity
to develop the new skills needed, countries will simply be left
behind. Indeed there are just two modern routes to achieving
high levels of growth and employment – flexibility without
fairness, which leaves people helpless in face of change, or
flexibility with fairness, where governments and firms equip
people to cope with change and tackle the insecurities that
surround it. The issue of the best modern policies for fairness
is one I will address in detail in a later speech.

But it is right both to create flexible markets and to equip
people to master change – through investment in skills and
training, through the best transitional help for people
moving between jobs, and – as I hope to demonstrate –
through the operation of a minimum wage and a tax-credit
system.

And flexible markets and active labour-market policies
are not incompatible opposites but can be essential allies of
each other as we seek high levels of growth and employment. So the issue is not one of abandoning fairness but of
achieving the right kind of flexibility. And what people
should oppose is not governments that insist on flexibility
but governments that fail to insist on matching that flexibility with fairness.

In other words, we should recognise that, with the right
kind of flexibility in British and European labour, capital and
product markets, economic efficiency and employment opportunity for all can advance together. So our goal – enterprise and fairness in a dynamic, flexible economy that delivers
full employment and prosperity for all – demands that we

match policies for stability, employment and fairness with flexible capital, labour and product markets.

Since 1997 we have, in pursuit of this:

- made our competition authorities independent and opened up product markets;
- revamped the physical planning system;
- encouraged our capital markets by cutting Capital Gains Tax and introducing new incentives for venture capital;
- encouraged enterprise with lower tax rates for small businesses;
- offered new incentives and resources to encourage greater investment, skills, and innovation; and
- devoted time and energy to promoting economic liberalisation in Europe.

At the same time as we have created a more flexible economy we have advanced fairness with the introduction of the National Minimum Wage, the Working Families Tax Credit and Jobcentre Plus – an employment service that offers personal help to people moving into and between jobs – reforms not at the expense of greater flexibility but consistent with greater flexibility.

But we can still go much further in product-, capital- and labour-market reform in Britain and in Europe to make our economy more flexible. When I argue for flexible capital and product markets I want open well-informed markets that ensure capital flows to productive uses so that the price mechanism works to balance demand and supply and labour and capital are used efficiently. So flexibility in product and capital markets means that instead of being suspicious of competition, we should embrace it, recognising that without it vested interests accumulate. Instead of tolerating monopoly or cartels which were never in the public interest, or appeasing special interests, we should systematically extend competition – forcing producers to be efficient, extending the choices available to consumers and opening up opportunity for the ambitious and the risk-takers.

To back up independence for the Competition Commission and the new proactive role of the OFT, we will take action where investigations reveal challenges that have to be met and demand that the same rigorous pro-competition policies are applied to the public sector as well as the private sector. As the DTI Secretary of State is showing: the old days of the 'sponsorship' department are over, freeing up resources to enhance the DTI's role in promoting competition and enabling markets to work better.

And it is right to demand the same liberalisation throughout Europe to make the single market work. Britain has learnt much from the steps taken in the European Union, before and after the Lisbon agenda, that promote liberalisation and economic reform. And we have supported wholeheartedly the attempt to restrict the wasteful use of state aids that prevents markets functioning well. Yet while in 1988 Cecchini estimated that single-market liberalisation would add 4.5 per cent to Europe's GDP, cut prices by 6 per cent and increase employment by 1.75 million, many of the gains have yet to materialise. The way forward is mutual recognition of national practices not harmonised regulations; and tax competition not tax harmonisation.

So we support:

- a more proactive EU competition regime furthering a strong and independent competition policy for Europe;
- investigations into particular European markets and sectors to drive up competition and prevent British firms from being excluded from European markets, from energy and telecommunications to agriculture;
- faster progress on the reform of airport slot allocation and liberalisation of postal services; and
- support for private-finance initiatives in Europe.

And Britain remains at the forefront of countries supporting the European Commission's demands for tougher state-aid rules to prevent unwarranted subsidies for loss-making industries and at the European Economic Reform Summit we will continue to push for a more aggressive approach to tackling unfair competition and state failure. In the UK we are removing the last of the permanent, ongoing subsidies – thus removing aids which have no market justification. But while it is right to remove state aids which distort the single market, it is also right to reform state aids to target market failures which need correction.

It took Britain more than a year to secure European permission to create regional venture-capital funds for localities desperately in need of strong local capital markets that work for small businesses. And it has taken months more for permission to abolish stamp duty for business-property purchases in areas urgently in need of local property markets that work and the new businesses and jobs that can ensue.

Here again, as I said in a speech on markets a few weeks ago, the case for state intervention is not to extend the role of the state but, by tackling market failure, to help make markets work better: instead of thinking the state must take over responsibility where markets deliver insufficient investment and short-termism in innovation, skills and environmental protection, we must enable markets to work better and for the long term.

An effective competition policy helps new and small businesses enter markets and prevents them being held back or penalised by large vested interests. And instead of being suspicious of enterprise and entrepreneurs, Labour should celebrate them – encouraging, incentivising and rewarding them, hence our reduction in Capital Gains Tax (from 40 pence to 10 pence) and our small-business tax reforms (from 23 pence to 19 pence and the lower rate from 10 pence to zero).

With their recommendations on small-business banking, the competition authorities have tried to cut the cost of investing for small businesses. The next stage is to help small and medium-sized businesses get fair access to public-sector procurement. Opening up markets to new suppliers intensifies competition as well as encouraging innovation. That is why we have asked the Office of Government Commerce to identify what more can be done to increase competition in markets where government has substantial purchasing power and to enable small businesses to compete for government contracts and deliver value for money.

I have said that instead of maximising regulation to restrict the scope of markets, we should systematically pinpoint regulation that does not serve the public interest and can be reduced. So as I examine measures for the Budget we will continue the process of cutting the cost and burden to small business of starting up, investing and growing, especially in areas of high unemployment. And as the government strengthens its assessments of the impact of regulation on small firms – which have included examinations of the retail and chemical sectors – we will also look at transport, pesticides, food and drink processing, and the collection of statistical data.

Because 40 per cent of new regulations originate in the EU, the European Economic Reform Summit this month should call for the same rigorous assault on unnecessary regulation throughout the European Union: an agreement to examine all new directives for their impact as well as taking stock of existing EU directives.

Achieving greater flexibility not just in product markets but in capital markets is essential for high levels of growth, and as we press ahead with the Cruickshank, Myners, Sandler and Higgs reforms and build on our cuts in Capital Gains Tax we should continue to examine where local capital markets have had least success, and continue to cut the barriers to entry faced by small businesses and to open up venture-capital markets in our regions.

State-aid rules – and thus the treatment of early-stage research – should be reformed to help Europe bridge the gap between our research and development performance and that of Japan and the USA. With the R&D tax credit we are trying to cut the cost of investing in innovative research, but state-aid rules should make it easier to address the market failures that obstruct research and innovation in its early and pre-commercial stages.

Capital markets can and must help us manage risk more efficiently, between sectors, over time and across national boundaries. While America has achieved a high degree of diversification across state borders, investment in Europe remains fragmented on national lines and there is a need to remove barriers to diversification of investments across borders, for example in pension and mutual funds.

So we will support the European Financial Services Action Plan as it improves mutual recognition of financial-services providers in insurance, banking and capital markets. It is also true that competition between trading systems in capital markets is vital to improve efficiency and reduce dealing spreads, and so cut the cost of capital and raise the returns from investment. And where EU regulation such as the proposed new Investment Services Directive threatens to weaken rather than strengthen competition we will fight to change it.

And instead of the old protectionism we must embrace open markets and thus free trade. Efforts to improve the flexibility of product and capital markets should not stop at the EU's borders. Greater openness to global trade and investment creates new opportunities for European produ-cers and consumers, and strengthens the incentives for re-form. A more flexible and dynamic Europe would, in turn, play a leading role in breaking down barriers to trade and investment in the rest of the world – a virtuous circle of reform and openness, leading to a stronger and more resilient economy from which the EU, and the global economy, would benefit. So we must drive forward the Doha agenda and also do more to strengthen the trading links between the EU and USA. Deepening what is already the world's largest trade and investment relationship would do much to stimulate flexibility and reform in Europe.

By looking for market solutions to market failures, we move beyond the old centrally imposed industrial policies – the corporatist policy of picking winners – in favour of a new regionally driven focus on local enterprise, local skills and local innovation. For it is not just how national economies adjust that matters but how local and regional economies and their markets adjust and respond that will determine whether full employment can be achieved in each region and on a sustainable basis. And that requires us to move beyond not only the first generation of regional policy that was centrally delivered first aid but the second generation of regional policy, which was London and then Brussels imposing centrally set rules focusing on incentives for incoming investors.

Today, in the third generation of regional policy, the focus is, rightly, moving from centrally administered subsidies to locally led incentives that encourage local skills, innovation and investment and boost the indigenous sources of regional economic growth. And to achieve this we also move from the old idea that regional policy is just the work of one or two departments. In the new regional policy for a more flexible economy each department must step up the pace of reform and devolution:

- from centrally administered R&D policies to the encouragement of local technology transfer between universities and companies and the development of regional clusters of specialisms;

- from a national 'one size fits all' approach to skills to devolving 90 per cent of the learning and skills Budget, so that we can promote regional excellence;
- from centrally run housing and transport policies to greater regional coordination . . . offering greater flexibility in response; and
- from centrally administered small-business polices to more local discretion starting with, in the East and West Midlands and the North-West, the small-business Budget locally administered with the Regional Development Agencies.

Because small-business creation is so important to the success of local economies it makes sense to examine why the rates of small-business creation vary so much between localities and regions and what we can do about it. In the UK just 5 per cent of adults think of starting a business; in the United States it is 11 per cent – so we have a long way to go. And there are also large variations in the rates of business creation between areas of the UK, with ten times the number of firm start-ups in the best-performing areas of the UK than in the worst performing.

So to remove the barriers preventing firms from starting up and growing in our most deprived communities, we have designated 2,000 new enterprise areas – where we encourage economic activity by cutting the cost of starting up, investing, employing, training, managing the payroll. Here we are bringing together industry, planning, employment and social-security policies to tackle local property-market, capital-market and labour-market failures – hence the new community investment-tax relief, the relaxation of planning regulations, the abolition of stamp duty, the engagement of the New Deal – government and business working together to bring investment, jobs and prosperity to areas that prosperity has still bypassed.

It makes sense for Europe to help this process forward. And while, as I argued last week, structural funds will inevitably be concentrated on the poorer regions of central and eastern Europe, more prosperous countries with large regional inequalities should be given the freedom to tackle capital-, labour- and product-market failures through a reform of state-aid legislation.

And we need to extend our approach of encouraging regional and local initiatives from R&D, skills, small-business, transport and housing policies to the critical area of employment and welfare policy. Because we seek local and regional labour markets that match labour demand and supply efficiently and help us meet our aim of full employment, the Work and Pensions Secretary, is focusing on how regional- and local-employment and social-security policies can help our labour markets get people back to work more quickly and help people move more easily from the old jobs that are becoming redundant to the new jobs that can give them greater security.

So while the preconditions for full employment are national stability, employability and an environment for investment and high productivity, the achievement of full employment and high levels of growth and prosperity depends upon regions and localities becoming better equipped to adapt to change. In particular, when there are negative economic shocks, it is all the more important that the economy can adjust and ensure that temporary output and job losses are minimised and do not become more permanent. And while it is true that in recent years in the United Kingdom earnings growth has been consistent with the inflation target, and what is called the NAIRU (non-accelerating inflation rate of unemployment) has fallen, it is still the case that UK labour-market flexibility – while greater than much of Europe – is lower than in the USA.

A dynamic economy needs adaptable and flexible labour markets where there is:

- first, mobility – a willingness to be more mobile, and firms and a labour market that support the ability to be so;
- second, what economists call functional flexibility – the skills to meet new and different challenges;
- third, employment flexibility – the ability of firms and individuals to adjust working patterns to new challenges; and
- fourth, at a local level the ability of our employment and wage systems to respond more quickly to shocks and imbalances between supply and demand.

And to meet the challenges of a global economy we have, in each of these areas, much further to go. While the rate of job turnover in Britain is higher than the seven years per job in the Euro area but lower than in America – five years against four years – it is also true that there is far less geographical mobility in response to change in Britain and in Europe than in the USA.

While around 25 per cent of the UK's workforce have degree-level skills, the UK, with 8 million men and women with low or no skills, 20 per cent of 18–24-year-olds, has a long way to go. While nearly 25 per cent of British employees work part-time compared with less than 15 per cent in the Euro area, and while working outside the five days a week is common in Britain – 13 per cent working on a Sunday compared to 11 per cent in the EU and as low as 4 per cent in some countries – adjusting to the global economic challenge will require firms and individuals to be more flexible. Indeed it is because our aim is not just achieving but sustaining full employment in our regions that we need not only stability but this flexibility to respond to shocks. And this is more important than ever in a single-currency area, with the

US experience demonstrating labour mobility and wage flexibility to be critical to the success of their single currency.

In the American single-currency area geographical mobility, which can help tackle skill shortages and help people find new opportunities, is twice the level of Britain and Europe today. It is often argued that mobility will be greater:

- the more flexible the housing market;
- the easier it is to commute; and
- the easier it is to attract economic migrants to high-demand areas.

Britain has a smaller privately rented sector than most countries. And the Deputy Prime Minister is examining how we can encourage more flexibility for those in social housing through initiatives such as choice-based letting and the new housing and mobility scheme to help tenants relocate to access employment. And because we also need to ensure we are building sufficient housing in areas of high employment, the Deputy Prime Minister has also set out ambitious plans to deliver a step change in housing provision and expand assistance for key workers to enable them to rent as well as buy in high-demand housing areas. Around 3.8 million tenants currently rely on housing benefit for help with their rent, but delays in processing new applications after a claimant returns to employment can lead to rent arrears and debt, dissuading some people from moving into work. So because housing benefit can constrain mobility, affecting an individual's ability to move into jobs and move between localities, we are piloting major reforms in housing-benefit administration and incentives that make it easier for the unemployed to return to work. The current Housing Benefit Pathfinders Scheme offers a flat-rate payment in the private rented sector and it makes sense to pursue the pilot of a flat-rate payment based on household circumstances and location.

International migration can help tackle skill shortages and aid adjustment to shocks. Migration into the UK through the work-permits system has risen from 50,000 in 1997 to 170,000 this year and is projected to rise to 200,000 by 2004. And while tackling illegal immigration, the Home Secretary and I have been considering further extensions to the successful work-permit system for legal migration.

The more skilled men and women there are, and the more they are willing to develop new skills, the more flexible and productive the economy is likely to be. And the more globalisation opens up the world economy to fierce competition across continents the more competitive advantage countries like Britain will gain from a higher level of skills. Yet despite our successes at university and college level, skills – particularly in basic and intermediate qualifications – are Britain's Achilles heel, the most worrying inflexibility of all within our labour market. And we are learning a great deal from successful industrial-training policies in other parts of Europe.

So the Education Secretary is right to forge a new partnership between government, employee and employer with a view to expanding our skills and making labour markets work more flexibly. Here, as elsewhere, a partnership between employers and workforces is the best means of combining flexibility with fairness. Building on the Union Learning Fund and other innovative partnerships, I believe we can do more to encourage and help trades unions expand their role in training and education. The increased registration for the University for Industry (providing courses for over 700,000 people already), the high levels of young people undertaking modern apprenticeships (now over 220,000 a year) and the success of the new Employer Training Pilots prove that the issue is not an unwillingness to get new qualifications and skills but the availability of training at the right time, price and standards.

So we are expanding the Employer Training Pilots now operating in six areas to around a quarter of the country – offering incentives for firms to give their staff paid time off to train towards basic skills and NVQ Level 2 qualifications. And a major shake-up in skills training will be announced this summer. From April, we are piloting devolved pooled budgets for adult learning in four areas of the country – providing greater incentives to employers and individuals to develop their skills, reducing bureaucracy and strengthening the regional and local dimension in skills development. Looking to the workforce of the future we are not only investing heavily to raise standards in schools but, from September next year, rolling out Educational Maintenance Allowances in England – providing young people from poorer families with up to £1,500 a year to encourage them to stay on at school and get the qualifications they need. And we have set up the National Modern Apprenticeship Taskforce, which will look at how to increase the opportunities for young people to participate in Modern Apprenticeships and how to engage employers more fully in the programme.

More flexible patterns of employment can remove unnecessary inflexibilities and enable more men and women to balance work and family and other responsibilities. And it is important to look at new ways of ensuring that firms have the flexible working patterns they need and families have the flexible arrangements they need. So the government is not only looking carefully at employment regulation, but also at how we can empower mothers in particular to secure the benefits of more flexible working arrangements.

So we will resist inflexible barriers being introduced into directives like the European Working Time Directive and we will support flexible interpretations of existing rules and remove unnecessary regulations and restrictions.

In recent years attitudes to part-time work have changed. Companies have found flexible working patterns help them be more productive. Families have found that flexible working arrangements help them balance work and family responsibilities.

So most people who work part-time today do so not because there are no full-time jobs available but out of choice. So while temporary employment is half the European Union average, 6 per cent compared with 13 per cent in the EU, 25 per cent of our total employment is part-time and employees already work far more flexible hours than most EU countries.

One reason is our tax-credit system and the Childcare Tax Credit. And we continue to seek ways of making it easier and less costly for employees to balance their work and family responsibilities and for businesses to recruit.

That is why building on:

- our rise, from April, in maternity pay to £100 a week;
- the extension in paid maternity leave to twenty-six weeks;
- the first ever paternity and adoption pay;
- a new right for parents of young or disabled children to request flexible working; and
- the first ever National Childcare Strategy . . .

. . . we will consider further reforms: new tax and national-insurance incentives to expand employer-supported childcare; paying Childcare Credit for approved home child care by carers who are not already childminders; and increased flexibility in parental time off, including giving fathers time off to attend ante-natal appointments.

Lone parents genuinely worry that without flexible working patterns they will end up neglecting their children and fear that the price of employment may make it difficult to discharge family responsibilities. To ensure the balance is better, the Childcare and Child Tax Credits are not only making work pay for the single parent – £10 an hour for a part-time job – but ensuring that a decent income does not require them to work excessive hours damaging to their family life.

And because employers recognise these anxieties, a new employer taskforce is now examining how, among other measures, working patterns can be more flexible and child-care provision better to suit the needs of lone parents. With a national discussion of how we help lone parents balance work and family responsibilities, we can offer companies a smart solution to their employment needs, help thousands of lone parents move out of poverty from welfare into work, and reach our target of 70 per cent of lone parents in employment. And similar initiatives will also be forthcoming for men and women who have previously lost out in the old economy – such as the ethnic minorities – but who, by more flexible recruitment patterns, could gain in a new economy where we should see diversity as a source of strength.

While there are more than 900,000 men and women over fifty now in work compared with 1997, more flexible recruitment patterns could make it easier for older workers to move between jobs and tomorrow we are holding a summit of employers aimed at more flexible recruitment incentives for firms to take on the 1 million disabled men and women who want to work to find suitable employment.

To reduce unemployment and to achieve full employment we must not only focus on the needs of particular groups of the unemployed but also focus on regional and local flexibilities and so tackle the regional and local variations in unemployment rates, in skills, in the ability to create new jobs and generate new businesses. And here we are able to learn from the success of active labour-market policies especially in the Nordic countries and the low-unemployment countries of the European Union.

Without the New Deal, youth long-term unemployment would be twice as high and today inflows to Jobseekers Allowance are at their lowest since records began in 1967.

Unemployment in the UK is 5.1 per cent compared to 6 per cent in the US and 8.5 per cent in the Euro area.

But after six years of a national programme I am more convinced than ever that if we are to get more of the long-term unemployed back to work, and more successfully match vacancies to jobs, a full-employment strategy now demands regional and local flexibility as well as a national framework of incentives and sanctions. And this is needed too to increase the New Deal's ability both to respond in the event of a local or regional shock and to help the unemployed move into work more rapidly.

Today vacancies – 2.5 million notified at Jobcentres every year, 5 million overall – are still at historically high levels in almost every region and nation of the UK. And in relatively low-skilled trades like in hotels and catering 350,000 vacancies were reported last year. Often large numbers of vacancies exist side by side with large numbers of unemployed in adjacent communities. Tottenham, for example, has some of Britain's worst long-term male unemployment among its 5,000 unemployed while neighbouring districts have seen nearly 90,000 vacancies in the last nine months, with many more in the wider London economy.

So it makes sense for Jobcentres to develop programmes more sensitive to, and tailor-made for, local and regional conditions and to have greater flexibility and discretion to move people quickly into work, to stop too many long-term unemployed falling through the net, and to tackle shocks when they arise. So we should consider extending the areas of job search for the newly unemployed and as we combine flexibility with help for people coping with change we are prepared to help with initial transport costs where appropriate.

And while in France nearly 40 per cent of unemployed have been unemployed for more than a year, in Germany more than 50 per cent in Italy more than 60 per cent, Britain's 27 per cent compares unfavourably with 6 per cent in the USA so, with our Step Up and other programmes that require the long-term unemployed to take jobs on offer, we will consider an even greater emphasis on responsibilities as well as opportunities in moving the long-term unemployed back to work.

In the global economy it has been easier in the past for nations to respond to shocks when wages are either highly centralised at a national level or highly decentralised at a local level. In Britain only 5 per cent of private-sector workplaces are covered by multi-employer collective-bargaining arrangements – and many have profit-related pay schemes, helping to make pay more responsive to the economic cycle. Wage-setting tends to be local, annual and normally at a plant or workplace level.

But a willingness to be flexible in both the private and the public sectors can be matched with a guarantee of fairness. Indeed as the government has implemented its reforms to the tax and benefit system, two of the critical guarantees that have been put in place for people in work are the minimum wage and the Working and Child Tax Credits. Critics of the minimum wage have argued that it reduces the flexibility of the labour market by inhibiting the workings of the price mechanism, with the potential to create stronger wage growth throughout the economy and reduce employment. But research suggests that the minimum wage has not led to increased unemployment or inflationary earnings growth across the economy. Adjusted through regular reviews by the Low Pay Commission, who consider the effect on pay, employment and competitiveness, wages can still respond effectively to labour-market changes and there is no reason why the minimum wage cannot continue to be uprated and rise this year.

But an even stronger guarantee of fairness at work is the tax credits which provide not only an even more generous floor but work to sustain incomes up the earnings scale:

- while the minimum wage today is £147 for a 35-hour week, the minimum for a family with two children – through tax credits – is a net £275, almost twice as much;
- the minimum for a couple in work without children is £183 and for a single adult over twenty-five is £154;
- a single parent working sixteen hours is guaranteed £179, the equivalent of £10.10 an hour after taxes;

compared with a minimum wage of £4.20 an hour. It is the guarantee provided by tax credits on top of the minimum wage – not just a minimal safety net but support right up the income scale – which makes it possible for regional and local wage flexibility to operate without undermining basic fairness. And this guarantee would matter even more in circumstances where, as happens in the United States single-currency area, real wages may have to adjust in response to a shock. Because of the tax credits, a fall in wages of £1 impacts to the tune of 30p on the earner – just one-third – with the generous Child Tax Credit making the same true for incomes extended up the income scale.

So what are the next steps?

First, we need to do more to help the newly unemployed and the long-term unemployed back into work and help our labour market work better and more rapidly.

Second, we need to take forward our tax-credit reforms which match flexibility with fairness.

Thirdly, all key public-sector workers in London receive some form of London premium. There are London arrangements for teachers, nurses and policemen, with officers in the Metropolitan Police receiving free travel in the London area. And there are attempts at special housing-cost arrangements for public-sector workers with 10,000 key workers helped through the Starter Homes Initiative. Yet while professionals have benefited from London weighting and other arrangements it is clear that many lower-paid workers have been at risk of losing out. A more considered approach to local and regional conditions that pays attention to the needs of recruitment and retention makes sense. Reliable, timely regional prices and cost-of-living data can help inform the debate. So the review of regional information and the wider examination of statistics by Chris Allsop will help us address some of these issues, providing greater impetus to our objective of promoting economic growth in all regions and reducing the persistent gap in growth rates between the richest and poorest areas of our country.

But evidence so far suggests that the tax and benefit reforms introduced since 1997 have already improved the flexibility of the UK labour market. The unemployment trap – the trap that made it not worth while for unemployed men and women to take a job – has been addressed, work now pays more than benefits, and the reforms have extended support for families with children up the income scale, ensuring not only that work pays but that more people are protected from the impact of economic shocks.

So by examining the challenges ahead, we open up a rich reform and modernisation agenda for our product, capital and labour markets, an agenda of economic reform not just for the future of Britain but for the future of Europe. And policies for flexibility need not be implemented at the expense of fairness but can move forward together, indeed in support of each other, in ways that ensure that genuine concerns in Britain and in Europe about the importance of social cohesion are not swept aside or forgotten but rather recognised and addressed in ways consistent with the realities of today's global economy and of tomorrow's.

And we have shown today that greater flexibility in both Britain and Europe is good for Britain and Europe. We have learnt from Europe's emphasis on skills, on the social foundations of markets, and on social cohesion. And through the Luxembourg employment initiative and then the Lisbon economic-reform agenda we continue to learn from each other. But we also learnt – and this is an important message especially for trade unionists committed to full employment – that to achieve full employment in Europe we have to learn from the best of American flexibilities and sweep aside the worst of European inflexibilities. Indeed, in the future, achieving a full-employment economy will need much of the flexibility of America applied to much of Europe. And I have suggested a programme of economic reform not just in Britain but in Europe – a programme upon which I will elaborate in greater detail in my Budget and beyond.

In its history – from our Industrial Revolution through Empire – Britain has stood out: a beacon to the rest of the world as a land of enterprise – of invention, of commerce, of creativity – and of fairness.

As we prepare for the world upturn and to meet the long-term challenges of globalisation, Britain has a unique opportunity to be, once again, a beacon to the world, advancing enterprise and fairness together – a dynamic, vibrant economy that is the first economy in the new era of globalisation to match flexibility with fairness and, in doing so, to attain the high levels of growth and employment that are the best route to prosperity for all.

6

ADVANCING THE PUBLIC INTEREST

The public interest is an important but also an elusive concept. Its definition itself is the subject of political debate. Gordon Brown's position in this debate is clear: 'opportunity and security for all'. Accepting this notion the question remains how this interest can best be served, and here the Labour leader and long-serving Chancellor of the Exchequer has given his own reply.

It is in two parts. One is insistence that there must be a common floor on which all citizens stand. Gordon Brown does not refer to the idea of basic income guarantees but his concern with poverty, notably child poverty, and with the belief that work must pay, has led him to a number of measures which are stepping stones to a secure income for all: the minimum wage, welfare-to-work measures, tax credits at least for working families are elements of what may be described as a policy of citizenship.

This is of crucial importance; but the other part of Gordon Brown's route to the public interest has become his personal trademark. He respects the history of both the political left and the right. The state has a role in correcting serious market failures, and markets have a role in remedying state failures. But in order to avoid the costly errors of repeated pendulum swings from one to the other, a more stable approach has to be developed. It consists in giving each, government and business, the state and the market, its place, but above all in developing new forms of partnerships between the two which provide stability and flexibility at the same time.

Gordon Brown's original contribution to Britain's long-term prosperity but also to the politics of socio-economic progress generally, lies in imaginative combinations of historically separate institutions and approaches. Arms-length public institutions are one method, the Bank of England being the first example. At the other end, binding in the private sector into long-term relationships with the public sector' has the same purpose. PFI, the Private Finance Initiative, is an example, as are PPPs, Public Private Partnerships of many kinds. One point to be added here is Gordon Brown's deep interest in the Third Sector, and in partnerships between public, private and philanthropic institutions (PPPs as it were) which include a 'public-interest test' for the latter.

Some may prefer a greater liberal emphasis on the independence of non-state actors, others may find it easier to rely on the benevolence of the state. There can be no doubt, however, that Gordon Brown has introduced a wide range of alternatives into our understanding of the public sphere, and more, that he has practised what he preached. His speeches on the public interest demonstrate his achievement but also stimulate further debate.

Lord Ralf Dahrendorf

In an important speech to the Social Market Foundation on 3 February 2003, entitled 'A Modern Agenda for Prosperity and Social Reform', the Chancellor set out his most thoroughgoing appreciation of how to determine the respective roles of the public and private sectors in advancing the public interest. In particular there is an attempt to define what the public interest is – in his words: 'policies which create a Britain where there is opportunity and security not just for some but for all and the equity, efficiency and diversity necessary to achieve it.' There are extended sections on the role of government in relation to the creation and operation of markets; definitions of where markets

should not be permitted; and thoughts about how best to harness
the creativity and innovation of the private sector in provision of
public services. The speech marks a major advance on the
arguments deployed so far in this debate. As the Chancellor
says, it is time to face up to fundamental questions that cannot be
sidestepped about the role and limits of government and markets – questions, in fact, about the respective responsibilities of
individuals, markets and communities, including the role of the
state. He notes that in almost every area of current policy
controversy – the future of the private-finance initiative, of health
care, of universities, of industrial policy, of the European economic-reform agenda, of public services generally – the question
is, at root, both what is the best relationship between individuals,
markets and government to advance the public interest; and also
whether it is possible to set aside, and move beyond, the old
sterile and debilitating conflicts of the past.

The Chancellor states the issue with great clarity: how can we
renegotiate the relationship between markets and government?
His view is that agreeing on where markets have an enhanced
role and where market failure has to be addressed is absolutely
central to the next stage of the new Labour project. To hold on
to old, discredited dogmas about what should remain in the
public sector and how the public sector operates, or to confuse
the public interest with producer interests, makes no sense for a
reforming party and, as technologies and aspirations change,
would lead to sclerosis and make it impossible to achieve the
government's goals. His plea is that the party 'must not adhere to
failed means, lest it fails to achieve enduring ends'. Equally, to
fail to put the case for a reformed public sector, where the case is
strong, not only leads directly to the allegation that new labour
merely imitates old Conservatism, but also makes it impossible to
achieve the efficient and equitable outcomes that the government is seeking. As long as it can be alleged that there is no
clarity as to where the market requires an enhanced role (in
which the government enables markets to work better by tackling

market failure), and where markets have no role at all, then the impression may be given that the only kind of reform that is valuable is a form of privatisation. If so, new Labour will have failed to advance the case for a renewed and reformed public realm for the coming decades.

Since 1997, our government's central objective, the heart of our vision for a prosperous Britain, has been to promote opportunity and security for all. Our first priority was to address our country's chronic long-term failures in macro-economic policy. And in government we had the strength to take difficult decisions, including to freeze public spending for two years, as we constructed a new monetary and fiscal regime. But a sound macro-economic framework is a necessary but not sufficient condition to achieve, in what is an increasingly competitive global economy, a Britain where there is opportunity and security not just for some but for all.

So successive Budgets have sought to promote, on the one hand, competition, innovation, and the enterprise economy, and on the other hand, the New Deal, tax credits and public-service reform as the routes to an efficient and fair Britain in which individuals can realise their potential. Achieving these objectives demands the courage to push forward with all the radical long-term reforms necessary to enhance productivity and to improve public services, and, as we do so, we must have the strength to face up to fundamental questions that cannot be sidestepped about the role and limits of government and markets – questions, in fact, about the respective responsibilities of individuals, for markets and communities, including the role of the state.

Indeed, in almost every area of current controversy – the future of the private-finance initiative, of health care, of universities, of industrial policy, of the European economic-reform agenda, of public services generally – the question is, at root, what is the best relationship between individuals, markets and government to advance the public interest and whether it is possible to set aside, and indeed move beyond, the old sterile and debilitating conflicts of the past.

Take the health service. The essential question in a world of advancing technology, expensive drugs and treatments, and rising expectations, is whether efficiency, equity and responsiveness to the patient are best delivered through a public health-care system or whether, as with commodities generally, market arrangements, such as the hospital selling and the patient buying, are the best route to advancing the public interest.

Take higher education. Our universities operate in an increasingly global marketplace and at the same time their excellence depends upon drawing upon the widest pool of talent – making change inevitable and necessary. And one of the central questions round the world is the extent to which universities should become, in effect, the seller, setting their own price for their service, and the prospective graduate the buyer of higher education at the going rate, whether through an upfront or deferred system of payment, and what are the consequences for equity and efficiency as well as choice of such arrangements.

Take the private-finance initiative. The argument is whether, at a time of unprecedented need for investment in our public infrastructure, for example in hospitals and schools, the private sector can provide the benefits of efficiency and value for money to promote what most agree is the public interest: schooling and health care free for all at the point of need.

Take industrial policy. The essential question is whether, when global competition is challenging every industry, the state should replace market forces where they fail – the old Labour policy; whether the state should refuse to intervene at all even in the face of market failure – the old Tory *laissez-faire*; whether we should second-guess the market through a corporatist policy of supporting national champions – a policy I also reject; or whether, as I would propose, the best industrial policy for success in a global economy is to help markets work better.

Or take European economic reform. The question is how far, in a world where business must respond quickly and people must adapt to change, Europe is willing to go beyond old assumptions that flexibility is the enemy of social justice and recognise that the right kind of flexibility in European labour, capital and product markets can advance not only economic efficiency but also social cohesion.

In each area the questions are, at root, whether the public interest – that is opportunity and security for all – and the equity, efficiency and diversity necessary to achieve it, is best advanced by more or less reliance on markets or through substituting a degree of public control or ownership for the market and whether, even when there is public-sector provision, there can be contestability. Every modern generation – since Adam Smith counterposed the invisible hand of the market to the helping hand of government – has had to resolve this question for its time: what are the respective spheres for individuals, markets and communities, including the state, in achieving opportunity and security for their citizens. In the United States in the 1930s the New Deal – and in Britain in the 1940s, in a different way, nationalisation and the Welfare State – established new paradigms. Whole areas traditionally left to markets became regulated or owned by the state in the avowed interests of efficiency and equity.

In the 1960s and 1970s Labour's story could be summed up by the story of the breakdown of that relationship as – in the way Anthony Crosland predicted – old forms of collectivism were seen to fail. And, when Labour refused to update our conception of the respective roles of markets and state, and take on vested interests, the government also failed.

In the 1980s there was an attempt – some of it largely successful, as in utilities, and some of it unsuccessful, as in health – to withdraw the state from areas where previously the public interest was seen to be equated with public ownership. But by 1997 major questions about the relationships between individuals, markets and communities, including the role of the state, remained unanswered. On the other hand, it is also true that in every single post-war decade – on both sides of the political spectrum – the centralised state was wrongly seen to be the main, and sometimes the sole, expression of community, often usurping the case for localities and neighbourhoods taking more responsibility for the decisions that affect their lives.

The question I want to focus specifically on today is how, for a new decade in which globalisation and technology are challenging traditional assumptions anyway, we renegotiate the relationship between markets and government. Agreeing on where markets have an enhanced role and where market failure has to be addressed is, in my view, absolutely central to the next stage of the new Labour project. To hold to old discredited dogmas about what should remain in the public sector and how the public sector operates, or to confuse the public interest with producer interests, makes no sense for a reforming party and, as technologies and aspirations change, would lead to sclerosis and make it impossible to obtain our enduring goals. We must not adhere to failed means lest we fail to achieve enduring ends. Equally, to fail to put the case for a reformed public sector where the case is strong not only leads directly to the allegation from our opponents that new Labour merely imitates old Conservatism but also makes it impossible to achieve the efficient and equitable outcomes we seek.

As long as it can be alleged that there is no clarity as to where the market requires an enhanced role, where we should enable markets to work better by tackling market failure, and where markets have no role at all, an uncertain trumpet sounds and we risk giving the impression that the only kind of reform that is valuable is a form of privatisation and we fail to advance – as we should – the case for a renewed and reformed public realm for the coming decades

By stating our vision clearly, however, we can bring to an end the sterile and self-defeating argument over PFI where producer interests have often been wrongly presented as the public interest; move forward from what has been a debate insufficiently explicit on the role of public and private providers in some of our public services; and, most of all, open up a broad and challenging agenda for prosperity and social reform. In the last parliament we overturned old Labour shibboleths, rejected an old-style Keynesian assumption that there was a trade-off between inflation and growth, and, in making the Bank of England independent and applying fresh rules, procedures and systems of accountability in a new monetary and fiscal regime, sought to make Labour the party of stability and economic competence.

Now we need to affirm a yet more radical break with Labour's past – and in this parliament go further. By drawing the proper distinction between those areas where markets require an enhanced role; where, by tackling market failure, we can enable markets to work better; and where markets cannot deliver opportunity and security for all, we can, with confidence, make new Labour the party not just of social justice but of markets, competition and enterprise and show that advancing enterprise and fairness together best equips our country to succeed in the global economy.

I have said that the respective role of markets and the public sector has been the underlying, even if sometimes the unspoken, divide at the heart of British political arguments for nearly a century. But let us be clear at the outset where there is at least consensus. Left and right have always agreed that there is a sphere of relationships – which encompasses family, faith and civic society – that should never be reduced to transactions, either buying and selling, or to diktat, state command and control. In his recent Dimbleby Lecture on the market state the new Archbishop of Canterbury, and in his recent book *The Dignity of Difference* the Chief Rabbi, Dr Jonathan Sacks – profound and influential thinkers who have led the debate – tell us that while there are areas where the market is legitimate, there are areas where to impose market transactions in human relationships is to go beyond the bounds of what is acceptable, indeed where to do so corrodes the very virtues which markets rely upon for success.

Markets, they would suggest, may be the best way of constructing exchanges, and thus providing many goods and services, but are not good ways of structuring human relationships. They also argue that while, generally, markets are good at creating wealth they are less good at guaranteeing fairness and opportunity for all – and certainly not normally good at dealing with their social consequences. And they conclude that many of the choices we make cannot be made through markets alone and to have faith in markets cannot justify us sidestepping fundamental moral questions. Quite simply it is an unacceptable market fundamentalism that leaves markets to take care of all their consequences.

The political philosopher Walzer talks of 'blocked exchanges' – some things that are not and should not be for sale and are off limits. In the same way, the economist Okun has said that the market needs a place and the market needs to be kept in place. Everyone but an economist, he says, knows without asking why money shouldn't buy some things.

But that agreement between left and right extends beyond a proper distinction between the sphere of relationships and that of transactions and recognition of what Michael Sandel calls 'the moral limits of markets'. Both left and right generally agree also that markets are best seen as a means and not ends. Of course some on the right have argued that because market exchanges are freely entered into, markets define freedom; and the left have often slipped into arguing that because markets cannot cope with their social consequences, they are a threat to equality, liberty and the realisation of human potential; but both left and right say that for them markets or the public sector are means not ends.

There should indeed be a legitimate debate between left

and right about values and the stress we place on opportunity and equity, while safeguarding the importance of liberty. But the debate between left and right need not be any longer a debate about whether there should be a market-based economy or not.

But beyond this consensus, it is the respective role of markets and the public sector that has been the greatest dividing line between left and right. For the left historically it has been a matter of dogma to define the public interest – opportunity and security for all – as diminishing the sphere of markets; and for the right it has been historically a matter of ideology to expand the role of markets.

Why? Because for the left markets are too often seen as leading to inequality, insecurity and injustice. In this view, enterprise is the enemy of fairness, and the interests of social justice are fundamentally opposed to the interests of a competitive economy. The left's remedy has therefore been seen to lie in relegating the impact and scope of the market – through greater public ownership, regulation and state intervention. Indeed for nearly a century the left in Britain wrongly equated the public interest with public ownership and at times came near to redefining one means – public ownership – as a sole end in itself.

For the right, on the other hand, it is the absence rather than the prevalence of markets that is to blame. This benign, neo-liberal view of markets sees them as sufficient to produce a combination of liberty, equality, efficiency and prosperity. And so as Professor Michael Barber records of a conversation with a Treasury official during the 1980s: 'It doesn't really matter what the issue is,' the civil servant said, 'we know that the question we have to ask is, "How do we create a market?" ' – the prescription on every occasion: deregulation, marketisation and the withdrawal of the state.

So for the left opportunity and security for all is prejudiced by reliance on markets. For the right opportunity and security for those who deserve it is only possible by greater reliance on markets. These views – too much market on the one hand, too little market on the other – have defined the terrain of political debate in Britain and elsewhere in the post-war period.

Yet for all their differences both views reflect the same doctrinaire approach to the question of the role of markets. Whether markets are seen as the cause or the solution to inequality of opportunity and insecurity, they have been seen by the left and right as universally so – the vices and virtues of markets applying everywhere or nowhere. The result is that neither left nor right has been able to contribute to a considered view, and therefore a viable policy agenda, for where markets can serve the public interest and where they cannot.

So we start from a failure on the part of the left: that the left has too often failed to admit not just that, in order to promote productivity, we need markets but also that we should normally tackle market failure not by abolishing markets but by strengthening markets and enabling them to work better. But we also start from a failure of the right: the right's failure to understand that there are some areas where markets are not appropriate and where market failure can only be dealt with through public action.

So the argument that is often put as public versus private, or markets versus state, does not reflect the complexity of the challenges we face: that markets are part of advancing the public interest and the left are wrong to say they are not; but also that markets are not always in the public interest and the right is wrong to automatically equate the imposition of markets with the public interest. The challenge for new Labour is, while remaining true to our values and goals, to have the courage to affirm that markets are a means of advancing the public interest; to strengthen markets where they work and to tackle market failures to enable markets to work better. And instead of the left's old, often knee-jerk, anti-market sentiment, to assert with confidence that promoting the market economy helps us achieve our goals of a stronger economy and a fairer society.

So in this speech I want to achieve three purposes. First, to show how a progressive government seeking a strong economy and fair society should not only support but positively enhance markets in the public interest. Second, applying that same public-interest test, to recognise that there are limits to markets – not only where, as a matter of morality, we have always accepted they have no place, but also in those areas as a matter of practicality where they do not and cannot be made to work, and hence where we should support public provision as the more equitable, efficient and responsive solution. Third, to set out how we can avoid the trap of simply replacing market failure with state failure and, applying the same public-interest test, achieve equity, efficiency and diversity by reforming and modernising the public realm for the decades ahead, in particular through devolution, transparency and accountability.

First, advancing markets where they are in the public interest. In 1994, after Tony Blair led the abolition of Clause Four of the Labour Party's constitution, our first decision, which I announced two days after, was to revamp Labour's competition policy. We did so because we recognised that competition – not the absence of it – was essential not just to an efficient economy but also to a fair society. Indeed in a break from a hundred years of Labour history I said that the public interest required a pro-competition policy that would deliver efficiency, choice and lower consumer prices. Some asked us why we were extending markets when all around us we see the failures of the market economy. I argued that where there was insufficient competition our aim should be to enable markets to work better.

I said then too that we needed not just a new pro-

competition policy but also a new industrial policy whose aim
was not to second-guess, relegate or replace markets but to
enable markets to work better. People asked me why I
proposed this when it was clear that in Britain short-termism
and low investment were glaring examples of chronic market
failure. My opponents within Labour argued that the last
thing we should do was to extend markets. The best industrial
policy, they said, was the old one: as markets fail, to replace
markets with state action – national investment banks, national enterprise boards; import controls to protect big companies; even nationalisation of financial institutions. But I said
that markets here failed because special interests were undermining their dynamism. Here again the new industrial policy
should be to enable markets to work better and successfully
extend them and harness the initiative, creativity, innovation
and coordination which can come from the decentralisation
and dynamism of properly functioning markets – that is,
where there is:

- first – if not perfect information – fair and accurate
  information possessed by the consumer;
- second – if not perfect competition – fair competition
  between many suppliers with low barriers to entry and
  producers who are not monopolists with the power to
  dictate prices; and
- third, with mobility, capital and labour, like consumers,
  free to go elsewhere.

And it is ever more important that markets are strengthened.
While twenty years ago, even ten years ago, it was just about
possible – if costly and wrong – to protect and insulate
companies, sectors or whole economies from global competition, there is now no longer any safe haven from the ineffi-
ciency and uncompetitiveness of the past. With hardly a good
or service not subject to intense global competition it is not

only unwise but impossible to shelter our goods and services markets by subsidies or by other forms of protectionism without long-term damage. Indeed, competitiveness abroad is best served by competition at home so in the modern global economy stronger markets become more and more necessary.

So our new approach leads to fundamental changes in direction from the old policy approach. Instead of being suspicious of competition, we should embrace it, recognising that without it vested interests accumulate, and, instead of tolerating monopoly or cartels which were never in the public interest, or appeasing special interests, we should systematically extend competition – forcing producers to be efficient, extending the choices available to consumers and opening up opportunity for the ambitious and the risk-takers. Instead of being lukewarm about free trade, free trade not protectionism is essential to opportunity and security for all, and instead of the old protectionism we advocate open markets. Instead of being suspicious of enterprise and entrepreneurs, we should celebrate an entrepreneurial culture – encouraging, incentivising and rewarding the dynamic and enthusing more people from all backgrounds and all areas to start up businesses – here again enabling markets to work better and strengthening the private economy. Instead of thinking the state must take over responsibility where markets deliver insufficient investment and short-termism in innovation, skills and environmental protection, we must enable markets to work better and for the long term – here again the case for state intervention is not to extend the role of the state but wherever possible to tackle market failure and help make markets work better. Instead of the old centralisation that characterised industrial policy – promoting 'national champions' or 'picking winners' or offering subsidies to loss-makers – our industrial policy should reject special privileges for anyone – embracing a level playing field for all – and should aim to deliver higher growth and jobs in every region with a new decentralising regional policy that addresses market failures in skills and innovation closer to home at the local level. Instead of extending regulation unnecessarily to restrict the scope of markets, we should systematically pinpoint services where regulation does not serve the public interest and can be reduced. Instead of thinking of employment policy as maintaining people in old jobs even when technological and other change is inevitable, it is by combining flexibility – helping people move from one job to another – with active intervention to provide skills, information and income support that is the best route to full employment. And instead of viewing flexibility as the enemy of social cohesion, we should recognise that the right kind of flexibility in European labour, capital and product markets is becoming even more essential for competitiveness and that while government does have a role to play in easing the transition for those affected by change, it should not involve itself in resisting change.

So what are the next steps in the economic-reform agenda that will shape our Budget decisions this spring and help us towards higher productivity and thus towards a Britain of opportunity and security for all?

First, in testing times for every national economy it is ever more important to pursue policies for monetary and fiscal stability. The recent volatility in global stock markets – with US markets (S&P 500) now down 44 per cent since their peak, UK markets (FTSE 100) down 49 per cent, France (CAC 40) down 58 per cent and Germany (DAX) down 66 per cent – has demonstrated once again that no country can insulate itself from the ups and downs of the world economy. I understand the concerns that uncertainty causes for investors and consumers alike. Indeed it is because we have always understood that monetary and fiscal regimes must work well in challenging times as well as good times that – with tough decisions in 1997 on deficit and debt reduction, including a two-year freeze on spending in the late 1990s – we sought to ensure that Britain is better placed than we have been in the past to deal with economic challenges and ongoing risks.

And at all times we will have the strength to take the tough decisions. Instead of being, as in previous downturns, first into recession and last out, the country that normally suffers most, Britain has continued to grow in every quarter over the past six years while other major economies have been in recession. The true test of economic policy is whether it can cope with difficult as well as good times and I am confident that tested in adversity our system will demonstrate its credibility and resilience. With our fundamentals sound, and debt low, we have met our fiscal rules, are meeting our fiscal rules and will continue to meet our fiscal rules. And with interest rates, inflation and unemployment at record lows, this is indeed the right time, building on that underlying stability, to push ahead with competition, enterprise and productivity reforms in our economy so that in an increasingly competitive and uncertain world we can secure higher levels of long-term growth.

So, secondly, in every product and almost every service we must do more to open up competition. Having already in the past six years gone a long way:

- independence for the competition authorities;
- as Dr Irwin Stelzer proposed, introducing trust-busting incentives and criminal penalties for those engaging in cartels;
- giving the Office of Fair Trading a proactive role in investigating markets;
- dealing with a range of professions where regulation has been an excuse for vested interests and exclusions from entry; and,
- in the EU, demanding improvements to the functioning of the single market . . .

. . . we have a long way still to go.

The independent Office of Fair Trading is currently investigating the markets in liability insurance, private dentistry, estate agents, taxis, and doorstep selling. It has reported on many industries, including most recently the market for prescription drugs, recommending reforms that expose them to the bracing winds of competition. We look forward to tough pro-competition decisions and for them to continue to scrutinise areas where we expect them to do more. But the competition test should apply to the public sector as well as the private sector. And I hope that the OFT will use to the full their new powers to investigate all those areas where not just the private sector but the public sector through regulation or its actions unjustifiably restricts competition.

This month we will publish our progress report on European economic reform with detailed proposals, based on the pro-market principles I have set down, for further labour-, product- and capital-market deregulation, for a new approach to state aids, for support for private finance initiatives in Europe, for action to prevent British firms from being excluded from European markets from energy and telecommunications to agriculture, and for extending the principles of a strong, proactive and independent competition regime to the EU. And we will progressively seek to tackle barriers to a fully open trading and commercial relationship between Europe and America – strengthening joint arrangements to tackle competition issues.

Third, we must take far more seriously the need for urgent progress in the post-Doha trade discussions. And in the case of Europe, sooner or later Europe's leaders must come together to tackle, at root, agricultural protectionism, which imposes enormous costs on taxpayers, consumers and the world's poorest people.

Fourth, around one-third of our country's productivity gains come from new entrants challenging and then replacing existing companies so the Budget will continue our work of removing barriers to business success – the government on the side of small business:

- helping to cut the cost of starting, investing, hiring and training;
- continuing our reforms of the business tax regime for enterprise and entrepreneurs and capital gains;
- opening up public procurement to small firms; and
- moving forward with measures to encourage the entrepreneurial culture.

Fifth, where markets by themselves cannot deliver the long-term returns from investing in skills and new technologies, and cannot safeguard the environment for the long term, it is right to act.

- So where firms, large or small, cannot themselves make the large investments needed in basic research, it is right for government to attempt to safeguard their intellectual property rights more fully and to share the costs.
- And it is right to build on the new employer-skills pilots and to forge a new partnership between government, employee and employer with a view to making labour markets work more flexibly.
- Where there are barriers to the unemployed getting back to work, it is right to extend both the opportunities and the compulsion of the New Deal, ensuring labour markets are more flexible as we tackle the social and economic causes of unemployment.
- Where capital markets are short-termist and fail in the long term we should press ahead with the Cruickshank, Myners and Sandler reforms and be prepared to build on our Capital Gains Tax reforms (short-term rates at 40p to long-term rates at 10p) to encourage the long-term view.

- And our approach to the environment must not only be to prevent environmental damage but to offer incentives to invest in environment-friendly technologies.

Sixth, this emphasis on market solutions to market failures – and rejection of old-style centrally imposed industrial policies – demands a new regionally based policy focusing on local enterprise, skills and innovation. And our new regional-policy consultation document urging greater devolution of powers from the European Commission will be published shortly. We are removing the last of the permanent, ongoing subsidies for operating costs in coal, shipbuilding and steel and as the DTI Secretary of State is showing, the old days of the 'sponsorship' department are over, freeing up resources to enhance the DTI's role in promoting competition and enabling markets to work better.

The measures for competition, trade, enterprise, science and skills, and regions take us along the road towards a Britain of opportunity and security for all. They mean a more efficient economy that delivers more opportunity. But the extent to which we go further and ensure opportunity and security for all depends upon a further set of political choices. Let me give a few examples.

For a party that does not care about opportunity for all, need be at best agnostic on those excluded from it. But for a party for whom equity matters a central element of a pro-competition policy is to remove all the old barriers that prevent new entrants, and – integral to a skills and education policy – draw on the talents of not just some but the widest range of people and their potential. In both cases the most equitable solution is also likely to be the most efficient.

A party unconcerned about equity would be agnostic about the need for regional policy or be against it. I have suggested that an effective regional policy is economically efficient but those who are most concerned about divisions between

regions and the inequalities that result will wish to demonstrate that balanced economic growth is not only in the
interests of the least prosperous regions but in the interests
of regions where prosperity can bring congestion, overcrowd-
ing and overheating.

Too often, in Britain, unlike America, opportunities to start
a business have seemed accessible mainly to a closed circle of
the privileged so those of us who believe in opportunity for all
will wish to go furthest in promoting enterprise for all. In the
poorest areas in Britain, where only one business is created
for every six in the wealthier areas, and where not only family
savings but also bank capital at the right price is often
unavailable even where men and women show initiative
and dynamism, our whole approach must radically change.
Enabling markets to work better for the enterprising demands that we remove the old barriers to enterprise that
discriminate against lower-income groups and hard-hit unemployment black spots where the enterprise culture is
already weakest and open up wider access to capital, management expertise, telecommunications and financial advice:
active intervention to widen economic opportunities irrespective of background. So in tackling these market failures –
especially failures in the availability of information and the
mobility of capital – a new agenda opens up that helps
markets work better and delivers opportunity for all. It is
our answer to those who allege that we can only pursue equity
at the cost of efficiency, a demonstration that equity and
efficiency need not be enemies but can be allies in the
attainment of opportunity and security for all. Here social
justice – equality of opportunity and fairness of outcomes –
not bought at the cost of a successful economy but as part of
achieving such a success – a point I made when I gave the
Smith Lecture six years ago, an agenda that must continue to
be at the centre of our thinking and policy-making.

I have sought to show that markets can sometimes fail. We

also know that public services can fail, too. The experience of telephones, gas, electricity and water was of public-sector monopolies created to guarantee supply of service but which had become, over time, not an empowerment for the consumer but a restriction of their choices. In opposition, Labour had to come to terms with and accept the privatisation of telecoms. We saw that with the right framework – regulation only where necessary and light touch wherever possible – we could create the conditions in which markets could work in the public interest and deliver choice, efficiency and a fair deal for consumers. Too often the Tory approach was pro-privatisation but not pro-competition – to privatise without liberalising or regulating in conditions where private vested interests replaced public vested interests and denied the consumer choice, thus undermining the public interest.

Our insight was to see that the Tory solution was a private-sector solution at the expense of markets and, in the end, of the public interest. In this and other areas we knew that if we could ensure competition, proper flows of information and mobility of labour and capital – and thus help markets work better – then the consumer would gain from the efficiencies that would result and the extension of choice achieved, and that, over time, the regulation necessary to ensure security of supply for all could be diminished. But interestingly the Tory solution was to equate support for private sector and private business with support for markets. They adopted a pro-private-sector policy which replaced public-sector mono-polies with private-sector monopolies and failed to develop a pro-market policy where there was genuine competition, the possibility of new entrants and proper flow of information to, and choice for, consumers. Indeed when they privatised they often failed to put in place the conditions for effective markets. Instead they privatised rather than liberalised and the old monopolies returned this time but in the private sector.

It has been for new Labour to insist in opposition and in government that utility reform must promote a market economy (and not just a privatised economy) and that we liberalise where possible and regulate where necessary so that the needs of the consumer are best advanced. So while some on the left still say we should be anti-market and renationalise, in these areas our values can best be advanced through markets working in the public interest. So this is our approach to utilities:

- We are opening up to greater competition utilities like water and postal services.
- As markets fully develop we will withdraw unnecessary regulation while never putting at risk opportunity and security for all.
- We will ensure that the new consumer watchdogs now in place – for example, Postwatch, Energywatch and Water Voice – represent and empower consumers effectively; and that regulators make regulatory impact assessments – including effects on competition – standard practice for all significant new proposals.
- And we will press in Europe for the same liberalisation for energy and utility services: at all times our approach shaped by our view that the public interest can best be guaranteed with market means of delivery through the price mechanism.

And we cannot either hold to old ideas about what should be in the public sector when there is no justification for it. This demands we look at services to consumers where traditionally the public sector has been used and where markets are seen to have failed – but where, in future, markets, with their dynamism, capacity for innovation and enhancement of choice, can better respond to new technology and rising aspirations. Already we have proposed a shareholder executive bringing together all government shareholdings. And we have insisted on all government assets being publicly accounted for. And where there is no justification for them being in the public sector – indeed where the answer to market failure has wrongly been seen to be public ownership – we must be honest with ourselves – as with a range of industries and services already from the government's shares in privatised companies and from QinetiQ to the Tote – about the changes necessary when the public interest is best advanced not by government ownership but by markets.

Enhancing markets will mean reducing government. But – as I suggested in a series of articles and speeches last autumn and as the Chief Economic Adviser to the Treasury also argued in his New Localism pamphlet last year – we must also have the courage to recognise where markets do not work. Our clear and robust defence of markets must be combined with a clear and robust recognition of their limits. Let me explain.

For most consumer goods, markets adjust to preferences and thus to demand and supply on a continuous basis. But what about situations where this not only does not happen but the market failures cannot be corrected through market-based government intervention to make the price mechanism work? What of situations where there are clear externalities and clear social costs that cannot, even with the use of economic instruments, be fully captured by the price mechanism? What of situations also where there are multiple distortions in the price and supply disciplines and where even the removal of one distortion to create a purer market may turn a second-best outcome into a third-best outcome?

Take health care – the successful delivery of which has proved to be a mammoth challenge in every modern industrial country. The economics of health care are complicated and difficult. No sensible person pretends to have all of the answers to all of the complex, interrelated and excruciatingly difficult policy problems that rapidly rising demand, expectations and costs create. The only thing that is certain is that, as technologies change and needs change too, changes will follow in health-care delivery, now and for the foreseeable future. But those of us in positions of responsibility cannot afford the luxury of inaction: we have to come up with the best system we can devise and be prepared to adapt it in the light of changing technology and the rapidly changing needs of our citizens. The modern model for the British NHS – as set down by the government and the Secretary of State for Health – embodies not just clear national clinical and access standards but clear accountability, local delivery of services, independent inspection, patient choice, and contestability to drive efficiency and reward innovation. The free-market position which would – on the proposals of the Conservative Health Spokesman – lead us to privatised hospitals and some system of vouchers and extra payments for treatments – starts by viewing health care as akin to a commodity to be bought and sold like any other through the price mechanism. But in health care we know that the consumer is not sovereign: use of health care is unpredictable and can never be planned by the consumer in the way that, for example, weekly food consumption can.

So we know:

- that the ordinary market simply cannot function and because nobody can be sure whether they need medicinal treatment and if so when and what, individuals, families and entire societies will seek to insure themselves against the eventuality of being ill;
- that in every society, this uncertainty leads to the pooling of risks; and
- that the question is – on efficiency grounds – what is the best insurance system for sharing these risks?

A year ago when the government examined the funding of health care we concluded that, with uncertainty about risk, insurers often have poor information on which to base their risk assessment of the customer; that as a result of these uncertainties – and, with many citizens considered too high a risk, too expensive and therefore excluded – there are serious inefficiencies in private pricing and purchasing. Indeed in the United States some insurance policies are now thought to have a 40 per cent loading simply to cover the administrative costs involved in risk-profiling and billing, and today premiums average around $100 a week, are rising by 13 per cent a year, and even then often exclude high-cost treatments. Forty-one million Americans are uninsured.

And in my Social Market Foundation lecture a year ago I argued that on efficiency and equity grounds private insurance policies that by definition rely for their viability on ifs, buts and small print and can cover only some of the people some of the time should not be preferred against policies that can cover all of the people all of the time. But I also argued on efficiency as well as equity grounds that the case for such a comprehensive national insurance policy was greater now than in 1948 when the scientific and technological limitations of medicine were such that high-cost interventions were rare or very rare – there was no chemotherapy for cancer, cardiac surgery was in its infancy, intensive care barely existed, hip and knee replacement operations were almost unknown.

I argued that today the standard of technology and treatment is such that, unlike 1948, some illnesses or injuries could cost £20,000, £50,000 or even £100,000 to treat and cure and I suggested that because the costs of treatment and of drugs are now much higher than ever, and the risks to family finances much greater than ever – not just for poorer families but for comfortably-off families up the income scale – therefore the need for comprehensive insurance cover of health care is much stronger than ever.

But the very same reasoning which leads us to the case for the public funding of health care on efficiency as well as equity grounds also leads us to the case for public provision of health care. Let me explain.

The market for health care is dominated by the combination of, on the one hand, chronically imperfect and asymmetric information, and the potentially catastrophic and irreversible outcome of health-care decisions based on that information and, on the other, the necessity of local clusters of medical and surgical specialisms. This means that while in a conventional well-functioning market the price set by the producer is the most efficient, in health not only is the consumer not sovereign but a free market in health care will not produce the most efficient price for its services or a fair deal for its consumer. Take the asymmetry of information between the consumer as patient – who may, for example, be unknowingly ill, poorly informed of available treatments, reliant on others to understand the diagnosis, uncertain about the effectiveness of different medical interventions and thus is not sovereign – and the producer. With the consumer unable – as in a conventional market – to seek out the best product at the lowest price, and information gaps that cannot – even over the long term – be satisfactorily bridged, the results of a market failure for the patient can be long term, catastrophic and irreversible. So even if there are risks of state failure, there is a clear market failure.

But market failures do not only exist because of asymmetry of information and the irreversibility of decisions but because local emergency hospitals are – in large part – clusters of essential medical and surgical specialities and have characteristics that make them akin to natural local monopolies:

- 50 per cent of admissions, 75 per cent of hospital beds taken up by emergency, urgent or maternity cases –

non-elective cases where patients are generally unable to shop around;

- the need for guaranteed security of supply which means that, generally, a local hospital could not be allowed to go out of business;
- the need also for clusters of mutually reinforcing specialities (trauma, pathology and emergency medicine, for example);
- a high volume of work to guarantee quality of service;
- the economies of scale and scope, making it difficult to tackle these market failures by market solutions; and
- as the US system has also demonstrated, it is also difficult for private-sector contracts to anticipate and specify the range of essential characteristics we demand of a health care system.

So the many market failures in health care, if taken individually, challenge the adequacy of markets to provide efficient market solutions. But what could happen when these market failures – the asymmetry of information between consumer and producer, clusters of local specialisms, and the difficulty of contracting – combine with a policy that puts profit maximisation by hospitals at the centre of health care? It is then that the consumer, the patient, would be at greatest risk of being overcharged, given inappropriate treatments for financial rather than medical reasons, offered care not on the basis of clinical need but on the basis of ability to pay, with some paying for care they do not need and others being unable to afford care they do need – as a two-tier health-care system developed.

One response would be to regulate a private health-care market, as we do in the case of utilities which are privately owned but independently regulated. But let us list what, in Britain, a private-sector health-care regulator would have to do to fully safeguard the public interest. It would fall to a regulator:

- to control entry to the market by setting, specifying and policing basic standards for quality, workforce, facilities, governance and customer service;
- to maintain an inspection regime to protect patients by ensuring these standards were met;
- to step in when inadequate service was provided;
- to ensure security of supply and training provision;
- to police the market to guard against abuse, monopoly pricing and unfair competition;
- to adjudicate in disputes;
- to ensure that information supplied to patients and consumers is honest and accurate; and
- it would fall to a commissioner to attempt to specify every aspect of the service it purchases in a contract.

It is hardly surprising that in every advanced private health-care system in the world clinical-negligence litigation is a great and growing problem; complaints of bureaucracy, legion; attempts by insurers to standardise entitlements and restrict choice, controversial; huge government subsidy, reluctantly seen as essential; and allegations of two-tier care, divisive. Conventionally, regulation copes best in situations where we are insisting on minimum standards. But when there is an explicit undertaking that medical treatment must be given at the highest level to every patient based on health need and not ability to pay, then one is led to the conclusion that, even if that task of market regulation could be practically accomplished, public provision is likely to achieve more at less cost to efficiency and without putting at risk the gains from the ethic of public service where, at its best, dedicated public servants put duty, obligation and service before profit or personal reward.

So equality of access can best by guaranteed not just by public funding of health care but by public provision. The case for non-market solutions for education and other public services can also be made and there is a debate that will continue about what equality of access means for the coming generation; but my point today is that we can make the case on efficiency as well as equity grounds that market failures in health care, as in some other services, are not easily subject to market solutions.

So in health:

- price signals don't always work;
- the consumer is not sovereign;
- there is potential abuse of monopoly power;
- it is hard to write and enforce contracts;
- it is difficult to let a hospital go bust;
- we risk supplier-induced demand.

And having made the case for the limits of markets in health care for both finance and provision, I do not accept:

- that the future lies in a wholly centralised service;
- that we should rule out contestability or a role for the private sector in the future; and
- that we need devalue or ignore the important issue of greater consumer choice.

Even in a world where health care is not organised on market principles with consumers paying for their care, it is in the public interest to have devolution from the centre and to champion decentralised means of delivery. This includes contestability between providers on the basis of cost and efficiency. And the Secretary of State for Health is matching the record increases in investment with further far-reaching reforms:

- devolution with multi-year budgets for primary care and hospital trusts;

- more payment by results;
- NHS foundation hospitals with greater management flexibility;
- increased choice for patients through booked appointments and using NHS Direct and walk-in centres; and
- to ensure that the money invested yields the best results, independent audit, independent inspection, and independent scrutiny of local and national provision

Reforms that are essential not only to promote contestability but to decentralise control to where it can be exercised most effectively in the interests of citizens and patients. And where the private sector can add to, not undermine, NHS capacity and challenge current practises by introducing innovative working methods, it has a proper role to play – as it always has – in the National Health Service. But it must not be able, when there are, for example, overall capacity constraints, to exploit private power to the detriment of efficiency and equity . . . which is why the areas where the Secretary of State for Health is introducing a greater role for the private sector are not those areas where complex medical conditions and uncertain needs make it virtually impossible to capture them in the small print of contracts but those areas where the private sector can contract with the NHS for routine procedures, where we can write clear accountable contracts to deliver NHS clinical standards, where private capacity does not simply replace NHS capacity and where we ensure that patients are given treatment solely on clinical need. Indeed, the case I have made and experience elsewhere leads us to conclude that if we were to go down the road of introducing markets wholesale into British health care we would be paying a very heavy price in efficiency and equity and be unable to deliver a Britain of opportunity and security for all.

And because we are clear about the limits as well as the uses of markets in health care, we can now put the debate about

PFI in its proper context. In my view the Private Finance Initiative is in the public interest. It must be right that government seeks to secure, over the long term, the most cost-effective infrastructure for our public services. PFI enables us to do this by binding the private sector into open and accountable long-term relationships with the public sector aimed at securing a proper sharing of risk and access to private-service managerial expertise and innovative ideas to secure better public services. The public sector has always drawn on the expertise and experience of the private sector. But, whereas in the public procurement of the past, private companies built and then walked away, PFI seeks to ensure that the companies involved are held transparently accountable for design faults, construction flaws, overruns and long-term maintenance so that value for money is achieved.

Those who say that PFI is privatisation have got it wrong because, while the private sector is rightly helping in public-service delivery, the public interest is paramount. PFI is thus quite distinct from privatisation – where, for example, in privatised health or education it would be the market and the price mechanism, not the public (sector), that defined and provided the service directly to those customers that can afford it and thus where the public sector can end up sacrificing both fairness and efficiency in the delivery of these core services. But under PFI the public sector can harness the efficiency that can come from contestability and the private sector in pursuit of better-quality public services and, throughout, retains control of the services it runs, enabling these services to be comprehensive, efficient and universal. So there should be no principled objection against PFI expanding into new areas where the public sector can procure a defined product adequately and at no risk to its integrity and where the private sector has a core skill the public sector can benefit and learn from – as in the provision of employment and training services, the renovation of schools and colleges, major projects of urban regeneration and social housing, and the management of prisons. And in each of these areas we can show that the use of private contractors is not at the expense of the public interest or need be at the expense of terms and conditions of employees but, if we can secure greater efficiency in the provision of the service, it is one means by which the public interest is advanced.

And this leads to my third theme. Even when a market is inappropriate, old command-and-control systems of management are not the way forward but, instead, we are seeking and should seek – in the NHS and other public services – a decentralised, not centralised, means of delivery compatible with equity and efficiency.

It is the assumption that the only alternative to command and control is a market means of public-service delivery that has obscured the real challenge in health care and other public services – the challenge to develop decentralised non-market means of delivery that do not have to rely on the price mechanism to balance supply and demand. Indeed it is only by developing decentralised non-market models for public provision that respond to people's needs, extend choice and are equitable and efficient that we will show to those who assert that whatever the market failure the state failure will always be greater that a publicly funded and provided service can deliver efficiency, equity and be responsive to the consumer.

This opens up a challenging agenda for modernisation and reform: more radical devolution of responsibilities from Whitehall as we give the role of Whitehall a sharper focus; greater attention to the conditions favouring a new localism in delivery with greater transparency, proper audit and new incentives. It demands an honest appraisal of the ethic of public service which, at its best, is public servants seeking to make a difference and, at its worst, just the defence of vested interests. In this new world we need to ask about the next steps in matching responsibility and reward in the civil service as we encourage professionals who welcome accountability and whose ethic is about maximising the difference they make; and we will need a better appreciation of the important role local, voluntary and charitable community organisations can play in future delivery. Our approach to public services has been to move away from the old system of controls:

- from a narrow centralism that dominated public-expenditure control from the days of the Plowden Report to devolution to regions, localities and communities;
- from a focus on inputs and process to a focus on outputs and results;
- from annual and incremental spending decisions that ignored investment needs to long-term, usually three-year, allocations based on proper policy analysis of consumption and investment requirements;
- from a crude departmentalism that put the consumers' needs second to how, by breaking down departmental boundaries, consumer needs can best be met; and
- from *ad hoc* policy initiatives and postcode lotteries that failed to meet public expectations for lower waiting times, better exam results and, generally, better service to national targets set in public-service agreements within which local authorities, hospitals, departments and others have the incentive to innovate and the discretion to do so.

The four principles of public-service delivery set down by Tony Blair correctly require a balance to be struck between national standards and local autonomy. And our long-term objective has always been to match the attainment of ambitious national standards with the promotion of local autonomy so we can achieve efficiency, equity and choice. Far from targets being a tool for centralisation, the modern company has lean headquarters that set clear targets, set the incentives and rewards, provide the freedom for local managers to deliver and then they collect the information so that results can be monitored and assessed; and so too in the public sector. Where objectives are clear well-defined targets can provide direction; where expectations are properly shaped, they provide the necessary ambition; where people can see and assess the impact of policy, and where national standards are achieved and can be seen to be achieved, targets can make for the consistency, accountability, equity and flexibility to meet local needs that the traditional delivery of public services has often seemed to lack. Without targets providing that necessary focus and discipline for achieving change, recent public-service improvements – from literacy and numeracy performance in the primary school to waiting times and cancer- and heart-care improvements in the NHS – could simply not have been achieved. And there is thus a critical role for targets, now and in the future, in shaping expectations of what can be delivered on what timescale and avoiding the trap of low ambition on the one hand and – when faced with decades of chronic investment – overpromising on the other.

We know that national targets work best when they are matched by a framework of devolution, accountability and participation – empowering public servants with the freedom and flexibility to make a difference: first, to tailor services to reflect local needs and preferences; second, to develop innovative approaches to service delivery and raise standards; and third to enable – as we should – a bonfire of the old input, interventionist, departmentalist controls over front-line public-service managers – which is too often what they still find frustrating. And so it is right to consider greater local autonomy, and its corollary, greater local democratic oversight.

What then are the next steps as we prepare for our next spending review and as targets are achieved and national

standards established? One way forward is that local communities should have the freedom to agree for each service their
own local performance standards – choosing their own performance indicators and monitoring both the national and
local performance indicators with, as a backstop, last resort,
national powers to step back in. Accountability would be
enhanced with local and national performance indicators
published and tracked, and – as pioneered in New York –
the local community expecting their local managers to con-
tinuously monitor and learn from their performance.

Further reforms flow from such improvements: greater
flexibility for local pay and conditions of service; the reduction of ring-fenced budgeting; the reform of both inspecto-
rates and monitoring regimes to recognise the benefits of
local discretion; work with service providers and user groups
on performance indicators to help community groups and
local residents, especially in poor areas, build their capacity to
hold local services to account. So the accountability of local
services providers to patients, parents and local communities
would be improved through greater transparency and a
deeper democracy, tailoring services to needs and choices
expressed both individually and collectively.

But we have also to get the balance right between responsiveness to choice and efficiency – and equity. Local autonomy without national standards may lead to increased
inequality between people and regions and the return of
the postcode lotteries. And the view we take on the appropriate balance between efficiency, diversity and equity will be
shaped by the values we hold. The modern challenge is to
move beyond old assumptions under which equity was seen
to go hand in hand with uniformity; or diversity appeared to
lead inevitably to inequality. Instead we should seek the
maximum amount of diversity consistent with equity. Indeed
we are, in my view, already developing non-market and non-
command-and-control mechanisms for service delivery and

championing diversity by devolving further and faster to local government, the regions and the voluntary sector, and I want to suggest next steps here too.

In local government with clear and concise information about each council's performance across its local services, with inspection regimes now more proportionate and with interventions concentrated on the small number of failing councils, the Deputy Prime Minister has moved us far from the destructive centralism – the universal capping, inflexible borrowing, the Poll Tax – of the 1980s and early 1990s. As we move forward we propose more freedoms and flexibilities – a 75 per cent cut in the number of plans; reduced ring-fencing; local PSA agreements that give localities more discretion; more targeted and thus more limited inspection; and more freedom with a fairer prudential regime for borrowing; greater freedom to trade; more scope to use self-generated income, including the freedom to benefit from new rates income from the growth of new businesses – freedoms and flexibilities that reflect a government that enables and empowers rather than directs and controls.

And in return for reform and results, and as an incentive to all the rest, the best-performing localities will soon have even more freedoms and flexibilities:

- the removal of both revenue and capital ring-fencing;
- the withdrawal of reserve powers over capping;
- sixty plans reduced to just two required – the best-value performance plan and a community plan; and
- a three-year holiday from inspection.

Freedom and flexibility matters just as much as we innovate with a new regional policy with its emphasis on indigenous sources of economic strength and thus a philosophy that requires genuine devolution of power from the centre. There has been more devolution to English regions in the last few years than in the preceding one hundred years and this localism involves the freedom to determine local needs in Regional Development Agency budgets worth £2 billion a year and in economic development, regeneration, tourism, planning, and – from April in selected pilots – the management of skills, training and business support. Soon 90 per cent of the £7-billion-a-year learning and skills budget, 50 per cent of the small-business-services budget and the vast majority of housing capital investment will be devolved to the freedom and flexibility of local decision-making as we pioneer non-centralist means of delivering these services.

The financial freedoms and flexibilities are matched by greater accountability through the role of regional chambers and, for those who in time choose to have them, elected regional assemblies. And having, in the NHS, already devolved 75 per cent of health budgets to primary-care trusts, we have also established strategic health authorities. And there is already discussion of democratic arrangements in these areas too. There is greater freedom and flexibility, too, for charities, voluntary and community organisations as they take a bigger role in the delivery of services.

At the heart of each of the new services we have played a part in developing – Sure Start for the under-fours, the Children's Fund, IT learning centres, Healthy Living Centres, the New Deal for jobs, the New Deal for Communities, as well as the Safer Communities Initiative, Communities Against Drugs, the Futurebuilders programme and Gift Aid – is a genuine break with the recent past: services, once centrally funded and organised, can and should now be led, organised and delivered by voluntary, charitable and community organisations.

This new direction – this agenda for prosperity and social reform – moves us forward from the era of an old Britain weakened by 'the man in Whitehall knows best' towards a new Britain strengthened by local centres awash with initiative, energy and dynamism. And the next steps should include not just further reform of local government but reform in the civil service as we map out the full implications of extending choice, equity and efficiency in individual public services.

Of course in each decade the relationship between individuals, markets and communities will evolve as technology and rising expectations challenge each generation's vision of what is possible and best. But I am suggesting today that, today and in the future, in the large areas of the economy I have highlighted, our mission must be relentless: to strengthen markets to maximise efficiency. And, in those areas where market failures are chronic, I am suggesting that we step up our efforts to pioneer more decentralised systems of public-service delivery. This agenda I propose – one where we advance enterprise and fairness together – not only meets the contemporary challenges of competitiveness and equity but is, in my view, wholly in tune with British traditions and enduring British values. Indeed this agenda for prosperity and reform is the modern means of applying enduring British values.

For centuries Britishness has been rightly defined to the world as a profound belief in liberty and in the spirit of enterprise, combined with a deep civic pride that has emphasised the importance of what Orwell called decency: fair play and equity. It is this long-standing commitment to both enterprise and fairness which has shaped our past that now should define not only our economic policy but Britain's modern mission as a nation. Some continents are defined to the world as beacons of enterprise but at the cost of fairness; others as beacons of fairness or social cohesion at the cost of efficiency. In our time, Britain can be a beacon for a world where enterprise and fairness march forward together. It is this very British idea and patriotic purpose, and its enormous potential for shaping our country's future prosperity, which should give us the strength to make all the tough and demanding reforms now necessary to create a Britain of opportunity and security for all.

When the Social Market Foundation published this speech on 18 May 2004, the Chancellor spoke at the launch, making some additional remarks on this topic, and taking forward some of the themes in the original. In particular he deals with the issue of personalisation of public services, trying to resolve what some perceived as a dilemma posed in the last speech – that the government's three goals for public services (greater personalisation, higher efficiency, and increased equity) were mutually incompatible. In this speech, the Chancellor argues that achieving equality of opportunity is a fundamental goal in a progressive society, and hence that each person has an equal entitlement not just to high standards of service, but to as equal a chance as another of developing themselves and their potential to the fullest. Because people begin from different starting places, in different circumstances and with different needs, public services need to be personalised in terms of their resources and range of provision. Achieving this vision of personalised public services – meeting the individual needs of all our citizens – requires continuing reform in the way we deliver public services. And this vision is not of personalised services just for the few, for those who can afford to buy them in the market. It is for all. The Chancellor therefore concludes that personalisation is not opposed to equity; it is at the very core of what equity means. Achieving the goal of equality of opportunity – enabling each person to achieve their own potential to the fullest – requires a tailored approach that takes into account each person's unique circumstances.

In the original speech I argued for a new clarity on one of the oldest and most important issues in political economy: the role and limits of the state and markets. I argued that markets are in the public interest, while not to be automatically equated with it, and that we should be advancing market disciplines across the economy – promoting greater competition, open trade, entrepreneurship and flexibility in labour and capital markets.

I said that where there are market failures we should work to make markets perform better – as in skills and training, in science and research and development, in financial markets, in regional policy and to tackle environmental damage.

And I suggested that where there are systemic problems with the operation of markets that cannot easily be corrected, such as in health care and other public services, the challenge is to develop efficient and equitable but non-centralist means of public provision.

Since that speech we have already announced major changes in policy that were prefigured or anticipated by the arguments of the speech. We have removed the last permanent industrial subsidies in coal, steel and shipbuilding. We have announced the sale of UK government privatised shareholdings. From a platform of an increased National Minimum Wage and tax credits, we have promoted regional and local pay flexibility. We have announced new deregulatory initiatives for the administration of small companies in, for example, VAT and audit. We have agreed a four-presidency deregulation initiative for the EU, with the aim of putting every regulation to the competitiveness test. We have proposed a further round of European economic reform – liberalising product, capital and labour markets. We have proposed how the European Union can reform its state-aid regime – abolishing wasteful state aids but also making sure the rules do not prevent measures which help make markets work better. We have implemented our new competition and enterprise regime and the OFT and Competition Commission have a new work programme with investigations into market conditions in areas from pharmacies and door-step selling to estate agents and the professions. And we have invested substantially more in the areas where if government does not act, voluntary, private or other agencies cannot be relied on to do so – in schools, adult learning, universities, colleges, health and infrastructure. And in adult learning we are seeking a new partnership between government, employers and employees. In health and the public services the programme of reform is proceeding faster than ever, and that reform will go on and on.

Tony Blair and I are working closely on both our spending round and the five-year departmental plans for the future: radical plans for investment matched by reform which we and the Cabinet are also working through together, reform plans that we will outline in the next few weeks, reforms on the basis of which Tony Blair will map out the road ahead. And working with the Secretary of State for Health in the field of health care, we are recognising just how much more progress on the reform agenda we can make.

Last year I argued for more devolution, more local accountability, more flexibility and more choice – more diversity of supply – in the delivery of services. But advances we are making now allow us to go even further. Take information available to the patient. In my speech last year I pointed out that professional and care relationships suffer from information asymmetries – information asymmetries that made the typical market model of service provision difficult to work in every health-care system, including in America as well as Britain. Whereas in a market there is always a temptation for the supplier to exploit information asymmetries, in public services we must attempt to face up to them in the interests of patient power. So increasingly we will empower patients.

In addition to producing better information for patients through star ratings, putting waiting times and other information on the NHS.UK website, we are piloting expert support for patients in exercising choice over their care. In our coronary and heart-disease choice pilots, for example, specialist nurse 'patient care advisors' are being provided to help patients. And we are now planning to roll out choice at referral, where PCTs and GPs will provide advice and support either directly to patients or with the help of voluntary organisations. We are also providing more information, particularly in primary care and for patients with chronic conditions where patients increasingly have considerable knowledge of their condition. Addressing these asymmetries – putting patients and users of other public services at the heart of the delivery of those services – is a crucial aspect of the government's desire to achieve a wider aim: to make public services more personal to the needs of the user.

Personalisation means opening up wherever possible a greater range of options to the service user and I believe it will serve us well to consider the future of the public services in this way: making public services responsive to the particular needs of their users so that his or her needs are better met:

- for the NHS patient, the opportunity to book an appointment time, to see their own electronic records, to choose a hospital;
- for the school pupil, allowing the individual to learn at his or her own pace and style;
- for the elderly or disabled person, the chance to design for themselves and then obtain the right package of care options;
- for the young person on the New Deal, access to an adviser who can provide help tailored to the particular circumstances of the individual and the employment conditions of the area;
- for the parent, a range of flexible childcare services and financial support to choose from;

- for the local community, the opportunity to discuss and influence community safety strategies and environmental improvements.

And in this way the work of the doctor, the nurse, the teacher and the provider focus more on the individual needs of the patient, pupil and user than ever before; public services can be shown to be superior to privately provided services in these areas; and a new model of non-centralised non-market public-service delivery can evolve – devolved, accountable, flexible, with the user in the driving seat.

For too long in the past chronic underinvestment made many resigned to the poor performance of too many public services, standardised and uniform services starved as they were of resources and of long-term direction and hope. But today we can see a new vision ahead of us – where instead of standardised and uniform services, public services meet people's diverse needs, in ways personal to those who depend upon them.

As Amartya Sen has famously argued, equality rooted in an equal respect and concern for our citizens demands not just greater equality of resources but also equal capability to function and develop their potential. Such capability can be developed through a new approach to public services – one that maximises responsiveness and flexibility to provide services that empower the individual to flourish and one that engages individuals themselves to be active partners in achieving these results.

Because achieving equality of opportunity is a fundamental goal in a progressive society, I believe each person has an equal entitlement not just to high standards of service, but to as equal a chance as another of developing themselves and their potential to the fullest. Because people begin from different starting places, in different circumstances and with different needs, public services need to be personalised in terms of their resources and range of provision.

Achieving this vision of personalised public services –
meeting the individual needs of all our citizens – requires
continuing reform in the way we deliver public services. This
is the process on which the government has embarked and on
which we continue to push ahead, as we shall show in the
spending review in the summer.

And this vision is not of personalised services just for the
few, for those who can afford to buy them in the market. It is
for all. For personalisation is not opposed to equity; it is at the
very core of what equity means. Achieving the goal of equality
of opportunity – enabling each person to achieve their own
potential to the fullest – requires a tailored approach that
takes into account each person's unique circumstances.

When I gave the speech to the SMF last year, some people
said that the government's three goals for public services –
greater personalisation, higher efficiency, and increased
equity – were mutually incompatible. They said that we faced
a dilemma:

- that if public services were to be efficient, they had to be
  inequitable, because only market mechanisms, which
  depend on ability to pay, can achieve efficiency; and
- that if services are to be equitable and universally available to all, then they cannot be personalised, but must
  inevitably be uniform, inflexible and standardised.

Yet, in my speech and now pamphlet, I showed how not just
equity but efficiency is better served through a publicly
funded and publicly provided NHS than a private market.

But now I believe we can go further than this. We can show
that public funding and largely public provision cannot only
be equitable and efficient but can provide personalised
services as well.

7

MODERN PUBLIC SERVICES

'When I was a boy,' Gordon said, 'my father told me story after story about the fear which illness brought to families as they faced up to the crippling costs of seeking treatment for loved ones.' Clearly, removal of that fear was a wonderful release and had a huge impact on people's lives. And a big impact on Gordon, as it had on me. As he spoke, I could hear my own parents telling me similar stories about their own experiences in their early years in the North East of England.

His pride shone through that his party had changed Britain so substantially, with such benefit for so many, after 1948. So did his passionate belief that our National Health Service played a crucial role in defining 'Britishness'. The NHS was, as described in the Bevan Lecture, a clear, enduring and practical expression of those shared values which shape our country. Equally clear was his determination that he and his colleagues in government, the 'successors of Bevan' who were likely to be in power for a good few years, should reform health services to ensure successful delivery for decades to come, meeting the challenges of changing demographics and new treatments.

Would I, he asked, be prepared to review the resources needed, long term, for UK health services to continue to provide comprehensive, high-quality services? For the first but not the last time, I encountered a steely stare as I suggested that these terms of reference would have to change. 'Continue to provide comprehensive, high-quality services', I said, seemed to make too many assumptions about the adequacy of the quality being delivered in 2000. Surely he wanted to aim much *higher? A warm smile returned. He did indeed have concerns about the service being delivered; he had a vision of a much better service and it was that which he wished to play his part in creating: innovative, using new technologies well and playing an important role in developing a healthy and skilled UK population.*

When, a year later, I presented the findings to him, his view was clear that the prudence of his early years as Chancellor had, indeed, been for a purpose. This was no mere slogan but an important part of his strategy falling into place. But what the findings showed was that some other countries had combined equality of access with better delivery. The defining difference of 1948 had been lost. And, by 2006, it is a measure of his own success that the Conservative Party has apparently accepted all he said. No longer can he claim that a free NHS at the point of need is the central dividing line between the political parties. The debate, and no doubt Gordon Brown's speeches, will move on to the issue of how to achieve successful implementation and reform. Have the processes and the measurement systems delivered? Has his trust in colleagues to produce results borne sufficient fruit? That is where the eventual judgement will be made.

Sir Derek Wanless

As a medical practitioner and heart specialist, I spent almost the entire first half of my professional career focused on learning, practising and developing my specific branch of medicine. I was soon to realise that achieving the potential and morals of medicine both now and in the future depends critically on having the appropriate system of health-care delivery and investing heavily in research. Having had first-hand experience with different systems around the world and working for a long time (more than forty years) for the NHS left me with no doubt about the unique nature and superiority of the NHS, both as a concept and in practical terms.

The speeches of the Chancellor, Gordon Brown, published in this book indicate clearly his commitment, coupled with deep understanding of the NHS as a whole, and the practicalities involved, including investing in basic science and applied research. Having listened to Gordon on more than one occasion, I am convinced that upholding the principles of the NHS and planning for the future is one of his main overall targets. As he repeatedly affirms, the NHS says a lot about the morals and aspirations of people of this country and is a unique model for the rest of the world and therefore must be preserved and developed in spite of the continuous changes and challenges.

Sir Magdi Yacoub, FRS

A recurring theme in the speeches of the Chancellor has been the question of the role to be played by the state in the provision of public services. However, this is also a debate about what kind of country we are, because it is a debate not just about the right choice of health-care system, or the technicalities of how best to finance public services, but about the national values the people of Britain hold to be important.

In the Aneurin Bevan Memorial Lecture given on 23 May 2002 the Chancellor argues that social policy has always to be rooted in the shared experience of the nation. Asserting that Bevan's philosophy was not abstract or theoretical, the Chancellor argues that Bevan's social-inclusion policies started from what he saw around him in Welsh communities, and were based on real needs found in the real lives of the real people he grew up with and worked with in South Wales. Taking off from this, the Chancellor argues that we need to find specific policy solutions to unique British problems which are rooted in people's experiences and histories. People from Bevan's community believed that the injustices they suffered should not just not happen to them, they should not happen to anyone. They had a vision, and in this powerful speech the Chancellor argues that this might translate, for our time, into five social-justice objectives, to be met by modern public services: a commitment to full employment; the collective provision of the best modern public services; an end to child and pensioner poverty; to ensure the best educational opportunity including higher education for the majority of young people; and to forge a new global deal for the developing world.

2002, now, is the right time to honour the memory of Aneurin
Bevan. Because the NHS, which he created just fifty years ago,
which has endured for fifty years, is this year being renewed, I
hope, for the next fifty years under the same principles he set
out with the same objective he set out: free to all at the point
of need, irrespective of wealth. And it is appropriate we are
meeting here today because Bevan's great book *In Place of Fear*
– which showed the insights and inspiration which led him to
create the NHS – was published exactly fifty years ago this
year.

In place of fear there should, he said, be security and, in his
words, serenity. Bevan's philosophy was not abstract or just
theoretical, but started from what he saw around him here in
Welsh communities; was founded on unshakeable beliefs; was
driven forward by a clear mission for change; and was built on
a passion for justice. That he started not from textbooks or
abstracts, but from real needs found in the real lives of the
real people he grew up with and worked with here in South
Wales, can be seen from the inspiration he received from the
Tredegar Medical Society – the contributions of miners and
steelworkers who employed their doctors and nurses and
whose collective endeavour, each contributing to the health
of all, became the inspiration for the National Health Service
we enjoy today.

And from his starting point of where people found themselves – as he said 'a free people will always refuse to put up
with preventable poverty' – Bevan built his philosophy not –
as the Conservatives accused him – around violating rights but
around righting wrongs: a demand for a correction of a
generation of injustices: 'the sense of injustice' that, as he
said, 'does not derive solely from the existence of inequality.
It arises from the belief that the inequality is capricious,
unsanctioned by usage and, most important of all, senseless.'
And what he called his philosophy's driving force was utterly
positive and life-enhancing: the promotion and liberation of

the potential of all – as he said in a memorable phrase, the conviction that 'free men can use free institutions to solve social and economic problems of the day, if they are given a chance to do so'. And his objective – as he said, quoting his favourite philosopher José Enrique Rodó: 'not to reduce all to the lowest common level but to raise all towards the highest levels'. His aim: not to level people down, but to enable people to lift themselves up.

High ideals about the extraordinary potential of ordinary people: enduring values to be reapplied by each generation – indeed, as he said, 'modernised' because 'policies are often blunted in use' and may have to be renovated or even discarded in each era to meet the needs of the times. And in our time I believe it means five social-justice objectives:

- first, a commitment to full employment;
- second, to renew the collective provision of not just basic but the best modern public services;
- third, to secure for the first time an end to child and pensioner poverty;
- fourth, to ensure the best educational opportunity including higher education for young people – not just for the privileged but, for the first time, for the majority; and
- fifth, to forge a wholly new global deal for the developing world – for few would deny that we have in our hands the power, never given to any other generation at any other time in human history – and thus the obligation – to banish ignorance and poverty from the earth.

So I believe that for Labour this is not a time to slow down or pause or to be complacent. For as long as there is poverty, unemployment and deprivation; as long as prosperity by passes a single family or community; as long as there is opportunity denied in education; as long as there is injustice not just in Britain but round the world; our work has only just begun.

I believe that the experience here in South Wales that shaped Bevan's beliefs and his political programme made Bevan's starting point the goal of full employment. As Michael Foot put it in his magnificent biography of Bevan, 'unemployment was the great issue on which all else hinged'. For Bevan, the mass unemployment of the 1930s was 'the biggest human problem parliament has ever had to handle'. Bevan came from a Wales which, both by inclination and by necessity, depended upon strong communities. Communities which had together endured war, depression, and would live through war again. Communities which together had suffered closure, unemployment, poverty and deprivation but, despite all that, communities that remained resilient and strong. Communities from which thousands had been forced to emigrate and travel tens of thousands of miles – but still, from whatever extremity of the world they found themselves in, they saw their village or valley as home. For our parents and grandparents, community was never artificial, never an afterthought, never an unreal or false togetherness for the sake of appearances. In a mining area where, not least when a mine's safety was an issue, the lives of each depended upon the support of all. Community – or what we sometimes call solidarity – was of the essence. We owe obligations to neighbours, even strangers, because they are part of what we are.

As here, so in Scotland and in the industrial communities, hard times – the harsh and bitter experience of industrialisation – taught the parents of the men and women I grew up with not just solidarity in preference to individualism but also compassion in preference to selfishness. Out of a sense of community – and a respect each for the other – came a hatred of injustice and a demand for social justice.

As William McIlvanney – a great Scottish writer – says, our

ancestors were not fools. They knew how much easier it was to be a Conservative than a Socialist; easier to conserve than to change; easier to succumb to vested interests than to take them on; easier to take your own share than fight for everyone to have a fair share; easier to see progress as moving up on your own than ensuring everyone moves up together. But Bevan's generation – as McIlvanney says – sensed their lives were part of a worthwhile struggle, believed that the injustice they suffered should not just not happen to them, it should not happen to anyone. And they rose above the bleakness of their daily struggle and blessed it by transforming their hardships into a vision: a society where there is not indifference but care; not cruelty but kindness; not endless competition but regular cooperation; not selfishness but sharing; not the pursuit of élitism but of excellence; not class but classlessness. And it was this that gave purpose to their lives. For them, as he says, democratic socialism was an honest attempt to fulfil what is best in human nature: people choosing quite deliberately to develop the best aspects of their nature and to keep in check the worst.

They were not, in the main, Marxists. For them, McIlvanney concludes, Marxism was a demand to be something you are not, which our individual natures could not honestly answer. Instead democratic socialists say you must be the most you can be while allowing others to be the most that they can be – an attempt to share as justly as we can with each other the terms of human existence. But this did not mean that for Bevan social justice was an abstraction. Social justice was houses free of damp, teachers in our classrooms, nurses in our hospitals . . . and, as a precondition, work for people. For unemployment he saw as not only immoral but an economic waste, hence the demand not that each be left isolated and stranded to fend for himself but that we organise a society where there is work for all – full employment.

So in Bevan's generation, so in ours. Since the time I went

to school and grew up beside a mining community – and for a whole generation – our political life has been dominated by unemployment – long-term unemployment, youth unemployment, the fear of unemployment, the poverty and insecurity caused by unemployment. Unemployment is an impassable barrier to people realising their potential and an implacable source of poverty. An unemployment, as Bevan said, that 'eats like acid into the homes of the poor'. Bevan's dream was to rebuild the towns and villages around him so that – in the words of an American – young children could again get up in the morning and look out of their windows to see whole communities going to work.

If the 1920s and 1930s of Bevan's time are remembered for adults standing around street corners, the 1980s will be remembered for young people sleeping rough in cardboard cities, young people without jobs, prospects or hope. It has not only been our party's dream for a century that full employment should be a central goal but that the driving force of any successful economic policy should be a commitment to full employment not just for a year or two but on a sustainable basis. For years in opposition we could do nothing about it. All we could do was protest. We marched for jobs, we rallied for the right to work, we petitioned for full employment. But out of government we could not deliver jobs.

After I became Shadow Chancellor in 1992 Labour set out proposals for taxing the excess profits of the privatised utilities to pay for jobs for the unemployed. If only one person had benefited from the New Deal that would have made it worth while. But in total 660,000 young people, two-thirds of a million of our fellow citizens, nearly 50,000 in Wales, have benefited. And when I tell you that, under Tony Blair, one and a half million men and women denied jobs under the Tories are now in jobs under Labour, I do not say this in a spirit of congratulation, but in a spirit of resolve. In the mid-1980s 350,000 young people had been out of work for more than a year. Today it is 5,000. Youth unemployment is down two-thirds; long-term unemployment by three-quarters, now the lowest since the 1970s. For the first time in years, the majority of lone parents are now able to work. Twenty-six thousand more people are in work in Wales today than in 1997.

But this is only a start. For one in six working-age households still has someone who is not working and our goal is full employment for our generation: employment opportunity for all. So we are:

- entrenching monetary and fiscal stability and discipline to help create jobs;
- pushing forward with a challenging economic reform agenda not just for stability but for productivity in Britain and Europe;
- investing in skills to improve employability;
- extending the New Deal, its opportunities and its responsibilities, to all the remaining 95,000 long-term unemployed, with – in twenty of the highest-unemployment communities of Britain – in return for the responsibility to accept the offer, guaranteed jobs with proper wages;
- and to help more long-term unemployed people in Wales into jobs, we have set up two employment zones, including the Head of the Valley's employment zone, to help tackle the problems in the areas where long-term unemployment has remained consistently high.

Because women have suffered most from injustice in employment opportunities, we are pushing forward with a new programme of 'choices' for lone parents – to push up employment rates from just over 45 per cent when we came to power to 70 per cent, underpinned by a national childcare strategy – extending, for the first time ever, the right of child care to all those who need it. And we are seeking to make a reality of the right to work for disabled men and women when they wish to work: disabled people cruelly denied their chances under the Tories, now under Labour given the right to develop their talents and fulfil their potential. And recognising that, in high-unemployment communities which prosperity has for too long passed by, we need more economic activity and enterprise, we will be working with the Welsh Assembly and Scottish Parliament to regenerate run-down high streets and industrial sites, cut the cost of investing in small businesses and in entrepreneurship, deliver special help for growing enterprises and provide funds for training and education in the new skills we need.

And we are not just determined to create jobs but, in a world of fast-moving change where people will tend to move between jobs and have to acquire during their working life new skills for jobs, we will make sure there are continuous and recurring opportunities for work, and will make work pay: next year building on the minimum wage, a new Working Tax Credit to tackle poverty in work. For the first time from next April a Minimum Income for all those in work over twenty-five, creating a tax system where the rates range from 40 per cent at the top to minus 200 per cent as we create fairness and justice in the workplace.

But the new Britain worthy of Bevan's vision will be built not only around a goal of full employment but around the goal of world-class public services. Just as it is only because people have forgotten the unemployed standing on street corners in the thirties that they undervalue the deliverance from evil that came with full employment and the Welfare State, so too it is only because some people have forgotten the chaos and patchwork of voluntary, charitable and municipal health care that Aneurin Bevan swept away – and the un-mitigated good that comes from a National Health Service – that anyone can contemplate its withering away. Yet many of you will look back, like me, and recall that so many of the opportunities we have had – the best schooling, the best of health care when ill, for many of us the best chances at university – so many of the opportunities we have enjoyed – owe their origin to the decisions of the 1945 Labour government to create a Welfare State that takes the shame out of need, to fund a National Health Service free to all, to build decent public services worthy of a civilised society – in health, transport, education and the important fight against crime – public services that are an expression of something more than the material – of an ethic of service that reflects our obligation each to the other in society.

A National Health Service, Bevan said in a famous speech introducing the National Health Service Bill in 1946, would . . .

> lift the shadow from millions of homes. It will keep very many people alive who might otherwise be dead. It will relieve suffering. It will be a great contribution towards the well-being of the common people of Britain. No society can legitimately call itself civilised if a sick person is denied medical aid because of lack of means. The essence of a satisfactory health service is that rich and poor are treated alike, that poverty is not a disability, that wealth is not an advantage.

For me the National Health Service is a clear, enduring and practical expression of these shared values which shape our country: the NHS built upon the conviction that the health of each of us depended upon a contribution by all of us. And let me say that I believe that the case for the NHS system of funding and thus a renewed and reformed NHS is not weaker but stronger now than even it was in Bevan's day. In 1948 when the NHS was founded, the scientific and technological limitations of medicine were such that high-cost interventions were rare or very rare. There was no chemotherapy for cancer, cardiac surgery was in its infancy, intensive care barely existed, hip and knee replacement was almost unknown. Now, the standard of technology and treatment is such that unlike in 1948 some illnesses or injuries could cost £20,000, £50,000 or even £100,000 to treat and cure. Because the costs of treatment and of drugs are higher than ever, the risks to family finances under a paying system are greater than ever not just for poorer families but for comfortably-off families up the income scale and therefore the need for comprehensive insurance cover of health care stronger than ever. Private insurance policies that, by definition, rely for their viability on ifs, buts and small print can cover only some of the people some of the time. Because none of us ever knows in advance whether it is you or your family that will need that expensive care – for acute or chronic illness – the best policy to cope with unpredictability is clearly an insurance policy that offers cover to all of the people whatever their income for all illnesses and diseases without the ifs, buts and small print of other policies.

So while some present the current NHS system of funding as an ideological hand-me-down from Bevan's days as Health Minister, to be supported only out of sentiment rather than hard-headed calculation; and while others dismiss the NHS funding system as an impossible dream – 'fine in principle, a failed experiment in practice', the NHS system of funding – comprehensive and inclusive insurance with treatment free at the point of need – is demonstrably the modern rational choice: the best insurance policy in the world not just for poor or low-income families in Britain, but for the vast majority of families in Britain. Not just for today but for tomorrow too, and more so than in 1948.

So we believe in a reformed and renewed NHS free at the point of need where, as we see in Wales, there is local devolution and then greater local choice; local accountability and improved service; a health service that has to be reformed and renewed to meet the three great challenges facing health care: the rising costs of new technology, the increase of 3 million by 2020 in the elderly population, and the ever rising expectations for higher standards of personal care. I believe, just as it was in 1948 when Bevan had to wage war against the Conservatives, a free NHS free at the point of need is now the central dividing line between the political parties in British politics and will be a central theme in Welsh and Scottish elections next year.

The Conservatives – in fact, their Shadow Chancellor Michael Howard, that well-known Welshman – now tell us that the NHS was a Stalinist creation, in other words that it was wrong in principle from the very start, and that when he said under the Thatcher government the NHS was safe in their hands he never really meant it. He and his party now explicitly refuse to commit themselves to an NHS free to all at the point of need. Their hatred of the NHS is such that they would prefer a private sector performing inefficiently to a public service delivering well.

I believe we should now expose the costs and inequity of private insurance under which typical family premiums cost £100 a week, are rising by 13 per cent a year and leave 40 million Americans uninsured; and the costs and inequity of charging for clinical services – £8,000 for a hip replacement, £40,000 for a heart transplant, £10 for a visit to a GP or to stay in hospital for a day – the unfairness of the sick paying for being sick. And I want to ask you today to help us ensure that, just as in Bevan's generation private health was decisively rejected in favour of the NHS system of funding, so too in our generation we reject a system under which poverty would bar the entrance to the best hospitals; where the only health care you could be sure of is the health care you were able to pay for; where, for today's Tories, one person on BUPA matters more to them than 50 million people covered by the NHS.

Let us affirm that it was Aneurin Bevan who helped us escape from a world where nurses had to leave the beds of their patients to run charity flag days to pay for their hospital buildings and their doctor's salaries. And we are not returning to that. And so let us affirm that it is because we recognise the unpredictability of health needs, the rising costs of health technology, and the equity and efficiency of the NHS tax-funded system that, for us, the renewed NHS – with the largest sustained increased investment in any decade of its fifty-year-long history – will remain a National Health Service: a public service free at the point of use with decisions on care always made by doctors and nurses on the basis of clinical need – the best insurance policy in the world.

But, for Bevan, democratic socialism was not just about work, however important, and the provision of public services, however critical. Democratic socialism was – yes – about teachers in classrooms, roofs above people's heads, doctors and nurses when needed, money in people's pockets. But power, wealth and opportunity in the hands of the many not the few meant something more. It was also about the liberation of human potential. Bevan's starting point was a fundamental belief in the equal worth of every human being. As he said in *In Place of Fear*: 'it is commonly said that we are all born unequal, but surely that is the wrong way of expressing it. It would be more correct to say that we are born with different potential aptitudes than that we are born unequal.' And as his favoured philosopher Rodó said, our duty is to help each and every one develop their potential to the full – in other words, to bridge the gap between what we are and what we have it in ourselves to become.

Bevan believed that nobody's potential should be written off at birth, seven, eleven or sixteen. As Bevan said in *In Place of Fear*, 'whether the special aptitudes, qualities or temperament we are born with turn out to be of later advantage, will turn upon whether they are sufficiently cultivated'. It was

simply a denial of any belief in equality of opportunity and a
waste of human potential if we were to assume that there is
one type of intelligence, one means of assessing it, only one
time when it should be assessed and just one chance of
succeeding. We have to act on the consequence of recognising these facts about human worth: that people have a
richness and diversity of potential, that their talents take
many forms – not just analytical intelligence but skills in
communication, language, and working with other people
– and that these talents can develop and flourish over a
lifetime. And should all be valued.

In the central scene in Trevor Griffiths' play *Food for Ravens*,
commissioned to mark the fiftieth anniversary of the NHS
and the centenary of Bevan's birth, the old dying Bevan talks
to the young enquiring Bevan: it is a moment, as Hywel
Francis has recorded in a recent speech, 'of magic, pathos
and controlled anger':

> Schooling for our people [said the old Bevan] has always
> been constructed misery, from which a true education
> has been deliberately excluded – obedience and crin-
> ging servility in; imagination and mental daring out.
> That's always been our sort of schooling, a human dog-
> training.
>   Once I asked a simple question, 'What do we put in
> place of fear?' If we let ourselves believe that reading and
> writing and painting and song and play and pleasure in
> the imagining, good food, good wine, good clothes and
> good health are the toff's turf, boy, haven't we lost the
> battle already? They're ours, our human right, all right?

There it is: the driving force in Bevan's philosophy – tackling
what was called the 'poverty of aspiration' and challenging
people everywhere to accept the equal right, what he called
the human right, of the poorest citizen to develop their

potential to the full. Not – as he says – the old one-off opportunity of schooling up till age sixteen: a single chance to get your foot on a narrow ladder – one opportunity at school till sixteen, a chance if missed that was gone for ever – followed by an opportunity for just 10, 20 or 30 per cent to go into higher education. But instead recurrent, permanent, lifelong opportunities at any time, education at any age at any place, and not just education but the liberation of potential with new opportunities in employment, the economy and across our society and culture.

While mining communities like yours and mine have always understood the importance of education as a means of financial and personal liberation, for too long since 1945 the Welfare State tried to compensate people for their poverty instead of ensuring the opportunities were delivered to tackle the causes of poverty, and providing routes out of poverty to the liberation of potential. So while we reject equality of outcome because it is statist, centralising, against human nature, and – as I said earlier – demands we be something we are not, an equality of outcome that would level down, we support an equality of opportunity that lifts people up and helps answer Bevan's worries about the poverty of aspiration. It is an equality which demands not just that individuals enabled by opportunity also accept responsibility to make the most of their talents for their community – rights and responsibilities the modern expression of community, of solidarity – but that we have a duty to remove all the old barriers – whether it be lack of nursery schools, under-investment in schools, old-fashioned élitism in our higher-education system or failure to take adult education seriously. The challenge, because we waste too much of the talent of Britain: to open up opportunities for education to an extent never before seen in this country so that every child will have the best possible chance in life. And because today the most important resource of a country is not its raw materials but the talents of its people – now the essential means of production – and because economies that work only for the few and do not bring out the best in all their people will ossify and be left behind – the equality of opportunity that we have always argued for as an ethical imperative is today also an economic necessity.

The old walls of privilege for some must be replaced with new paths of opportunity for all. We said in our manifesto that we would put schools and hospitals first. This summer, in the Spending Review, we will honour our commitments not just to health but to education – which will receive the priority it requires to deliver further substantial improvements in standards in our schools, colleges and universities. Having raised the share of education in our national income during the last parliament, we are pledged to increase significantly the share of national income devoted to education over the course of this parliament – not just because education is crucial for social justice but because it is key to improving the productivity of the British economy. We must promote opportunity not just for some of the people some of the time but opportunity for all of the people all of the time.

And one focus in our Spending Review will be not just on resources but on reforms to break down the educational barriers that, at whatever point in the life cycle, deny opportunity and hold people back. Because for Britain to be the best society it can we must tackle the challenge of low aspirations – by reminding young people of the new opportunities to go as far as their talents will allow them, to make the most of themselves, and to be all that they can be, to fulfil the potential they have, just as we remind them of their responsibilities – the modern expression of community and solidarity – to others to use their talents well.

The first barrier is poverty – for child poverty is a scar on the soul of Britain. So Labour's goal is to halve child poverty in ten years on the road to abolishing child poverty in our generation.

Our approach is universal and progressive – it starts with Child Benefit for every family, but is designed to help families most when they need help most and when their children are youngest. So payments for the first child, which in 1997 started at £11 and rose to £28, now start at £15.75, for 5 million families are nearly £26, and for the poorest families are £48.25 a week – a near doubling of cash support since 1997.

And as the next step in meeting our poverty targets, we are bringing together all these related payments for children in a new Child Tax Credit, paid through the tax system, introduced next April – a new seamless system of support, built on universal Child Benefit, with one single payment – improving work incentives and ensuring for the first time that all child payments are paid to the main carer.

And it is exactly the same progressive universalist principles that we are applying to pensions with our £1.5 billion rise in pensions next year: the universal state pension rising each year, pensioners with modest occupational pensions and savings gaining up to an extra £14 a week from the pension credit rising each year faster than earnings, with a Minimum Income Guarantee rising in line with earnings that takes thousands of pensioners out of poverty – our aim that in our generation we abolish pensioner poverty and ensure every pensioner has dignity and security in retirement.

So from removing the barrier of poverty, the second barrier to remove is that too many children go to school not ready to learn. By 2004 Sure Start will be helping 400,000 children, ensuring they are given the opportunity to flourish and are ready to learn when they get to school. I want Sure Start in the UK to be as central to defining Britain as a country of opportunity as Head Start in the USA. And with nursery places already increasing by over 200,000 since 1997, by 2004 all three- and four-year-olds will have access to nursery schools – the early learning that was once the privilege of a minority now under Labour becoming available for all.

Third, the task is now to achieve for secondary schools what we are achieving for primary schools – setting higher standards, and demanding results in return for the new resources. If we can reach out to the fifth of children denied opportunity before they leave school, we will all gain; fail and we all fail. But even then we have more to do. Today in Britain most of the children of rich families go to university but most of the children of poor families do not. In fact, 76 per cent of children of the wealthiest fifth of our families go into higher education, while only 14 per cent of the children of the poorest fifth do. And our aim is not to reduce the numbers from rich families but to increase the number from poor families. This is not only right and fair; it is essential to our economy – with higher productivity and higher-paid jobs increasingly dependent on higher levels of education. For too long too many in this country have believed college and university are not for them, a sad reflection of a poverty of aspiration. That day must end. The Secretary for Education is right to examine measures that will help broaden intake so we will help more pupils stay on at school after sixteen and get the necessary qualifications for university or college:

- extending the successful experiment of providing targeted financial grants via Educational Maintenance Allowances, which has raised school staying-on significantly to cover more sixteen-, seventeen- and eighteen-year-olds – and in Wales the assembly is introducing a similar scheme; and
- in doing so ensuring that all young people have access to the advice and support they need to make the most of college and university opportunities.

And we in the UK administration are looking at the success of the Welsh Assembly's student-grant scheme as it develops.

We want to give new support for the colleges supporting 4 million students now in further education. And to back up 'Learndirect' to improve workplace adult skills we will, in a new pilot experiment, ask employers, in return for our financial support for paid leave, to offer their employees time off to obtain the qualifications they need, and we will continue to back TV learning. And we will encourage a programme of open access in which teams go regularly to all schools to explain both the opportunities and importance of university to young people early on in their secondary education.

For as we tackle the inadequacy of provision and the poverty of aspiration it is time to leave behind for ever what Aneurin Bevan would have called the old Britain of the old-boy networks where too often the privilege you were born to mattered more than the potential you were born with. It is time to leave behind the old Britain where too often the school your parents went to counted more than the skills you were prepared to acquire. And it is time to leave behind the old Britain which too often valued the connections you had when what matters is the contribution you can make.

But a tribute to Aneurin Bevan would be incomplete, especially in front of Michael Foot, and wholly inadequate if we did not understand that the challenges we have to address for Britain – poverty, inequality, access to education and health, the challenges of economic and social development – we have to address for the world. As Bevan said so eloquently in *In Place of Fear*, 'if it is by now irrefutable that most, if not all, the peoples of the world are linked together in an endless variety of reciprocal activities, then the condition of each of us becomes the concern of all of us.'

Martin Luther King put it this way: 'we are each strands in an inescapable network of mutuality, together woven into a single garment of destiny', not here as self-interested individuals sufficient unto ourselves, with no obligations to each

other, but all part of a community bound together as citizens
with shared needs, mutual responsibilities and linked destinies – not only across our nation but also across our world,
our fates and interests bound together. Bevan's vision was not
national, it was international: not just international but cos-
mopolitan – his belief not just that an injury to one is an injury
to all but that an injustice anywhere is a threat to justice
everywhere. A minister in the post-1945 government and then
Foreign Affairs Spokesman for Labour in the fifties, he was
one of a generation of leaders who had known both the
greatest of depressions and the greatest of wars and who had
resolved that the failed policies of *laissez-faire* which resulted in
vast inequities and recurring depression from the 1870s to the
1930s and had contributed to war and conflict should not be
repeated. Untrammelled, unregulated market forces had
brought great instability and even greater injustice. In the
post-war era governments had to work collectively if they were
to achieve both stability and justice. For Bevan's generation
knew that just as peace could not be preserved in isolation,
prosperity could not be maximised in isolation, that prosperity like peace is indivisible. And that prosperity, to be sustained, had to be shared. Bevan said in *In Place of Fear*: 'either
poverty will use democracy to win the struggle against property, or property, in fear of poverty, will destroy democracy'.
Or as John F. Kennedy put it, if a free society cannot help the
many who are poor, it cannot save the few who are rich.

And having built in Bevan's time for the post-war world of
distinct national economies new international institutions
and a commitment to growth and prosperity for all, now
we must do it for the post-national global economy – where
economically no nation is an island; and where the new
frontier is that there is no frontier. And the way forward
for tacking poverty and injustice in the new global economy is
not to retreat from globalisation – to a 1930s-style *laissez-faire*
or to protectionism or old national controls but to ensure by

cooperation and modernising our international institutions that it is possible to envisage a world free of hunger, poverty and deprivation and meet development goals:

- that by 2015 we halve poverty;
- end avoidable child mortality, cutting it by two-thirds; and
- achieve universal education, giving every girl and every boy in every part of the world the right to schooling.

Look at the challenge: the 113 million children – two-thirds of them girls – who are not going to school today because they have no schools to go to; the 200 million young people working as child labourers; the 150 million children who are malnourished, living on the knife's edge of bare existence; and the 30,000 children facing death each day from diseases we could prevent. In total 600 million children in developing countries living in the most disfiguring, grinding poverty imaginable – condemned to failure even before their life's journey has begun.

The global campaign for debt relief in which many of you through churches, NGOs and local organisations have been engaged is now lifting the burden of unpayable debt from twenty-six of the most highly indebted countries, cancelling $62 billion in debt. And as we have seen with Uganda, pupil–teacher ratios as a result of debt relief will fall from 100:1 to 50:1 and every child at school will have a roof above their head.

But what drives us forward are not the achievements we can point to – important as they are – but the gains still to be made. And I want to propose what is a new deal for the global economy, that is also a new deal for the world's poor, that ensures no country genuinely committed to good governance, poverty reduction and economic development is denied the chance to cut infant mortality and poverty and achieve schooling for every one of its children. The new deal is that in return for developing countries pursuing corruption-free policies for stability and for creating a favourable environment for investment, developed countries should agree to increase vitally needed funds to achieve the agreed Millennium Development Goals. Let me briefly mention the four areas in which progress is urgent.

First, hunger is a fact of life for too many children. And in some countries – and not just Malawi – it is tragically getting worse not better. Even when there is adequate food available, poverty often prevents poor people from feeding their children. And as Tony Blair's African partnership recognises, Africa is getting poorer. So the British government proposes today not only to take short-term immediate action – as our International Development Secretary is doing – to help those countries currently affected by food shortages, including Malawi, Zimbabwe and Zambia, but that we finally recognise the importance of the trade round for long-term food security – opening up agriculture in all our countries to fair competition, opening up trade in everything but arms.

Second, because we have been far too slow in advancing our education goals – because as things stand eighty-eight countries will not achieve primary education for all by 2015 and indeed because instead of raising educational aid as a share of national income the world has been, disgracefully, cutting it – our government's proposal today is that the richest countries back the new World Bank initiative with the funds it now needs to fast-track our commitment to meeting the goal of primary education for all by 2015 and to ensuring that in all countries education is not subject to fees but free for everyone.

Third, half child deaths are from four avoidable diseases – acute respiratory-tract infection, diarrhoea, malaria and measles – a loss of millions of children's lives unnecessarily each year. So building on this year's new global health fund for drugs and treatments in HIV/AIDS, malaria and TB, I propose that just as we fast-track investments in education for countries who have a plan, so too for health we should fast-track support for helping to build health-care systems.

Fourth, because too often the world has set goals like the Millennium Development Goals and failed to meet them; because, too often, we have set targets, reset them, and recalibrated them again; because too often our ambitions, in the end, only measure our lack of achievement, this time, it can be – and must be – different.

So to build a virtuous circle of debt relief, poverty reduction and sustainable development for the long term, I propose we step up our commitment to making debt relief a success, by driving forward with HIPC implementation and pledging to ensure its full financing – something that will need a further $1-billion contribution from the richest countries. And I propose we do far more than that. That we accept that the cost of meeting the Millennium Development Goals is $50 billion a year more; and that to achieve this we ask Europe and America to maximise their development spending by examining as a matter of urgency the means by which the currently planned $12-billion-a-year boost to aid can be made to go much further and its benefits maximised.

Every time we lift one child above the squalor of the slums . . . every time we rescue one teenage soldier pressed into combat or one young girl pushed into prostitution or forced labour . . . every time we cure one mother afflicted by disease, and give her and her children a chance in life . . . we are making a difference. But if we can lift not just one child, but millions of children, and then all children, out of poverty and hopelessness, we will have achieved a momentous victory for the cause of social justice on a global scale and the values that shape our common humanity.

Every child the best possible chance, every young person the prospect of education, every adult the reality of a job, every pensioner dignity in retirement, every citizen the best public services, every country playing its part in a just and inclusive world. Not just some but everyone – whatever their birth, background or race – has the chance to achieve their potential. Five national and international goals which show the sheer scale of our ambitions for Britain – goals that for economic as well as equity reasons we cannot postpone or defer, goals that taken together can advance a new progressive consensus for Britain that no opponent could ever erode; goals for our country worth fighting for, goals that show there is purpose in politics, inspired by the same principles that shaped the creation of our labour movement a century ago.

Here tonight in South Wales I ask you to look back on not just the life of Aneurin Bevan but on the lives of our pioneers: men and women in communities like this who one hundred years ago got together in small groups, initially against the odds, to form the labour movement we know today. And their sacrifices, their struggles, their hard-won gains, their great achievements – full employment, an NHS, a Welfare State, a belief in equality and justice – and their conviction that power need not be won at the expense of principle but could not be won without unity and solidarity, must inspire us, here from Wales this evening, to rededicate our efforts to achieve in our time the realisation of their dream:

- a society based on need rather than greed;
- a society where individuals stand free of paternalism and privilege;
- a society where each person has the chance to realise their potential to the full;
- not just here in Britain but in our world.

There are good causes worth fighting for – the same yesterday, today and tomorrow. There is a purpose in politics. We can build a Britain worthy of our pioneers; we can build a Britain worthy of our ideals.

8

DELIVERING LOCAL PUBLIC SERVICES

'All politics', said Tip O'Neill, 'is local.' It is there that the energies are, where problems are best understood and solved, where individuals not otherwise politically engaged can be enlisted in the service of others. The neighbourhood, the parish, the congregation, the youth club are where people experience directly and immediately the power of working together to achieve what none of us can do alone. They are where the virtues of community are born and sustained among people we know, in the midst of whom we live. Community is society with a human face.

Throughout much of the twentieth century, political interest lay elsewhere, in the nation and its two great institutions: the state and the market. The pendulum swing between right and left lay between the two, the left favouring the state, the right, the market. Yet despite the best efforts of governments of either orientation, intractable problems remained: concentrations of urban blight, poverty, educational underachievement, deprivation and other social pathologies. Noting this, people began to ask whether there might not be something missing in this entire way of conceiving the political.

Seeking wisdom in the past, they began re-reading the great thinkers of the eighteenth and nineteenth centuries: Edmund Burke, Thomas Jefferson, Alexis de Tocqueville, John Stuart Mill. There they discovered a surprising emphasis on the local – long derided for most of the twentieth century as small-minded and parochial compared to the gleaming schemes of government action that alone seemed to offer hope of social transformation. They were struck by Burke's emphasis on the 'little platoons' where loyalties and responsibilities were formed, and by de Tocqueville's 'habits of association' which he believed to be the safeguard of democratic freedom and the antidote to individualism.

This led to an enthralling debate, mostly in the United States, about what was called in some circles 'civil society', in others 'communitarianism'. There were great landmarks on the way. First came Peter Berger and Richard John Neuhaus's 1977 pamphlet To Empower People, *with its emphasis on 'mediating structures' – families and communities – larger than the individual but smaller than the state. This was followed by Michael Sandel's* Liberalism and the Limits of Justice *(1982) and Robert Bellah's* Habits of the Heart *(1985), both critical of the shallowness of a politics of atomic individuals without attachments or a sense of belonging. More practically, there was Osborne and Gaebler's* Reinventing Government *(1992), with its powerful examples of how individuals and local networks sometimes brought about change in ways no government could.*

The political vision that emerged was as much about neighbourhood as nation, responsibilities as rights, local involvement as government action. It was an activist politics, recognising that one of the best ways of creating change is to empower those most immediately affected by it. In my own work on the subject, The Politics of Hope, *I spoke about altruism not just self-interest as a force in politics, and drew a distinction between the social contract that creates a state and a social covenant that sustains a society.*

The Chancellor has had a deep interest in this entire debate. He has read the books, engaged with the ideas, thought through ways of translating them into policy, tested them in practice, and set them in the context of a highly articulated political vision. He has understood how empowering localities creates active citizens with a strong sense of the common good. He has seen the transformative energies that communities and voluntary associations can generate. He knows that politics involves not only people trusting politicians, but also politicians trusting people to solve their own problems, while giving them access to resources that only a government can provide.

These speeches testify to a politics of high ideals, in which there is more to citizenship than self-interest: there is also service to others. They bespeak an all too rarely articulated truth: that what matters in politics is not only what we achieve through it, but also what we become by it.

Sir Jonathan Sacks

A consistent theme in many of the Chancellor's speeches is a determination to devolve power for service delivery to local communities. Whether it is in the speeches on Britishness, on how best to advance the public interest, or more recently in his speeches on liberty, responsibility and fairness, there is a consistency of approach which is at odds with the allegations made by his political opponents that he is an instinctive centraliser. His belief is that effective service delivery for families and communities cannot come from central command and control.

A speech given by the Chancellor in Hull on 11 October 2002, entitled 'Empowering Local Centres of Initiative, is a good summary of the argument, which also foreshadows the drive to double devolution: a proper strategic division of responsibilities is to be introduced, on the basis that 'the man in Whitehall does not know best', and on the basis that effective service delivery for families and communities requires local initiative matched by local accountability. Instead of people looking to Whitehall for solutions, people will themselves take more control of the decisions that most affect them – a real devolution of power to voluntary groups and local centres of initiative, across all regions and communities.

The first generation of regional policy, before the war, was essentially ambulance work getting help to high-unemployment areas. The second generation in the 1960s and 1970s was based on large capital and tax incentives delivered by the then Department of Industry, almost certainly opposed by the Treasury. It was inflexible but it was also top-down. And it did not work.

The new approach to regional economic policy, wholeheartedly promoted by the Treasury, is based on two principles. It aims to strengthen the long-term building blocks of growth, innovation, skills and the development of enterprise by exploiting the indigenous strengths in each region and city. And it is bottom-up not top-down, with national government enabling powerful regional and local initiatives to work by providing the necessary flexibility and resources.

. . .

So to build a long-term and strategic partnership between central and local government, and to deliver improved public services, this government has begun to reverse the trend towards ever greater centralisation. We have:

- boosted financial support for councils, through real-terms increases in revenue and in capital expenditure for four years in a row;
- matched devolution with greater accountability and with new constitutions for local government following local consultation;
- recognised the key role of local government by introducing statutory community strategies, supported by a new power to promote community well-being through coordination and partnership with other local actors;
- introduced local public-service agreements with councils, which link resources and greater flexibilities to stretching outcome targets for both national and local priorities. By this time next year we will have concluded

local PSAs with virtually all upper-tier authorities. And in
2004 we will launch a new round of local PSAs that will
boost partnership working and local innovation still
further.

These are important measures, but they are only the first steps
in developing this new partnership. We must now be ready to
do more to achieve our goals. The White Paper last December
set out our vision of local authorities as strong community
leaders responsible for high-quality public services. And we
have made good progress since then in developing further
reforms that will let councils make more decisions for themselves free from central control. So we are introducing a
range of new financial freedoms – new powers for local
authorities to trade, retain fines, develop new services and
decide council-tax exemptions and discounts – allowing responsible councils to innovate and respond to local needs.
    We are making councils themselves responsible for decid-
ing how much they can prudently borrow, providing greater
freedom for councils to invest in local services. We are
removing unnecessary red tape and bureaucracy and will
cut the numbers of plans and strategies that the government
requires councils to produce by 50 per cent. We are developing a more coordinated and proportionate inspection
regime to generate real performance improvements for all
local authorities. And we are restricting ring-fencing of central grants to cases which are genuine high priorities for
government and where we cannot achieve our policy goal
by specifying outcome targets.
    But with freedom comes responsibility and the need for
greater accountability to local communities. That is why the
Treasury has worked with the Deputy Prime Minister to
introduce a new comprehensive performance assessment
– for the first time providing clear and concise information
about each council's performance across a range of local

services. The assessment will enable us to make our inspection regimes more proportionate, to target support where it is most needed, and to identify the small minority of failing councils in need of tough remedial action. And to encourage all councils to deliver the best public services, high-performing councils will receive substantial extra freedoms to enable further service improvements. Our best local authorities will see a dramatic reduction in the amount of their funding that is ring-fenced, plan requirements reduced to the absolute minimum and inspection cut by around 50 per cent. We will also withdraw reserve powers over capping, as a first step towards dispensing with the power to cap altogether.

This is our vision of a modern partnership between central and local government – a new localism where there are flexibility and resources in return for reform and delivery – local authorities at the heart of public services, equipped with the freedom they need, and accountable to the communities whose needs they serve. This is the shape of a government that enables and empowers rather than directs and controls. Many social problems once addressed only by the state gaining more power can be solved today only by the state giving much of its power back to the people. And this is why there is renewed interest in voluntary organisations – devolving more power from government altogether, and into the hands of local communities. It is because we are committed to matching local devolution with agreed national goals that we can encourage local innovation without putting at risk our shared commitment to the highest-quality public services available not just to few but for all.

A few illustrations will show how Britain is changing. With Sure Start – new local partnerships to run services for the under-fives – we break new ground. For the first time, services for the under-fours not only involve private, voluntary and charitable organisations, but can be run through and by them

– not implementing a standardised central plan, but reflecting the needs of local communities and families. And this is just one of the new social initiatives at the heart of a new relationship now being forged between individual, community and state. Our children's policy is evolving not just through better financial support for mothers and fathers, balancing work and family responsibilities, but with a national and local network of Children's Funds, seed-corn finance to enable and empower local community, charitable and voluntary action groups to meet children's needs.

Through the New Deal, we are working in ever closer partnerships with third-sector organisations; our Healthy Living Centres bring together public, private and voluntary sectors; we have introduced new Computer Learning Centres run not centrally but locally as we work to ensure that no one is excluded from the computer revolution – even more not being run by government agencies but by community organisations and partnerships. And of course voluntary action extends to community economic regeneration. Today the Phoenix Fund is pioneering new community finance initiatives and the boards of New Deal for Communities have strong voluntary and community-sector involvement. The whole purpose of Communities Against Drugs, and the Safer Communities Initiative, is to engage voluntary, community and local organisations at the centre of the war against drugs and crime.

What do all these initiatives have in common? In the not-so-distant past, each of these public efforts would have been initiated, planned and run by the state. Today, instead, they are the domain of local leaders, local and community organisations, private-sector leaders working in partnership for the public good. In Britain today there is not one centre of initiative but many centres of local initiative ready to flourish in all parts of the country. So in the provision of these services the old days of 'the man in Whitehall knowing best' is and should be over: men and women in thousands of communities round the country – the mother in the playgroup, the local volunteers in Sure Start, parents in the fight against drugs – know much better. So instead of people looking to Whitehall for solutions in locality after locality, more and more people will themselves take more control of the decisions that most affect them – a devolution of power, an empowerment of local centres of initiative that is now ready to spread across regions, local government and communities, large and small.

The government's approach to localism empowers people – bringing public, voluntary and private sectors together, encouraging innovation to deliver our shared goals of high-quality public services for all. Others appear to be simply advocating privatisation under another name – public services taken over by private companies with the best provision guaranteed just for the few not the many. Instead, for us, a new era – an age of active citizenship and an enabling state – is within our grasp. And at its core is a renewal of civic society where the rights to decent services and the responsibilities of citizenship go together.

. . .

The speech by the Chancellor at the National Council for Voluntary Organisations' Annual Conference on 18 February 2004 develops the theme of partnership in the delivery of public services. Entitled 'Civic Renewal in Britain', the speech reaffirms the government's determination to devolve funding and power to deliver public services, but it also confirms that the government feels that the voluntary and charitable sectors (often referred to as 'the third sector') are ready to partner local councils and neighbourhood organisations so as to better serve our communities. The speech also offers an apology for past mistakes and misjudgements about the third sector; an acceptance that the uniqueness of voluntary and community organisations has not always been recognised by government. The Chancellor feels that in the past some on the left wrongly saw the voluntary sector as a threat to the things that they believed only government should be doing; while others on the right misused the goodwill of a caring voluntary sector as an excuse to relieve government of its proper responsibilities. He feels that both failed to recognise the uniqueness and richness of the third sector, and in different ways had it completely wrong – and unfortunately as the political battle swung back and forth, voluntary organisations were too often caught in the middle.

In an important passage, the Chancellor argues that the third sector must never be seen as a cut-price alternative to statutory provision, or seen as a way of ducking the responsibilities of families or society. Nor should it be seen as a second-class alternative to state provision. For it is now recognised, for example in many Sure Start projects, that even when the public interest is established it is often better for it not to be guaranteed by a public-sector organisation but by those who on the ground can advance the public interest better. He continues: 'governments should have the humility to recognise that voluntary organisations can provide solutions that governments cannot offer. And it is because your independence as a voluntary sector is the essence of your existence, the reason you can serve, the explanation of why you can be so innovative, that you can make the difference that others cannot.'

My theme today is that of new challenges, new responses – civic renewal flourishing in a changing Britain. I know that a recent survey suggested the amount of time spent in Britain on unpaid activities fell from 2.3 billion hours in 1995 to 1.6 billion hours five years later – a drop of more than 30 per cent. So some suggested we have a caring deficit. But in fact a recent MORI poll showed that 59 per cent of 15–24-year-olds want to know more about how to get involved in their communities. I believe we have a goodwill mountain just waiting to be tapped.

I want today to set out why I believe in the independence and strength of a thriving voluntary and community sector in Britain both now and in the future – a strength and independence that we all should and do value. And in setting out my views I want to discuss with you how for the future we can help strengthen that independence and vitality by complementing the measures we are taking and will continue to take to incentivise the giving of money with measures to incentivise the giving of time.

. . .

Now, the community I grew up in – even though it was one made famous as the birthplace of the theorist of the free market Adam Smith – revolved not only around the home but the church, the youth club, the rugby team, the local tennis club, the scouts and boys' brigades, the Royal National Lifeboat Institution, the St John's and St Andrew's Ambulance Society . . . community not in any sense as some forced coming-together, some sentimental togetherness for the sake of appearances, but out of a largely unquestioned conviction that we could learn from each other and call on each other in times of need, that we owed obligations to each other because our neighbours were part also of what we all were: the idea of neighbourliness woven into the way we led our lives.

And while some people say you have only yourself or your family, I saw every day how individuals were encouraged and strengthened, made to feel they belonged and in turn contributed as part of an intricate local network of trust, recognition and obligation, encompassing family, friends, school, church, hundreds of local associations and voluntary organisations.

And while it is easy to romanticise about a Britain now

gone, I believe that there is indeed a golden thread which runs through British history not just of the individual standing firm against tyranny but also of common endeavour in villages, towns and cities – men and women with shared needs and common purposes, united by a strong sense of duty and a stronger sense of fair play. And their efforts together produced not just a rich tradition of voluntary organisations, local democracy and civic life but also a uniquely British settlement that, from generation to generation, has balanced the rights and responsibilities of individuals, communities and state.

The British way has always been much more than self-interested individualism. And this was always recognised, even by those philosophers associated with free-market ideas like Adam Smith and Samuel Smiles. They knew that prosperity and improvement must be founded on something more and something greater than harsh organised selfishness: instead a sense of social obligation – often infused with religious values – and a broad moral commitment to civic improvement. And while it is true that voluntary organisations have risen and fallen over time, it is also true that, in our own time, new organisations from playgroups and mothers-and-toddlers' groups to pensioners or third-age groups and the hospice movement have grown to become vital threads in our national fabric.

And this is my idea of Britain today . . . not the individual on his or her own living in isolation 'sufficient unto himself' but the individual at home and at ease in society. And in this vision of society there is a sense of belonging that expands outwards as we grow from family to friends and neighbourhood; a sense of belonging that then ripples outwards again from work, school, church and community and eventually outwards to far beyond our home town and region to define our nation and country as a society.

Britain – because there is such a thing as society – as a

community of communities. Tens of thousands of local neighbourhood civic associations, unions, charities, voluntary organisations. Each one unique and each one very special, not inward-looking or exclusive. A Britain energised by a million centres of neighbourliness and compassion that together embody that very British idea – civic society.

It is an idea that best defines a Britain that has always rejected absolutism and crude selfish individualism and always wanted to expand that space between state and markets. But it is not a sentimental attempt to hark back to the past nor a rejection of modernity but its practical fulfilment – a Britain where social change redefines community but does not abolish community. And it is an idea that Rabbi Jonathan Sacks captures best and most eloquently when he talks of British society, not in terms of a contract between people that defines our rights but a British covenant that sets out the shared values which can inspire us to neighbourliness and service to others.

And today civic society finds its greatest embodiment in the strength of your voluntary organisations – a genuine third sector established not for self or for profit but for mutual aid and, most often, to provide help and support for those in need.

We know from the theory and evidence on what is called 'social capital' that societies with strong voluntary sectors and civic-society institutions have lower crime, greater social cohesion and better-performing economies than those without. But we in government should be honest and humble, recognising that even as you play a vital role in delivering services because you are better than anyone at doing so, it is your independence that is the source of your strength. And let me explain why not just you but I, from not just history but everyday, on-the-ground experience of living in Britain, believe that to be the case.

For it is true that the uniqueness of voluntary and community organisations has not always been recognised by government. In the past let us be honest that some on the left wrongly saw the voluntary sector as a threat to the things that they believed only government should be doing; while others on the right misused the goodwill of a caring voluntary sector as an excuse to relieve government of its proper responsibilities. Both, failing to recognise the uniqueness and richness of the third sector, had it completely wrong. And yet unfortunately as the political battle swung back and forth, voluntary organisations were too often caught in the middle.

I hope the political establishment has learnt from these mistakes, from the conflicts and sterile battles for territory of the past. The voluntary sector must never be seen as a cut-price alternative to statutory provision, never seen as a way of ducking the responsibilities of families or society. Nor should it be seen as a second-class alternative to state provision. For it is now recognised that even when the public interest is established it is often better for it not to be guaranteed by a public-sector organisation but by those, quite simply, who on the ground can advance the public interest better. That is why today – with for example Sure Start – local voluntary organisations with their unique local knowledge not only provide the service but run many of the projects.

And governments should have the humility to recognise that voluntary organisations can provide solutions that governments cannot offer. That instead of – if I might put it this way – the man from Whitehall always knowing best, it is the woman from the WRVS or Sure Start or Community Service Volunteers or any of the NCVO organisations, that knows better. And it is because your independence as a voluntary sector is the essence of your existence, the reason you can serve, the explanation of why you can be so innovative, that you can make the difference that others cannot.

So I believe, with you, that the great strength of voluntary action – and why we should value your independence – is your capacity for the individual and unique rather than the impersonal or standardised approach. Your emphasis on the individual need, aspiration and potential – and on a one-to-one, person-to-person approach, on being at the front line. As has so often been said, you do not rebuild communities from the top down. You can only rebuild one family, one street, one neighbourhood at a time; or as faith-based organisations, who are so important, often put it – one soul at a time. As one Jewish saying puts it: 'if you have saved one life, you are saving the world'.

And voluntary action, while often conducted through national organisations is, characteristically, local; volunteers and local-community workers, working on the ground, at the coal face, at the heart of local communities, far better positioned than ever a government official could be, both to see a problem and to define effective action. It is about being there.

John Dilulio – former head of the White House Office of Faith-based and Community Initiatives – quotes a conversation between Eugene Rivers, a minister in Boston, worried about his hold on a new generation of young people, and a local youth who has not only become a drug dealer but has a greater hold now over the young people. 'Why did we lose you?' asks the minister of the drug dealer. 'Why are we losing other kids now?' To which the drug dealer replies, 'I'm there, you're not. When the kids go to school, I'm there, you're not. When the boy goes for a loaf of bread . . . or just someone older to talk to or feel safe and strong around, I'm there, you're not. I'm there, you're not . . .'

In the face of drugs, crime, vandalism, social breakdown, voluntary and community organisations – there on the ground, one to one, person to person – really do matter and make the difference that others cannot.

And so too does the second great strength of voluntary action, your freedom to innovate. Long before government took notice, voluntary organisations saw wrongs that had to be righted. Indeed, it is because you innovate that societies most often change. And – often more so than the state – voluntary organisations can be flexible, can pilot, can experiment, can try things out, and can more easily move on.

And just as you did in the past with, for example, the settlement movement or the new campaigning organisations which sprung up in the 1960s, today you are pioneering in new directions: from the hospice movement to anti-AIDS campaigns, from environmental groups to the playgroup movement, from advocates for disabled people to the global coalition against the debt burden of developing countries.

. . .

I am conscious that when we talk of public-service delivery we have a further responsibility not just to ensure voluntary organisations can help – as they have done successfully with Sure Start – and to shape the services they run, but to build upon what I felt was a ground-breaking 2002 Cross Cutting Review on the role of the voluntary and community sector in service delivery – which, I can say, helped us in government, right across departments, to understand much better the issues which voluntary-sector organisations face in public-service delivery.

And when you identified a fundamental problem – basic capacity needs in it, sustainable funding, financial management and skills, and the need for an 'infrastructure map' – we tried to respond. And from this summer, grants and loans will be available through the Futurebuilders fund to help build capability and I can tell you that, recognising that there are skill shortages in management and business planning, the Home Secretary is also finalising work with you on a new capacity and infrastructure framework, including funding to help improve skills, use of IT, performance management and governance in the sector. And I hope that as we discuss all the new challenges ahead, the same spirit and practice of partnership will flourish to the benefit of all.

My late father always said that each of us could make a difference. We could all leave, in his words, 'our mark for good or for ill'. He said that it was not IQ or intelligence or, for that matter, money that defined whether you made the best mark in your society. He believed in Martin Luther King's words, that everybody could be great because everyone can serve. So I certainly grew up influenced by the idea that one individual, however young, small, poor or weak, could make a difference.

Robert Kennedy put it best: 'Let no one be discouraged by the belief there is nothing one man, one woman can do against the enormous army of the world's ills, misery, ignorance, and violence,' he said. 'Few will have the greatness to bend history, but each of us can work to change a small portion of events. And in the total of all these acts will be written the history of a generation'.

Together, your organisations are ensuring not only that service remains an honourable tradition in Britain but that as

old person helps young person;
young helps old;
neighbour helps neighbour;
mentor helps mentored;
business helps community; and
voluntary organisations help, enable and empower
    individuals,

service can make us a stronger, more caring, more resilient society: a Britain with a strong and independent and forward-looking voluntary and community sector . . . a Britain true to its values . . . a Britain ready to face the future.

9

ENDING CHILD POVERTY

I met Gordon Brown for the first time in 2000, at a reception for the National Council for One Parent Families that was held at 11 Downing Street. I doubt that anybody without personal experience of lone parents' stigmatisation by the previous administration can imagine the slight air of unreality that hung over that gathering. One fellow lone mother muttered to me as she took a drink from a passing tray, 'Can you believe we're here?' I quite saw her point.

When I became a lone parent in 1993, following the break-up of my first marriage, the then government's view of 'single mothers' was that they cost the taxpayer far too much money (in spite of the fact that they were poorer as a group than pensioners). Though only 3 per cent of lone parents were under twenty years old, and 60 per cent of us had been married or cohabiting with a partner when we had our children, senior members of the Major administration stereotyped us as feckless teenagers who were 'married to the state' and whose children had been conceived as a means to secure a council flat. While these cowardly, rabble-rousing attacks did not help re-elect those who made them, they left their mark none the less: those of us struggling to bring up children on our own felt demoralised and alienated. Gordon Brown's invitation to hold a reception for lone parents in 11 Downing Street therefore sent a powerful message: poverty was a problem to be solved, not a well-merited punishment for failure to conform to some government-sanctioned ideal of family life.

Although (as you may have read somewhere) I no longer stand in personal need of financial help from the government, I watch every Budget with a view to how it would have improved my life between 1993 and 1997, when I lived in terror of the nappies running out before benefit day. Gordon Brown's Childcare Tax Credits and increases in maternity pay would have made a real difference to my family's life then, most importantly in enabling me to get back to work sooner.

Poverty is a bad place to live on your own, but the worst place on earth if you have a child with you. We will never know how much talent and ability has been stifled in poverty over the centuries, but we can be sure that we will continue to live with ill health, crime and addiction until we succeed in eradicating it from as many children's lives as possible. The same year that I met Gordon Brown, he made a speech in which he expressed perfectly why the eradication of child poverty is surely the most important political goal: 'We must never forget that poverty – above all the poverty of children – disfigures not just the lives of the poor, but all our society.'

J.K. Rowling

Anyone who knows Gordon Brown well, or who came across him in his early days, knows of his deep-seated commitment to root out poverty and in particular to ensure that all our children are given the best chance of developing their potential.

The discovery, on coming into government, that Britain had one of the highest rates of child poverty in the developed world was clearly a shock to many involved in the development of social policy. How could it be that the world's fourth-largest economy could permit a situation to exist whereby over 4 million children – more than a third of all children – lived in a poor family? The research showed that many of them would remain poor for a large part of their childhood – up to a quarter of all children were persistently poor. Most of the children living in poverty, 60 per cent, lived in a household where no one has a job. Overall in the UK, children – 20 per cent of all children – lived in a workless household. Each year around 100,000 children were born into families which were pushed into poverty by the birth of their child.

On 8 July 2004 the Chancellor gave the Joseph Rowntree Foundation Centenary Lecture, entitled 'Our Children Are Our Future'. It covers the background and the philosophy under-pinning all aspects of the action being taken by the government on child poverty. It is also a powerful argument for doing more to create equality of opportunity and equity of outcome for this crucial sector. And it is also a recognition that action at this level needs a new compact between the state and those who benefit from the measures. In the speech the Chancellor clearly en-dorses the radicalism of the approach being taken in Sure Start under which services for the under-fives not only involve volun-tary and charitable action at a local level – even more so than there has been in the past – but also the running of these local groups is being passed to community control, with hugely im-pressive benefits which the Chancellor clearly recognises.

The speech is also noteworthy for its appraisal of what more needs to be done in this area. The Chancellor explains that (even) after seven years of government he is not less idealistic but more idealistic about what can be achieved. He wants Sure Start to be rolled out to all parts of the country, and building on this, perhaps even to tackle an even greater challenge – the poverty of aspiration amongst children and young people and their parents.

It is a privilege to be here today to deliver the Joseph Rowntree Foundation Centenary Lecture and let me begin by paying tribute to one hundred years of service to our community by the Rowntree Foundation: born out of Joseph Rowntree's concern and Christian outrage about poverty and deprivation; built by the dedicated commitment of people who had a vision of the world not as it was but as it could be; and today widely acknowledged to be at the heart of what I can call the nationwide crusade for justice for the poor, with not just an established and well-deserved reputation for authoritative research that consistently shines a spotlight on the needs of our country's families but a path-breaking role in finding practical solutions – that started with pioneering developments in housing and community regeneration and now extends into not just housing and community regeneration but innovative forms of care for the young, the elderly and the disabled.

So in a century of service, the Rowntree Foundation, always rooted in values of public service, always driven forward by ideas and often painstaking research, always a tangible national expression of compassion in action – taking its rightful place as one of the great British national institutions. So I want today at the outset to congratulate all of you – board, staff, supporters, campaigners – on your years of progress and achievement. And I hope you can be proud that your concern – poverty; your mission – to shock the nation into action against poverty; and your driving ambition – the eradication of poverty – for far too many years a call for justice unheard in a political wilderness, is the ambition now not just of your organisation but the ambition of this country's government. And let me also say today that I am humbled not just to deliver this lecture to this Foundation but to address a gathering of so many people who have served our communities and country with such distinction, men and women here today in this audience so distinguished in their own spheres of service –

charity workers, social workers, community activists, academics, researchers, NGO leaders. You have not only worked year after year to tackle social evils but have worked tirelessly in some of the most difficult circumstances, keeping the flame of compassion alive often in some of the least propitious times and in some of the darkest and most challenging corners of our community. So especially for those who have toiled at the front line – often with few resources and little support – let me place on record my appreciation of the service so many of you give – of the work you do, the contribution you make, the dedication you show and the real difference you make.

Let us think back to the conditions Joseph Rowntree surveyed one hundred years ago: the first building blocks of the modern Welfare State yet to be established, the Lloyd George People's Budget still a few years away, but Victorian and Edwardian society starting to discover the full scale of poverty in their midst; and Winston Churchill – who went on to introduce the first minimum wage – appalled by the huge gap between what he called the excesses of accumulated privilege and the gaping sorrows of the left-out millions. And about Joseph Rowntree we could have no doubt: an idealist not a dreamer; an enthusiastic reformer not a reluctant donor; and in his lifetime and through the Foundation he created we can genuinely say that he led the way in four areas vital to the development of our social services and the fabric of our community life.

First, his plea – and I quote – that we 'search out the underlying causes of weakness or evil in the community rather than remedying their more superficial manifestations'. You might call it tough love: his rightful insistence that we tackle the sources of poverty and not just their consequences; that we should focus on the eradication of the evil of social injustice and not just compensate people for its existence.

Second, Rowntree's insistence on an evidence-based

approach. Indeed his Foundation is a monument to one man's conviction that the lives of countless fellow citizens can be improved by the intelligent application of knowledge and then policy to one of the greatest social evils and one of the greatest moral challenges of the day.

And that led, thirdly, to an understanding of the multiple causes of poverty, and the multidimensional nature of poverty. And although there have been many changes in the last one hundred years – for when he began there was no sickness benefit, no state pensions, no unemployment benefit and no National Health Service – I am struck by the fact that the multiple challenges that Rowntree identified in his 'Founder's Memorandum' still remain relevant today – the challenge of poverty itself, of bad housing, poor education, neighbourhood renewal. And you could say that he understood what was meant by multiple deprivation long before the term was even invented. And finally it led him – and the Foundation – to pioneer an understanding of the life cycle of poverty. In 1904, Rowntree described that tragic life cycle – of poverty during childhood, poverty for parents when they had children and poverty during old age: a life cycle of poverty broken only by the short periods when you were an adult before your children were born or an adult whose children had grown up and left home.

And the striking truth about what we found in 1997 was how firmly and how widely this 'life cycle of poverty' had returned. And I believe that Rowntree would agree that addressing the multiple causes of poverty and the life cycle of poverty in our times, demands we be far bolder than the philanthropists of 1904. Let us recall that in 1942 – nearly forty years after the Rowntree Foundation was set up and in response to some of its pioneering work – Sir William Beveridge identified five evils – want, idleness, ignorance, squalor and disease – which a new Welfare State had to confront. But because we are interested in the potential of every person, our goal today – inspired by Rowntree – must be even more ambitious than the one Beveridge set us in 1942 when he listed his five evils:

- instead of simply attacking idleness and unemployment, our goal is the genuinely challenging goal of full and fulfilling employment;
- instead of simply attacking ignorance, our goal is the more ambitious goal of lifelong education for all;
- instead of simply attacking squalor, our goal is high-quality affordable housing for all and not just houses but strong and sustainable communities;
- instead of simply tackling disease, our goal is not just an NHS there when you need it but health and social policies that can prevent as well as cure disease and promote good health; and
- instead of just securing freedom from want – which meant sufficiency and minimum standards – our goal is the development of the potential of all to secure prosperity for all.

And in addressing these great challenges, our objective must be to ensure not only dignity for the elderly in retirement and the chance for all adults to realise their potential but that every child has the best possible start in life. And it is on the needs of children and the challenges ahead that I want to concentrate my remarks on policy today.

. . .

The return in the last three decades of the life cycle of poverty – indeed the great and unacceptable concentration of poverty amongst households with young children – is the greatest indictment of our country in this generation and the greatest challenge of all. The facts are that in the two decades before 1997 the number of children growing up in workless households – households where no one had a job – rose to almost 20 per cent. One in every five children did not have a parent earning any income from work. The numbers of children in low-income households more than doubled to over 4 million. And you must never forget that the UK – one of the richest countries of the industrial world – suffered worse levels of child poverty than nearly all other industrialised nations. Indeed, anyone reading reports on the condition of Britain will be shocked by one straightforward but disgraceful fact. When we came into government one in every three babies born in Britain were being born into low-income households; born not into opportunity but into poverty.

This is the 'condition of Britain' question we had to confront one hundred years after the Joseph Rowntree Foundation was set up. And it is the 'condition of Britain' question still with us fifty years after Beveridge and the creation of the Welfare State. Not only was child poverty endemic by 1997 but social mobility had slowed – in some respects, had gone into reverse. And while more room existed at the top, a child from the lowest social class was a quarter as likely to make it to that place at the top as the child from the highest social class. But during these years when child poverty grew, so too did our understanding of all that we had to do to tackle child poverty – and in particular just how crucial the first months and certainly the first years of a child's life are in determining life chances. Indeed recent research suggests that much of children's future prospects can be predicted within twenty-four months of them being born. Leon Feinstein has shown how psychological and behavioural differences varying strongly by social class can be seen in children as young as twenty-two months and continue to have a systematic – and increasingly significant – effect on employment and earnings patterns right through to later life. Research undertaken in the US shows that pre-school experiences in language and literacy are strong predictors of later development in language and literacy. And the

Effective Provision of Pre-School Education project in the UK found that children who participated in some sort of early learning made significantly more progress than those who didn't. Abigail McKnight concludes that individuals who experience childhood poverty tend to suffer a penalty in labour-market earnings in adult life, and that the size of this penalty has grown over time. For we now also know from your research that an infant who then grows up in a poor family is less likely to stay on at school, or even attend school regularly, less likely to get qualifications and go to college, more likely to be trapped in the worst job or no job at all, more likely to be trapped in a cycle of deprivation that is lifelong . . . less likely to reach his or her full potential: a young child's chances crippled even before their life's journey has barely begun.

I believe that action to eradicate child poverty is the obligation this generation owes to the next. Children may not have votes – or the loudest voices . . . or at least their voices are not often heard in our politics – but our obligation is, if anything, greater because of this.

. . .

So in 1999, determined to ensure that each child has the chance to realise his or her potential, the government set an ambitious long-term goal to halve child poverty by 2010 and eradicate it by 2020. Tackling child poverty is, for us, the critical first step in ensuring that each child has the chance to develop their potential to the full. And as a first step, we have sought to reduce the number of children in low-income households by April 2005 at least a quarter. So far, measured by absolute low income, 2 million children have been lifted out of poverty; so far too, measured by relative low income, half a million children have been lifted out. And I think there is general agreement that having allocated resources to raise our Child Tax Credits for the poorest families, we are on track to meet our target of reducing child poverty by a quarter by April next year. But we are not complacent in any way nor will we relax our efforts or allow them to be stalled. The next step – our goal of, by 2010, reducing child poverty by half – is even more challenging and how we reach this goal is the subject of the remaining observations I want to share with you.

I can tell you today that in the Spending Review next week we will set out the detail of the target for 2010 – to halve the number of children in households in relative low income compared to 1998. As many of you have proposed to us, next Monday we will also set out an additional target to halve the numbers of children suffering from material deprivation – children lacking basic necessities the rest of us take for granted. And because we know from your research that the quality of housing is critical in tackling poverty, we will – as part of this new material-deprivation measure – be monitoring the quality of a child's housing conditions. Acting, I believe, in the spirit of Rowntree.

And so let me point you to the policy changes that I believe are now necessary if we are to meet this anti-poverty target, the means by which we seek to develop the potential of millions of British children.

. . .

While universal Child Benefit is the foundation, it is the introduction of the Child Tax Credit – now benefiting 6 million families and 10 million children – that allows us, while giving more to every child, to give most to those who need it most, and is thus the front line of our attack on child poverty. So with the addition of the Child Tax Credit the nine out of ten families who would in 1997 have received just £11 in Child Benefits now receive more than twice as much – £27 a week. For the poorest families tax credits go even further: with one child under eleven, financial support which was £28 in 1997 is now £58.22 – a near doubling in real terms. And a family with two children under eleven can now receive in children's benefits over £100 a week.

Indeed, progress is being made to meeting our child-poverty target because the poorest 20 per cent of families have received not 20 per cent of all additional money but over 40 per cent. And, as a result, while all families with children are on average £1,350 a year better off now than they were in 1997, the poorest 20 per cent of families are £3,000 a year better off. For the rest of this parliament we will continue to uprate the child element of the Child Tax Credit in line with earnings – and I can tell you today that in future Pre-Budget Reports and Budgets we will assess progress towards our 2010 goal. As a government we have also come to realise that if we are to meet our child-poverty goals and ensure that there is equality in opportunity but also fairness in outcome, assets matter as well as income. So to each child born after September 2002 an initial contribution to their own individual Child Trust Fund of £250, with twice as much – £500 – for the poorest third of children; and then again a contribution at seven and then perhaps at later ages to enable all young people to have more of the choices that were once available only to some. With the new Child Trust Fund worth twice as much for the poorest child; with the Child Tax Credit worth four times as much for the poorest child; and with five times as much for the poorest infant – our anti-poverty commitment is based on a progressive principle that I believe that all decent-minded people can and should support: more for every child, even more help for those who need it most and at the time they need it most, equality of opportunity and fairness of outcome applied in new times and with tax credits the principal new means.

And as we develop our policies on financial support over the coming years, I recognise from your research and policy proposals that we have not done enough in a number of important ways and that there are major issues which now need to be addressed including:

- first, the costs faced by larger families and the consequences for benefits and tax credits; and
- second, the housing costs faced by the low-paid, and this requires us also to evaluate the way housing benefit interacts with the tax and benefit system and the impact of the pilots for paying flat-rate housing benefit.

So looking ahead we will continue to address the issue of children's benefits but we have also always been clear about the importance of the contribution of family employment to meeting our child-poverty targets. And of course we must get the balance right between supporting mothers to stay at home, particularly in the early years, and creating opportunities for employment. Again it is because of tax credits – which create a new tax system whose rates start at 40 per cent at the top but go to as low as minus 200 per cent for the lowest-income earners – that a lone parent with one child working thirty-five hours at the minimum wage is now £73 a week better off in work than on benefit. And a couple with one child and one parent working thirty-five hours at the minimum wage is now around £38 a week better off in work than on benefit. Because the starting wage for the unemployed man or woman returning to work is typically only two-thirds of the average hourly rate, the Child and Working Tax Credits have been designed not just to help people into work but to help people in work move up the jobs ladder and into higher incomes. Under the old system of family credit, 740,000 households faced marginal tax and benefit withdrawal rates of over 70 per cent; now the new credits have cut this figure by nearly two-thirds, helping people keep more of every extra pound they earn.

In total, 1.8 million more people are in jobs now than in 1997, with unemployment reduced to its lowest level in thirty years. But if we are to meet our child-poverty targets we must advance further and faster to full employment in every community and we must make it a priority to reach the still-large number of households with children where no adult works. And of crucial importance in meeting our child-poverty target for 2010 will be employment opportunity for lone parents. It is a striking fact that lone-parent households contain a quarter of all children but account for nearly half of those in poverty. As a result one and a half million of the country's poorest children are today living on benefit in lone-parent families where no one has a job. Since 1997 250,000 more lone parents have gone into work. Because of the New Deal, the minimum wage, the Working Tax Credit and other initiatives, the lone-parent rate of employment in the UK has increased to 53 per cent. But in the US lone-parent employment is more than 60 per cent, in Sweden above 70 per cent and in France in excess of 80 per cent. Our target is 70 per cent lone-parent employment by 2010. And let me explain the significance of this ambition. If we meet our target to raise lone-parent employment, this one success alone could reduce the number of British children living in poverty by around 300,000. And if we went even further to French levels we could reduce the number of children in poverty by a total of approaching half a million.

Now research shows most lone parents would like to combine paid work with the vital job of being a parent. But they face real barriers to doing so. And those who work with lone parents – and lone parents themselves – have rightly called on us to do more to help them get the skills they need for work and to ease the transition between income support and paid work. So while all lone parents are now invited in for work-focused interviews, we are also piloting new lone-parent 'work discovery weeks' – run by employers in London, Glasgow, Liverpool, Manchester, Leeds and Birmingham – that are providing introductory and preparatory courses for work in some of our best-known retail stores, hotels and companies – and are backed up by help with child care. Where local employers identify a demand for skills lone parents in these six cities also have access to free NVQ Level 3 training – and funds to buy work clothes or equipment. And because we recognise that the time of transition from benefits to employment can be difficult, from October lone parents will benefit from a new job grant of £250 when they move into work and they will enjoy a four-week extension of Housing Benefit.

So what does the success of our recent measures mean in practice for tackling child poverty? It means that with the new help with Housing Benefit, lone parents on a typical rent of £50 a week and working part time will receive at least £217 a week for around sixteen hours' work a week. The effective hourly rate is not the minimum wage of £4.50 but £13.50 an hour – making them far better off working part-time than not working at all. And so we have come to recognise that central to tackling child poverty – as well as to the importance of helping families balance work and family life – is the provision of adequate child care. And while we have since 1997 created over a million more childcare places, the greatest help for low-income families has been the third element of tax credits that we have introduced – the tax credit for covering the costs of child care – up to £95 each week for families with one child in qualifying child care and up to £140 for those with two or more children. When we started in 1997 it was claimed by just 47,000 families; it is now benefiting 320,000, with maximum help given to lone parents. And while we ensure that by 2008 nearly 2.5 million children a year will have access to good-quality child care, again for poor families the next stage in the extension of the Childcare Tax Credit is of greatest importance – from April 2005 extended to a wider range of eligible child care including, in some cases, at home. And the tax credit will be supported by a new incentive for employers – to give their employees up to £50 a week, free of income tax and National Insurance, to help with childcare costs.

So tax credits have been and will continue to be the key to

tackling child poverty. But as a government we also have a duty and role to play in encouraging the development of the potential of Britain's children through the provision of high-quality public services – and Bruce Katz has this morning shown why one of our priorities must be to drive up the performance of public services in our most deprived neighbourhoods and thus break long-established cycles of deprivation. And I do not underestimate the critical role that new investment in housing can play. Of all the services that contribute to the development of potential, a good education – the subject of the government's five-year plan today – is clearly the most fundamental. So as I announced in the Budget, we are investing over three years an additional £8.5 billion in education; raising average spending per pupil from the £2,500 a year we inherited to £5,500 by 2008 – and, as a sign of our commitment to tackling disadvantage – by even more in the 1,400 schools that benefit from our extra support for leadership and excellence to combat deprivation.

We have, indeed, a long way to go in ensuring for today's poor children a decent start in life but it is important to record that the greatest improvement so far in reading, writing and maths has been in the primary schools of the poorest areas. And I can tell you that the next stage is to help at an early stage the very pupils most in danger of falling behind – and with extra money for their books, and their classrooms, equipment and staffing drive up their literacy and numeracy. I can also inform you that secondary schools with more than 35 per cent of their fourteen-year-olds eligible for free meals are now making the biggest gains in maths and science results at Key Stage 3. Indeed the number of secondary schools with less than 25 per cent of their pupils achieving five or more good GCSEs has fallen from over 600 in 1997 to 224. And today's five-year plan sets out our next steps – with the very pupils most in need offered more personalised learning, including new vocational options, and greater access to it.

I can tell you also that in the Spending Review there will be new, more challenging floor targets for the poorest areas. And as part of the review of the local formulae used to distribute schools funding – due to take place later this year – I would like to identify even more effective ways to target resources at tackling deprivation: measures to help children in the bottom-income quintile catch up, particularly in primary school, and measures to enable schools to meet the higher costs of educating children from poorer backgrounds who may have lower levels of early educational attainment and who may have far less parental support.

Tragically Britain has, for decades, had one of the poorest staying-on rates of the industrialised world. In Britain more young people leave school early, more leave without qualifications and more never reappear in the world of education. So again to tackle both poverty and lack of opportunity – and to seek to tackle perhaps an even greater challenge, the poverty of aspiration amongst children and young people and their parents – we have reformed the careers service, introduced summer schools, encouraged better links between schools and universities and colleges. And we have piloted an Education Maintenance Allowance: up to £1,500 a year on top of Child Benefit and the Child Tax Credit for those young people who need financial help to stay on in education and get the qualifications they need. And so successful has the allowance been in raising staying-on rates that from September this year it will be available nationwide; and as it goes nationwide be made available not just for school and further-education courses but for training too – once again helping all young people, but doing more for those who need help most so that no child is left behind.

I said at the outset that while we are committed to social security from the cradle to the grave, too many children have already lost out within months of being born – condemned to poverty because not enough has been done to help them from the cradle to the nursery school. Indeed for fifty years while there was undoubtedly much innovation in the voluntary and charitable sector, Welfare State support for the country's youngest children consisted of maternity services, vaccinations and a requirement to appear at school at age five. Yet while the provision remained inadequate the evidence grew that the first four years of a child's life are critical to their personal development; that children who went to nursery or other early education before they attended school were likely to have significantly improved social, emotional and cognitive development; that the longer children attend pre-school – and the higher the quality of the service – the greater the positive influence; and that such intervention was particularly beneficial for the poorest children. And so it is clear that a strategy of counteracting disadvantage must begin right from the start of a child's life and that the earliest years – once the lowest priority – are now rightly becoming among the highest priority: not just the biggest gap in provision and next frontier for us to cross, but one of the single most important investments the Welfare State can make.

The Sure Start Maternity Grant – once just £100 – has been raised to £500, a five-fold rise in five years. Reversing a long-standing policy that more Child Benefits went to older rather than younger children, we doubled the Child Tax Credit for the first year of a child's life. To help parents stay at home with their children, maternity leave and pay has been substantially extended and paternity pay now exists for the first time. And earlier than planned, nursery education is now available for all three-year-olds as well as all four-year-olds.

Now, in the past to identify a problem – the need to expand provision for infants from birth to three – would probably have led simply to the creation of a new state service. But I believe that what today is happening in the area of under-five provision shows how what we do – in the spirit of Rowntree –

is based upon evidence; how the best approach is multi-dimensional – across the services – and the range of provision mixed; and how, instead of a narrow focus on what central government can do, voluntary and community organisations, and parents, and government – local and national – through not just one service but a range of services – child-health services, social services, and early learning – are now all part of the solution.

I often say that Sure Start is today one of the best-kept secrets of government, but it is also one of the unsung successes of the voluntary and community sector. And there are now over 500 Sure Start or children's centres providing services for 400,000 children across the country, including a third of all children under four living in poverty. And you have only to visit local Sure Start projects – as I did in Bristol a few weeks ago and then in Birmingham last week – to capture a very real sense of the difference they are making: and already evidence from individual projects in some of Britain's most deprived areas shows that Sure Start is having a notable effect on children's language development and social skills, and on the interaction of parents and their children.

What is then exciting about Sure Start and the approach it represents? I believe that what is exciting is what Rowntree himself would have approved of – and what Rowntree Foundation research has pointed towards: first, a coordinated approach to services for families with young children, tackling the multidimensional causes of poverty – physical, intellectual, emotional and social – by adopting an integrated approach with child care, early education and play, health services and family support at the core of Sure Start. It reflects a growing recognition that housing, health, transport, social services, youth and many other services are vital in tackling child poverty and developing young people's potential. And the new Public Service Agreements we will be publishing alongside our commitment to new investment for these services will reflect this.

Second, the emphasis within this approach on health and inequality highlighted by today's report of the Health Care Commission. And later this year there will be a new public-health White Paper – refocusing our attention on preventive health – which will emphasise once more the importance of tackling the unacceptable health inequalities – including infant life chances – which distort our country.

Third, Sure Start is emphasising the central role of parents in tackling child poverty – and that is why parents are enlisted in the very running of the Sure Start projects. We must never forget that it is parents who bring children up, not governments, and our emphasis is on the opportunities now available to parents and the responsibilties they must discharge. So we are not only increasing the financial support available to parents – and exploring options for future further increases in maternity and paternity pay – but making available wider support for parents, including expanding parenting classes and providing access to practical parenting advice in a wider range of locations.

Fourth, the central role of voluntary community and charitable organisations from mothers-and-toddlers' groups to the playgroup and childcare movement to a vast and impressive range of specialist organisations throughout our country. It is a humble recognition of the limits of government – that child poverty cannot be removed by the action of government alone but by government, working with parents, voluntary, charitable and community organisations – and a celebration of the vital role of the voluntary and community sector in every city and town of our country. And let us not forget that alongside traditional voluntary organisations – like the churches and uniformed organisations for young people – that have been declining in numbers, there has been a mushrooming of young mothers' groups, playgroups, and

groups and clubs associated with children locally and nationally. And let us be clear about the radicalism of our approach.
For Sure Start also enacts an important new principle into
action – that services for the under-fives not only involve
voluntary and charitable action at a local level – even more so
than we have done in the past – but either in partnership or in
sole control, the very running of these local groups can be
and is being passed to community control. And it is a
recognition that we must all accept our responsibilities as
parents, neighbours, citizens and community leaders, in the
battle against child poverty.

And of course there is a fifth innovation: the far greater
emphasis on early learning – so early that it can start with the
local school contacting the mother not in the months before
the child's fifth birthday but just a few weeks after the child is
born – backed up by innovations like Bookstart offering
children the books they might not otherwise have, to start
in their first months to learn to read.

And we can see now how, combined with the improved
income support for the under-fives that I have described, the
additional cash resources for early learning and the support
for the specialist groups – many represented here – that deal
with disability, special needs and other challenges, a new
more comprehensive approach not just to tackling child
poverty but to developing the potential of every child is
taking shape. And as we approach the Spending Review next
week and advance to the Pre-Budget Report, I can tell you
that what I have described this morning can only be the start
of what we have yet to do. Building on Sure Start, the next
stage is to fund the creation of new Children's Centres across
the country – again providing a combination of good-quality
child care, early-years education, family support and health
services. By 2006 650,000 children will be covered by Sure
Start or Children's Centres. And there will be new funding –
despite our other representations – to ensure 1,700

Children's Centres by 2008 – one in each of the 20 per cent most deprived wards in England, as we advance towards our goal of a Children's Centre for every community.

But Sure Start – and related services – point the way for a new agenda for services for young children: greater encouragement for local initiatives and community action in the war against child poverty; offering government money to back non-government initiatives to tackle disadvantage; partnership with both the biggest voluntary and community organisations and the smallest; the emphasis on prevention, not simply coping with failure; greater parental involvement in the running of services. And anyone who like me has attended a Sure Start conference – and seen the dynamism, energy and determination of parents, volunteers and carers in action – can begin to understand the transformative power that organisations from the playgroup movement to the childcare campaigns can have. And I look forward to the 'little platoons' in our communities becoming veritable armies demanding we do more.

So new finance, like tax credits; new initiatives, like the New Deal for lone parents; new dimensions, like support for child care; new services, like Sure Start; new approaches, whole services managed by the voluntary sector; new directions, engaging parents in the running of programmes. All weapons in the war against child poverty, all evidence that parents, voluntary organisations and government can, acting together, make a real difference. All evidence, also that informed by knowledge, working with the best of caring organisations, public action can transform young lives. Go to a Sure Start programme, as I did a few days ago – and see the bright new investments that are starting to change the face of some of the most deprived areas of our country. Listen to a mother, once feeling trapped in her home, telling you how Sure Start has introduced her to other mothers with similar stories to tell. Hear the views of children of lone parents – telling of their pride that their mother now has a job. And hear the responses of parents on the Child and Working Tax Credits – describing how what they can spend on their children has been raised by £50 a week.

And so I tell you: after seven years of government I am not less idealistic but more idealistic about what we can achieve working together. Because we now have evidence of what can be done by Sure Start in some areas of the country, we want to apply the lessons to all parts of the country. And because we have evidence of the good that is done for some children, then we want to extend these opportunities to all children. And what started, for us, seven years ago as an article of faith about what might be achieved is now a conviction based on clear evidence about what can and must be done. Because what has been done shows us what more can be done, because the evidence of small successes shows what even larger successes are possible, it must make us more even more ambitious to do more. So my experience of government has not diminished my desire to tackle child poverty but made me more determined to do more. For what has happened so far does not begin to speak to the limits of our aspirations for developing the potential of Britain's children, but challenges us to learn from the changes now being made and strive in future years to do even more. So on Monday I will be able to announce the next stage in our policies for tackling child poverty and for helping the development of the potential of every child – and I believe as a country we are ready to do more to tackle old injustices, meet new needs and solve new challenges.

But what we can achieve depends upon the growth of a nationwide sentiment of opinion – indeed, a shared and concerted demand across communities, across social classes, across parties, across all decent-minded people – that the eradication of child poverty is a cause that demands the priority, the resources, and the national attention it deserves.

It is not usual for government to welcome the growth of pressure groups that will lobby, demonstrate, embarrass, expose and then push them to action. But I welcome the New Alliance for Children – the broad coalition of community organisations, voluntary and charitable sector determined to push further to end child poverty. For the emerging evidence – and the growth in a nationwide public opinion – emboldens me to believe it can indeed be this generation of campaigners, charity workers, child carers, Sure Start organisers, working together, that will right the social wrongs that impelled Joseph Rowntree to action and ensure every child has a fair start in life.

So let us continue to follow the lead given by the pioneers who brought the Rowntree Foundation into being. And inspired by a generation of reformers like Rowntree who had a vision; driven forward – as the Rowntree Foundation has always been – by the evidence of what is happening around us; never losing sight of the vision that inspired a whole generation; our eyes fixed firmly on the goal that if every child has the best start in life, we can build a better Britain.

10

MOVING BRITAIN FORWARD

One is struck when reading Gordon Brown's speeches by both the passion and the clarity of purpose which drive his political commitment.

In an age when electoral choice is so often portrayed as just one more decision a consumer makes, it is refreshing indeed to see the social democratic vision for opportunity and security for all so eloquently expressed.

What makes these speeches all the more powerful is the fact that as Chancellor of the Exchequer, Gordon Brown, has put his ideas into action. The result is a Britain where so many more people are employed and have hope for the future for their families.

In the chapter on public services, Gordon Brown first makes the overwhelming case for preserving the National Health Service and the means by which it has been funded. He argues powerfully that, far from the NHS being a dinosaur from another age, it stands up very well against other Western nations' health systems as comprehensive, equitable and accessible.

Gordon Brown accepts that in the twenty-first century citizens are looking for services which are personalised, but argues that that together with efficiency and equity can be achieved through the NHS.

I agree : there is no reason why a public health system cannot meet all three objectives well. The same vision drives my government in New Zealand to fund the public health service so that all our citizens' reasonable health needs can be met within it, and so that any consideration of seeking private care is a personal choice for those with the means to do it rather than an imperative for those needing essential treatment.

It is good to see the vision of Aneurin Bevan invoked in these speeches. In New Zealand we recognise him as one of a remarkable generation of Labour leaders who created a new Britain in the immediate post-war era. Their simple commitment to fulfilling the potential and guaranteeing the security of every citizen had a transformational effect of Britain, in particularly in opening up opportunity through education to working-class children in an unprecedented way.

Even so, and despite the sterling efforts of Britain's subsequent Labour Governments in the 1960s and 1970s, Labour elected in 1997 still had work to do – at home and abroad.

In the past nine years, Labour has not only run a strong, job rich economy and invested heavily in public services in Britain; it has also put its philosophy into action through its overseas development assistance, with Chancellor Gordon Brown being a driving force behind that commitment.

Speeches like those in this chapter and through the book enable us to see the policies Gordon Brown supports, promotes, and funds within the context of their strong philosophical base. There is a clear logic behind and coherence about his programme. Gordon Brown believes there is a purpose in politics, and that purpose has motivated him to give the best years of his life to the noble cause of the betterment of the people of Britain.

Twelve thousand miles away in New Zealand, I as Labour Prime Minister read Gordon Brown's speeches with considerable interest, and believe that they resonate not only in our country which has been influenced so much by British political traditions, but also throughout the social democratic family world wide.

Helen Clark

In January 2006, Gordon Brown delivered the keynote speech to the Fabian Society annual conference. In this remarkable speech, much of the subsequent press comment focused on the rather narrow question of whether Britain should do more to celebrate Britishness, perhaps thorough greater use of flags, public holidays and the like. But in fact this speech, properly read as an extension of the Hugo Young Memorial Speech given a month earlier, sets out some interesting ideas for the future, and perhaps more than a hint of what might be in the manifesto for a fourth-term Labour government.

In this speech the Chancellor argues that our success as a nation, our ability to meet and master not just the challenges of a global economy but also the international, demographic, constitutional, social, and security challenges ahead, requires us to rediscover and build from our history and apply in our time the shared values that bind us together and give us common purpose. He develops the argument that there is a fundamental relationship that links liberty, responsibility and fairness to a modern definition of patriotism, and to Britishness. And taking off from that, the Chancellor sets out a range of policy initiatives aimed at addressing the major challenges facing our country – our relationships with Europe, America and the rest of the world; how we equip ourselves for globalisation; the future direction of constitutional change; a modern view of citizenship; the future of local government, ideas of localism; our community relations and the balance between diversity and integration; and the shape of our public services.

Being clear what Britishness means in a post-imperial world is essential if we are to forge the best relationships with the developing world and in particular with Africa. But take Europe also: there is no doubt that in the years after 1945, faced with relative economic decline as well as the end of empire, Britain lost confidence in itself and its role in the world and became so unsure about what a confident post-imperial Britain could be that too many people defined the choice in Europe as either total absorption or splendid isolation; and forgot that just as you could stand for Britain while being part of NATO, you can stand for Britain and advance British national interests as part of the European Union.

Let me also suggest that it is because that loss of confidence led too many to retreat into the idea of a Britain that was little more than institutions that never changed – so for decades, for fear of losing our British identity, Britain did not face up to some of the great constitutional questions, whether it be the second chamber, the relationship of the legislative to the executive or the future of local government. Take also the unity of the United Kingdom and its component parts. While we have always been a country of different nations and thus of plural identities – a Welshman can be Welsh and British, just as a Cornishman or -woman is Cornish, English and British – and may be Muslim, Pakistani or Afro-Caribbean, Cornish, English and British – there is always a risk that, when people are insecure, they retreat into more exclusive identities rooted in nineteenth-century conceptions of blood, race and territory – when instead we, the British people, should be able to gain great strength from celebrating a British identity which is bigger than the sum of its parts and a union that is strong because of the values we share and because of the way these values are expressed through our history and our institutions.

And take the most recent illustration of what challenges us

to be more explicit about Britishness: the debate about asylum and immigration and about multiculturalism and inclusion, issues that are particularly potent because in a fast-changing world people who are insecure need to be rooted. Here the question is essentially whether our national identity is defined by values we share in common or just by race and ethnicity – a definition that would leave our country at risk of relapsing into a wrongheaded 'cricket test' of loyalty.

Equally, while the British response to the events of July 7th was magnificent, we have to face the uncomfortable fact that there were British citizens, British born, apparently integrated into our communities, who were prepared to maim and kill fellow British citizens, irrespective of their religion – and this must lead us to ask how successful we have been in balancing the need for diversity with the obvious requirements of integration in our society. But I would argue that if we are clear about what underlies our Britishness and if we are clear that shared values – not colour, nor unchanging and un-changeable institutions – define what it means to be British in the modern world, we can be far more ambitious in defining for our time the responsibilities of citizenship; far more ambitious in forging a new and contemporary settlement of the relationship between state, community and individual; and it is also easier too to address difficult issues that some-times come under the heading 'multiculturalism' – essentially how diverse cultures, which inevitably contain differences, can find the essential common purpose without which no society can flourish.

So Britishness is not just an academic debate – something just for the historians, just for the commentators, just for the so-called chattering classes. Indeed in a recent poll, as many as half of British people said they were worried that if we do not promote Britishness we run a real risk of having a divided society. And if we look to the future I want to argue that our success as Great Britain, our ability to meet and master not just the challenges of a global economy but also the international, demographic, constitutional and social challenges ahead, and even the security challenges, requires us to rediscover and build from our history and apply in our time the shared values that bind us together and give us common purpose.

I believe most strongly that globalisation is made for a Britain that is stable, outward-looking, committed to scientific progress and the value of education. And that by taking the right long-term decisions Britain can stand alongside China, India and America as one of the great success stories of the next global era. But it is also obvious to me that the nations that will meet and master global change best are not just those whose governments make the right long-term decisions on stability, science, trade and education, but whose people come together and, sharing a common view of the challenges and what needs to be done, forge a unified and shared sense of purpose about the long-term sacrifices they are prepared to make and the priorities they think important for national success. And just as in wartime a sense of common patriotic purpose inspired people to do what is necessary, so in peacetime a strong modern sense of patriotism and patriotic purpose which binds people together can motivate and inspire. And this British patriotism is, in my view, founded not on ethnicity nor race, not just on institutions we share and respect, but on enduring ideals which shape our view of ourselves and our communities – values which in turn influence the way our institutions evolve.

Yet as Jonathan Freedland has written in his *Bring Home the Revolution*, Britain is almost unique in that, unlike America and many other countries, we have no constitutional statement or declaration enshrining our objectives as a country; no mission statement defining purpose; and no explicitly stated vision of our future. So I will suggest to you today that it is to our benefit to be more explicit about what we stand for and what are our objectives, and that we will meet and master all challenges best by finding shared purpose as a country in our enduring British ideals that I would summarise as – in addition to our qualities of creativity, inventiveness, enterprise and our internationalism, our central beliefs are a commitment to – liberty for all, responsibility by all and fairness to all. And I believe that out of a debate, hopefully leading to a broad consensus about what Britishness means, flows a rich agenda for change: a new constitutional settlement, an explicit definition of citizenship, a renewal of civic society, a rebuilding of our local government and a better balance between diversity and integration. And around national symbols that also unite the whole country, an inclusive Britishness where, as a result of our commitment to liberty for all, responsibility by all and fairness to all, we make it possible for not just some but all people to realise their potential to the full.

So what do we mean when we talk about Britishness? Remember when we were young, we wrote out our addresses: our town, our county, our country, our continent, the world, like James Joyce jokingly at the start of *Portrait of the Artist as a Young Man*: Stephen Dedalus, Class of Elements, Clongowes Wood College, Sallins, County Kildare, Ireland, Europe, The World, The Universe. I will say something more about the importance to identity of neighbourhoods, towns, villages and communities and about our global responsibilities. But, while a few years ago only less than half – 46 per cent – identified closely with being British, today national identity has become far more important: it is not 46 per cent but 65 per cent – two-thirds – who now identify Britishness as important. And recent surveys show that British people feel more patriotic about their country than almost any other European country.

So what is it to be British? What has emerged from the long tidal flows of British history – from the 2,000 years of successive waves of invasion, immigration, assimilation and trading partnerships; from the uniquely rich, open and outward-looking culture – is a distinctive set of values which influence British institutions. Even before America made it its own I think Britain can lay claim to the idea of liberty. Out of the necessity of finding a way to live together in a multinational state came the practice of toleration and then the pursuit of liberty. Voltaire said that Britain gave to the world the idea of liberty. In the seventeenth century, Milton in *Paradise Lost* put it as 'if not equal all, yet all equally free'. Think of Wordsworth's poetry about the 'flood of British freedom'; then Hazlitt's belief that we have and can have 'no privilege or advantage over other nations but liberty'; right through to Orwell's focus on justice, liberty and decency defining Britain. 'We can get a parliament from anywhere,' said Lord Grattan, 'we can only get liberty from England'.

So there is, as I have argued, a golden thread which runs through British history – that runs from that long-ago day in Runnymede in 1215; on to the Bill of Rights in 1689 when Britain became the first country to successfully assert the power of parliament over the king; to not just one but four great Reform Acts in less than a hundred years – of the individual standing firm against tyranny and then – an even more generous, expansive view of liberty – the idea of government accountable to the people, evolving into the exciting idea of empowering citizens to control their own lives.

Just as it was in the name of liberty that in the 1800s Britain led the world in abolishing the slave trade – something we celebrate in 2007 – so too in the 1940s in the name of liberty Britain stood firm against Fascism, which is why I would oppose those who say we should do less to teach that period of our history in our schools. But woven also into that golden thread of liberty are countless strands of common, continuing endeavour in our villages, towns and cities – the efforts and popular achievements of ordinary men and women, with one

sentiment in common – a strong sense of duty and responsibility: men and women who did not allow liberty to descend
into a selfish individualism or into a crude libertarianism;
men and women who, as is the essence of the labour movement, chose solidarity in preference to selfishness; thus
creating out of the idea of duty and responsibility the Britain
of civic responsibility, civic society and the public realm.

And so the Britain we admire of thousands of voluntary
associations; the Britain of mutual societies, craft unions,
insurance and friendly societies and cooperatives; the Britain
of churches and faith groups; the Britain of municipal provision from libraries to parks; and the Britain of public service.
Mutuality, cooperation, civic associations and social responsibility and a strong civic society – all concepts that after a
moment's thought we see clearly have always owed most to
progressive opinion in British life and thought. The British
way always – as Jonathan Sacks has suggested – more than self-
interested individualism – at the core of British history, the
very ideas of 'active citizenship', 'good neighbour', civic pride
and the public realm. Which is why two-thirds of people are
adamant that being British carries with it responsibilities for
them as citizens as well as rights.

But the twentieth century has given special place also to the
idea that in a democracy where people have both political,
social and economic rights and responsibilities, liberty and
responsibility can only fully come alive if there is a Britain not
just of liberty for all, and responsibility from all, but fairness to
all. Of course the appeal to fairness runs through British
history, from early opposition to the first Poll Tax in 1381 to
the second; fairness the theme from the Civil War debates –
where Raineborough asserted that 'the poorest he that is in
England hath a life to live as the greatest he'; to the 1940s
when Orwell talked of a Britain known to the world for its
'decency'. Indeed a 2005 YouGov survey showed that as many
as 90 per cent of British people thought that fairness and fair

play were very important or fairly important in defining Britishness. And of course this was the whole battle of twentieth-century politics – whether fairness would be formal equality before the law or something much more, a richer equality of opportunity. You only need look at the slogan which dominated Live Aid 2005 to see how, even in the years from 1985 to 2005, fairness had moved to become the central idea – the slogan in 2005 was 'From Charity to Justice': not just donations for handouts, but, by making things happen, forcing governments to deliver fairness.

Take the NHS, one of the great British institutions – what 90 per cent of British people think portrays a positive symbol of the real Britain – founded on the core value of fairness that all should have access to health care founded on need not ability to pay. A moment's consideration of the importance of the NHS would tell us that you don't need to counterpose civic society to government and assume that one can only flourish at the expense of the other or vice versa. Britain does best when we have both a strong civic society and a government committed to empowering people, acting on the principle of fairness. And according to one survey, more than 70 per cent of British people pride ourselves in all three qualities – our tolerance, responsibility and fairness together. So in a modern progressive view of Britishness, as I set out in a speech a few weeks ago, liberty does not retreat into self-interested individualism, but leads to ideas of empowerment; responsibility does not retreat into a form of paternalism, but is indeed a commitment to the strongest-possible civic society; and fairness is not simply a formal equality before the law, but is in fact a modern belief in an empowering equality of opportunity for all.

So in my view the surest foundation upon which we can advance economically, socially and culturally in this century will be to apply to the challenges that we face, the values of liberty, responsibility and fairness – shared civic values which are not only the ties that bind us, but also give us patriotic purpose as a nation and sense of direction and destiny. And so in this vision of a Britain of liberty for all, responsibility from all and fairness to all we move a long way from the old left's embarrassed avoidance of an explicit patriotism. Orwell correctly ridiculed the old left view for thinking that patriotism could be defined only from the right: as reactionary; patriotism as a defence of unchanging institutions that would never modernise; patriotism as a defence of deference and hierarchy; and patriotism as, in reality, the dislike of foreigners and self-interested individualism. We now see that when the old left recoiled from patriotism they failed to understand that the values on which Britishness is based – liberty to all, responsibility by all, fairness for all – owe more to progressive ideas than to right-wing ones. But more than that, these core values of what it is to be British are the key to the next stage of our progress as a people: values that are capable of uniting us and inspiring us as we meet and master the challenges of the future. So we in our party should feel pride in a British patriotism and patriotic purpose founded on liberty for all, responsibility by all, and fairness to all. And, as we address global challenges, the modern application of these great enduring ideas that British people hold dear offers us a rich agenda for change, reform and modernisation true to these values.

First, start with the constitution and test the current condition of Britain against our principles of liberty for all, responsibility by all and fairness to all. And just as each generation needs to renew the settlement between individual, community and state, so too we should recognise that we do not today meet our ideal of liberty for all if we are to allow power to become over-centralised; we do not achieve responsibility by all if we do not encourage and build a strong civic society; and we do not achieve fairness to all if too many people feel excluded from the decision-making process.

So the British way forward must be to break up, in the name of liberty, centralised institutions that are too remote and insensitive, and so devolve power; to encourage, in the name of responsibility, the creation of strong local institutions; and, in new ways in the name of liberty, responsibility and fairness, to seek to engage the British people in decisions that affect their lives. So I believe it is imperative that we reinvigorate the constitutional reform agenda we began in 1997. And I cannot see how the long-term success, legitimacy and credibility of our institutions or our policies can be secured unless our constitutional, social and economic reforms are explicitly founded on these ideas. Just as on the first day I was Chancellor I limited the power of the executive by giving up government power over interest rates to the Bank of England, I suggested during the general election there was a case for a further restriction of executive power and a detailed consideration of the role of parliament in the declarations of peace and war. And, of course, founding our constitution on liberty within the law means restricting patronage, for example, in matters such as ecclesiastical and other appointments so that we prevent any allegation of arbitrary use of power. I would apply this same approach to constitutional questions such as the issue of House of Lords reform, where, in my view, the two principles that should guide our approach are the primacy of the House of Commons and the need for the accountability of the second chamber. At the same time the next stage of our discussions of human rights should, as people such as Francesca Klug have argued, also take more fully into account the very British idea that individual rights are rooted in ideas of responsibility and community.

We must apply also our principles of liberty for all, responsibility by all and fairness to all to the future of our civic society and the responsibilities of citizenship, and we will therefore want to do more to encourage and enhance voluntary initiative, mutual responsibility and local community action. For

two centuries Britain was defined to the world by its proliferation of local clubs, associations, societies and endeavours –
from churches and trades unions to municipal initiatives and
friendly societies. And I believe that we should, for this and
the coming generation, do more to encourage and empower
new British organisations that speak for these British values. A
modern expression of Britishness and our commitment to the
future is the creation of the British National Youth Community Service: engaging and rewarding a new generation of
young people from all backgrounds to serve their communities; demonstrating our practical commitment to a cohesive
and strong society. So just as from America the Peace Corps –
and before it, in Britain, British Voluntary Service Overseas –
harnessed for the 1960s and beyond a new spirit of idealism
and common purpose, in 2006 a new British National Youth
Community Service can galvanise and challenge the energies
and enthusiasm of a fresh generation of teenagers and young
people. For example, gap years should not be available just
for those who can afford to pay, but to young people who
cannot afford to pay themselves but want to make the effort to
serve their communities at home and abroad. And we should
think of gap months, gap weeks as well as gap years. Time to
serve the community, not just for people going on to higher
education but for people whatever their skills.

   And we should consider how we can link up with Asia,
Africa and America and I will meet the airlines to ask what
more they can do to help sponsor this idea. In return for
service for their country in the USA in the 1940s the GI Bill
helped thousands through college and university and we
should consider and debate another idea: helping those
who undertake community service with the costs of education, including help with Education Maintenance Allowance
and tuition fees for those undertaking community work. The
Russell Commission has recommended a prominent role for
British business in this new community endeavour. I am

meeting all faith groups to discuss community service. And shortly I will meet business organisations. And I thank businesses who have already signed up as pioneer sponsors for this idea and today I invite and urge businesses to match-fund £100 million – £50 million each from government and business – for long-term funding for this new idea. Britain can lead the world with a modern national community service.

Responsibility by all in Britain today means also corporate social responsibility – business engagement in voluntary activity, translating the widespread social concern that exists among employers and employees alike into effective action for the common good. And with corporate social responsibility not as an add-on but at the core of a company's work, Britain can lead the way in a modern approach to corporate responsibility. We set up Futurebuilders to help existing charities adapt to the modern world. I believe we need to examine how we might do more to encourage new charities and social enterprises, locally and nationally, to start up, develop and flourish, perhaps with a fund for seed-corn finance. Take mentoring, which is about befriending people, especially, in a more isolated society, the most vulnerable. While underdeveloped in Britain in contrast to other countries, mentoring is a modern expression of civic society at work. And we should explore innovative ways – through the internet, TV, local organisations and personal contact – of recruiting and training mentors and linking those who need help and advice to those who can help and advise.

Next, test our principles of liberty, responsibility and fairness and apply them to how we think about local government. And if, as I argue, the British way is to restore and enhance local initiative and mutual responsibility in civic affairs, we should be doing more to strengthen local institutions. While all governments have proved to be cautious in devolving power, I hope we can say that – as the Scottish Parliament, Welsh Assembly and mayor in London bear witness – this government has done more to devolve power than any other. But we must now look to further devolution of power away from Westminster, particularly to a reinvigoration of local government and to schools, hospitals and the self-management of local services, the emphasis on empowerment, communities and individuals realising their promise and potential by taking more control over their lives. And in doing so we must recognise that people's local sense of belonging is now focused on the immediate neighbourhood. So I welcome the debate on what some call 'double devolution' – on how we reinvigorate democracy at the most local of levels. For example, neighbourhood councils could help harness that sense of belonging and involve people directly in decisions about the services that they use every day. Just as neighbourhood policing – being pioneered here in London as well as elsewhere – is showing, greater local engagement and improved public services can go hand in hand: the police able to respond more quickly to local concerns and local people taking greater responsibility for working with the police to tackle these concerns.

And I believe a genuinely British approach to representative and participatory democracy should explore new ways of involving people in decisions. In various places in Britain and around the world local, regional and even national governments have been experimenting with new ways of involving the public in decision-making – not the usual suspects, the vested interest – but groups of citizens who come together, sometimes in small groups such as citizens' juries, sometimes in large deliberative exercises, to examine important issues of public policy. And I look forward to the considerations of the Power Commission.

A commitment to the British values of liberty, responsibility and fairness also means taking citizenship seriously. From the quality of citizenship lessons in our schools; to building on the introduction of citizenship ceremonies; to defining not just the rights of citizenship, but the responsibilities too; to finding the best ways of reconciling the rights to liberty for every individual with the needs for security for all; and, of course, an issue we will discuss in detail today – getting the balance right between diversity and integration. July 7th has rightly led to calls for all of us, including moderates in the Islamic community, to stand up to extremism. At one level, when suicide bombers have connections with other countries and can, in theory, use the internet or be instructed through mobile phones, we know that defeating violent extremists will not be achieved through action in one country alone or one continent, but only globally, through all means: military and security means but also debate, discussion and dialogue in newspapers, journals, culture, the arts and literature. And not just through governments but through foundations, trusts, civil society and civic culture, as globally we seek to distance extremists from moderates. But, at another level, terrorism in our midst means that debates, which sometimes may be seen as dry, about Britishness and our model of integration clearly now have a new urgency.

I believe in your discussions today you will conclude that it does entail giving more emphasis to the common glue – a Britishness which welcomes differences but which is not so loose, so nebulous, that it is simply defined as the toleration of difference and leaves a hole where national identity should be. Instead I have no doubt that a modern commitment to liberty, responsibility and fairness will lead us to measures that bring all parts of the community together to share a common purpose and linked destinies. Clearly we will have both to tackle prejudice, bigotry and the incitement to hatred and to do far more to tackle discrimination and promote inclusion. I believe we must address issues about the incitement to hatred just as I believe that there should now be greater focus on tackling inequalities in job and educational opportunities, driving up the educational attainment of pupils from ethnic minorities and a more comprehensive New Deal effort to tackle unacceptably high unemployment in areas of high ethnic minority populations. Indeed, we should do more to help integration. Take the example of those who cannot find work because of language difficulties. Here we should look at expanding mandatory English training. And for those who are trapped in a narrow range of jobs where their lack of fluency in English makes it hard for them to make progress in their careers, we should examine the case for further support. And to back up this effort there should be a national effort for volunteers as well as professionals to mentor new entrants. And we should also think of what more we can do to develop the ties that bind us more closely together.

The Olympics is but one example of a national project which is uniting the country. But think for a moment: what is the British equivalent of the US Fourth of July, or even the French Fourteenth of July for that matter? What I mean is: what is our equivalent for a national celebration of who we are and what we stand for? And what is our equivalent of the national symbolism of a flag in every garden? In recent years we have had magnificent celebrations of VE Day, the Jubilee and, last year, Trafalgar Day. Perhaps Armistice Day and Remembrance Sunday are the nearest we have come to a British day that is – in every corner of our country – commemorative, unifying, and an expression of British ideas of standing firm in the world in the name of liberty, responsibility and fairness?

And let us remember that when people on the centre left recoiled from national symbols, the BNP tried to steal the Union Jack. Instead of the BNP using it as symbol of racial division, the flag should be a symbol of unity, part of a modern expression of patriotism. So we should respond to the BNP by saying the union flag is a flag for Britain, not for the BNP; all the United Kingdom should honour it, not ignore it; we should assert that the union flag is, by definition, a flag for tolerance and inclusion.

And we should not recoil from our national history – rather we should make it more central to our education. I propose that British history should be given much more prominence in the curriculum – not just dates, places and names, nor just a set of unconnected facts, but a narrative that encompasses our history. And because citizenship is still taught too much in isolation I suggest in the current review of the curriculum that we look at how we root the teaching of citizenship more closely in history. And we should encourage volunteers to be more involved; to help schools bring alive the idea of citizenship with real engagement in the community. Rediscovering the roots of our identity in our shared beliefs also gives us more confidence in facing difficult questions about our relationship with the rest of the world. And – instead of a Britain still characterised by doubts about our role in the world, and in particular, grappling uncertainly with issues of integration in a European trade bloc; instead of a Britain seeing the battle as Britain versus Europe, not Britain part of Europe; instead of thinking the European choice is between non-engagement and total absorption; a Britain failing to see we can lead the next stage of Europe's development – I believe that, more sure of our values, we can become a Britain that is an increasingly successful leader of the global economy; a global Britain for whom membership of Europe is central; and then go on to help a reformed, more flexible, more outward-looking Europe play a bigger part in global society, not least improving the relationship between Europe and the USA.

And, of course, true to our ideals of liberty, responsibility and fairness, Britain leading the way in new measures to make the world safer, more secure and fairer – not just debt relief, the doubling of aid and, reflecting our openness as a nation, by securing a world deal on trade. But, from that foundation, proposing, true to our internationalism, a new way forward: a global new deal – universal free schooling for every child, universal free health care for every family – where the richest countries finally meet our commitments to the poorest of the world.

So a modern view of Britishness founded on responsibility, liberty and fairness requires us to:

- demand a new constitutional settlement;
- take citizenship seriously;
- rebuild civic society;
- renew local government;
- work for integration of minorities into a modern Britain; and
- be internationalist at all times.

BIOGRAPHICAL NOTES ON THE CONTRIBUTORS

Kofi Annan is the seventh Secretary-General of the United Nations, and the first black African to hold the position. Mr Annan's priorities as Secretary-General have been to revitalize the United Nations through a comprehensive programme of reform; to strengthen the organisation's traditional work in the areas of development and the maintenance of international peace and security; to encourage and advocate human rights, the rule of law and the universal values of equality, tolerance and human dignity found in the United Nations Charter; and to restore public confidence in the organisation by reaching out to new partners and, in his words, by 'bringing the United Nations closer to the people'.

Helen Clark MP is Prime Minister of New Zealand. She joined the NZ Labour Party in 1971, has been an MP since 1975 and in the cabinet since 1987. She was elected Leader of the Labour Party in December 1993 and served as Leader of the Opposition until the general election in November 1999, when Labour was elected to government, and she has led her party to two further election victories since then.

Linda Colley is a British historian, widely known for her 1992 study *Britons: Forging the Nation, 1707–1837*, which explored the development of a British national identity following the 1707

Acts of Union. She was a Fellow of Christ's College, University of Cambridge, before taking a position at Yale University in 1982, and later being Richard M. Colgate Professor of History there. From 1998 she held the Senior Leverhulme Research Professorship in History at the London School of Economics, moving to become Professor of History at Princeton University in 2003.

Lord Ralf Dahrendorf is a German-British sociologist, philosopher, political scientist and politician. From 1969 to 1970 he was a member of the German parliament for the Freie Demokratische Partei, and a Parliamentary Secretary of State in the Ministry of Foreign Affairs. In 1970 he became a Commissioner in the European Commission in Brussels. From 1974 to 1984 he was Director of the London School of Economics. He returned to Germany to become Professor of Social Science at Konstanz University (1984–86). He became Warden of St Anthony's College at Oxford University in 1986. He sits in the House of Lords as a crossbencher.

Al Gore is an American politician, businessman and author, who served as the 45th Vice President of the United States from 1993 to 2001. He ran for President in 2000 following Bill Clinton's two four-year terms, and was defeated in the Electoral College vote, while winning the popular vote. He currently serves as President of the American television channel Current and Chairman of Generation Investment Management, sits on the board of directors of Apple Computer, and serves as an unofficial advisor to Google's senior management.

Alan Greenspan is an American economist and former Chairman of the Board of Governors of the Federal Reserve of the United States. First appointed chairman in 1987, he was reappointed at successive four-year intervals until retiring in 2006, and is considered by many to be the leading authority on American domestic economic and monetary policy. Following his retirement as Fed chairman, he accepted an honorary position at the UK Treasury.

Wangaari Maathai founded the Green Belt movement in Kenya in 1977, which has planted more than 10 million trees to prevent soil erosion and provide firewood for cooking fires. The programme has been carried out primarily by women in the villages of Kenya, who through protecting their environment and paid employment for planting the trees are able to better care for their children and their children's future. In December 2002 Wangaari Maathai was elected to Parliament, and became Deputy Minister in the Ministry of Environment, Natural Resources and Wildlife in January 2003.

Nelson Mandela, in his own words, personifies struggle. He is still leading the fight against apartheid with extraordinary vigour and resilience after spending nearly three decades of his life behind bars. He has sacrificed his private life and his youth for his people, and remains South Africa's best-known and loved hero. He was inaugurated as the first democratically elected State President of South Africa on 10 May 1994, retiring from public life in June 1999.

Trevor Phillips was appointed Chair of the Commission for Racial Equality in March 2003. A former president of the National Union of Students, he has been a broadcaster, a member of the Greater London Authority, and is the author of many newspaper articles and comment pieces as well as co-writer of *Windrush: The Irresistible Rise of Multiracial Britain,* and *Britain's Slave Trade.*

J.K. Rowling is the author of the Harry Potter books. After she graduated from Exeter University, she found work as a secretary, and later spent time teaching English in Portugal before moving to Edinburgh, Scotland, with her daughter. She currently resides in Scotland with her husband and three children. She is active and passionate in her support of single-parent families.

Sir Jonathan Sacks is the Chief Rabbi of the United Hebrew Congregations of the Commonwealth and is widely recognised as one of the world's leading contemporary exponents of Judaism. A gifted communicator, the Chief Rabbi is a frequent contributor to radio, television and the national press. He is the author of a number of books, and a frequent contributor to the national press and also to 'Thought for the Day' on BBC Radio 4's *Today Programme*.

Sir Derek Wanless was Group Chief Executive of NatWest from 1992 until 1999. In April 2002 he produced the report *Securing Our Future Health: Taking a Long-Term View* for the Chancellor of the Exchequer. He undertook further work on this topic for the UK government in April 2003, and has recently completed a study *Securing Care for Older People* for the King's Fund. He is currently a director of Northern Rock plc and Business in the Community, a Commissioner at the Statistics Commission and a Trustee of the National Endowment for Science, Technology and the Arts.

Sir Magdi Yacoub is an eminent heart surgeon, who was consultant cardiothoracic surgeon at Harefield Hospital (1969–2001), Director of medical research and education (from 1992), and was involved in the development of the techniques of heart and heart-lung transplantation. In 2002 he was selected to spearhead a government recruitment drive for overseas doctors. Although retired, he continues to act as a high-profile consultant and ambassador for the benefits of transplant surgery.

FURTHER READING

Annan, Kofi, *We the Peoples: The Role of the United Nations in the 21st Century*, United Nations Millennium Report, 2000

Arnold, Matthew, *Poems*, 1853; *Poems*, 2nd Series, 1855; *Merope*, 1858; *New Poems*, 1867; *On Translating Homer*, 1861 and 1862; *On the Study of Celtic Literature*, 1867; *Essays in Celtic Literature*, 1868, 2nd Series, 1888; *Culture and Anarchy*, 1869; *St Paul and Protestantism*, 1870; *Friendship's Garland*, 1871; *Literature and Dogma*, 1873; *God and the Bible*, 1875; *Last Essays on Church and Religion*, 1877; *Mixed Essays*, 1879; *Irish Essays*, 1882; *Discourses in America*, 1885; *Essays in Criticism*, 1865 and 1888; *Culture and Anarchy*, 1888

Balls, Ed, Foreword to *New Localism: Refashioning the Centre-Local Relationship*, by Dan Corry and Gerry Stoker, New Local Government Network, 2002

Bellah, Robert, *Habits of the Heart*, 1985; *The Good Society*, 1992

Berlin, Isaiah, 'Two Concepts of Liberty', Inaugural Lecture, Oxford, 1958

Bevan, Aneurin, *In Place of Fear: A Free Health Service*, 1952

Beveridge, William, *Unemployment*, 1909; *Social Insurance and Allied Services*, 1942

Blendon, Robert J., Cathy Schoen, Catherine M. Desroches, Robin Osborn, Kimberly L. Scoles and Kinga Zapert, *Inequities In Health Care: A Five-Country Survey*, Health Affairs 21, 2002

Bono, speech to Labour Party Conference, Brighton, September 2004

Boswell, James, *Life of Samuel Johnson*, 1791

Burke, Edmund, *Philosophical Inquiry into the Origin of Our Ideas of the Sublime and Beautiful*, 1756; *Reflections on the Revolution In France*, 1790

Bush, George W., 'Remarks by the President on Global Development', The White House, 14 March 2002

Butler, R.A., *The Art of the Possible*, 1971

Campbell, Joseph, with Bill Moyers, *The Power of Myth*, 1988

Carlisle, Thomas, *An Occasional discourse on the Negro Question*, 1849

Churchill, Winston, House of Commons speech, 1 March 1955

Coalition Government Report, *Full Employment*, 1944

Colley, Linda, *In Defiance of Oligarchy: The Tory Party 1714–1760*, 1982; *Britons: Forging The Nation, 1707–1837*, 1992

Crosland, Anthony, *The Future of Socialism*, 1956; *The Conservative Enemy: A Programme of Radical Reform for the 1960s*, 1962; *Socialism Now and Other Essays*, edited by Dick Leonard, 1974

Dahrendorf, Ralf, *Class and Class Conflict in Industrial Society*, 1959

Darwin, Charles, *Voyage of the Beagle*, 1839; *On the Origin of Species by Means of Natural Selection*, 1859; *The Descent of Man*, 1871

Davies, Norman, *Europe: A History*, 1996; *The Isles: A History*, 1999

Eskimo poem of Netsilik origin called 'Magic Words', as recorded in Jerome Rothenberg's *Shaking the Pumpkin* and in Robert Bly's *News of the Universe*

Feinstein, Leon, 'The Relative Economic Importance of Academic, Psychological and Behavioural Attributes Developed in Childhood', in *What Do We Know about Brain Development and Childhood Interventions?*, Centre for Economic Performance, London School of Economics, July 2000

Ferguson, Adam, *Essay on the History of Civil Society*, 1767; *Principles of Moral and Political Science*, 1792

Foot, Michael, *Aneurin Bevan: A Biography*, 1973

Freedland, Jonathan, *Bring Home the Revolution*, 1999

Gaitskell, Hugh, 'Public Ownership and Equality', in *Socialist Commentary*, 1955

Giddens, Anthony, BBC Reith Lectures, 1999

Goodhart, David, 'Too Diverse/Discomfort of Strangers', *Prospect*, February 2004

Gore, Al, *Earth in the Balance: Forging a New Common Purpose*, 2000; *An Inconvenient Truth*, 2006

Gray, Thomas, *Pindaric Odes*, 1757; 'Elegy Written in a Country Churchyard', in Arthur Quiller-Couch (ed.), *The Oxford Book Of English Verse: 1250–1900*

Green, T.H., *Lectures on Liberal Legislation and Freedom of Contract*, 1881

Griffiths, Trevor, *Food for Ravens*, television film for BBC Wales, 1997

Gutmann, Amy, *Democracy and Disagreement*, 1998

Hammarskjöld, Dag, *Markings*, translated by Sjoberg & Auden, 1964

Hazlitt, William, *Principles of Human Action*, 1805; *Political Essays*, 1819; *Table Talk*, 1821; *The Spirit of the Age*, 1825

Heffer, Simon, *Nor Shall My Sword: The Reinvention of England*, 1999

Himmelfarb, Gertrude, *The Roads to Modernity*, 2004

Hobhouse, L.T., *Liberalism*, 1911; *Labour Movement*, 1893; *Theory of Knowledge*, 1896; *Morals in Evolution*, 1906; *Development and Purpose*, 1913; *The Elements of Social Justice*, 1922

Hobson, J.A., *Problems of Poverty*, 1891; *Problem of the Unemployed*, 1896; *Evolution of Modern Capitalism*, 1894; *John Ruskin: Social Reformer*, 1898; *The Industrial System*, 1909; *Towards International Government*, 1914

Hume, David, *Treatise of Human Nature*, 1739; *Essays Moral and Political*, 1741; *Political Discourses*, 1752; *History of England*, 1754–62

Hutcheson, Francis, *A System of Moral Philosophy*, 1755

Ignatieff, Michael, 'Identity Parades', *Prospect*, April 1988

Jenkins, Roy, *Churchill: A Biography*, 2001

Joyce, James, *A Portrait of the Artist as a Young Man*, 1916; *Ulysses*, 1922

Kant, Immanuel, *An Answer to the Question: 'What is Enlightenment?'*, 1784

Kinnock, Neil, *The Future of Socialism*, Fabian Pamphlet no. 509, 1986

Kennedy, President John F., statement upon signing order establishing the Peace Corps (Executive Order 10924), 1 March 1961; Inaugural Address, 20 January 1961

Kennedy, Robert, Day of Affirmation Address, University of Cape Town, 6 June 1966

Keynes, John Maynard, *The General Theory of Employment, Interest and Money*, 1936; *Economic Consequences of the Peace*, 1919; *Treatise on Probability*, 1921; *Tract on Monetary Reform*, 1923; *Treatise on Money*, 1930; *Essays in Persuasion*, 1931

King Jr, Martin Luther, 'I Have a Dream' speech, Washington DC, 28 August 1963; 'Letter from a Birmingham Jail', 16 April 1963; sermon delivered at Ebenezer Baptist Church, Atlanta, Georgia, February 1968; 'The Drum Major Instinct' sermon, Ebenezer Baptist Church, 4 February 1968

Lawson, Nigel, *The View From No. 11: Memoirs of a Tory Radical*, 1992; Mais Lecture, 1984

Lincoln, Abraham, First Inaugural Address, 4 March 1861

Macaulay, Thomas Babington, *History of England, from the Accession of James II*, 1852

Maathai, Wangaari, *The Canopy of Hope: My Life Campaigning for Africa, Women, and the Environment*, 2002; *The Green Belt Movement – Sharing the Approach and the Experience*, 2004

Mandela, Nelson, *Nelson Mandela Speaks: Forging a Democratic, Non-racial South Africa*, 1993; *Long Walk to Freedom: The Autobiography of Nelson Mandela*, 1994

Marr, Andrew, *The Day Britain Died*, 2000; *My Trade: A Short History of British Journalism*, 2004

Marshall, George, Harvard speech, 5 June 1947

Marshall, T.H., *Citizenship and Social Class*, 1992

McNair, John, *James Maxton: Beloved Rebel*, 1955

McIlvanney, William, *Docherty*, 1975

McKnight, Abigail, *Trends in Earnings Inequality and Earnings Mobility, 1977–1997: The Impact of Mobility on Long-Term Inequality*, DTI Employment Relations Research Series, No. 8, February 2000

Mill, John Stuart, *A System of Logic*, 1843; *On Liberty*, 1859; *Utilitarianism*, 1863; *Three Essays on Religion*, 1874

Milton, John, *Paradise Lost*, 1667; *Paradise Regained*, 1671; *Samson Agonistes*, 1671

Montesquieu, Charles de Secondat, baron de, *The Spirit of the Laws*, 1748

More, Sir Thomas, *Utopia*, 1895

Morris, William, *Letters on Socialism*, 1888

Morrison, Toni, *James Baldwin: His Voice Remembered;* 'Life in His Language' featured in the *New York Times*, 20 December 1987

Mount, Ferdinand, *Property and Poverty: An Agenda for the Mid-80s*, 1984; *The Recovery of the Constitution: The Second Sovereignty Lecture*, 1992; *The British Consitittion Now: Recovery or Decline?*, 1992; *Mind the Gap: Class in Britain Now*, 2004

Nairn, Tom, *The Break-up of Britain: Crisis and Neo-Nationalism*, 1977

Okun, Arthur, *Equality and Efficiency: The Big Tradeoff*, 1975

O'Neil, Onora, 'A Question of Trust', BBC Reith Lectures, 2002

Opinion Leader Research, published in *New Britain*, a Smith Institute pamphlet, 1999

Orwell, George, *The Lion and the Unicorn: Socialism and the English Genius*, 1941; *The English People*, 1947

Osborne and Gaebler, *Reinventing Government*, 1982

Owen Robert, *A New View of Society*, 1814

Paine, Thomas, *Common Sense*, 1776; *The Rights of Man*, 1792; *Age of Reason*, 1795

Pope John Paul II, '*Pacem In Terris*: A Permanent Commitment', Message of His Holiness for the Celebration of the World Day of Peace, 1 January 2003

Pope Paul VI, *Encyclical Populorum Progressio* (On the Development of Peoples), 1967

Phillips, Anne, *Which Equalities Matter?*, 1999; *The Politics of Presence: Political Representation of Gender Race and Ethnicity*, 1998

Phillips, A.W., 'The Relation between Unemployment and the Rate of Change of Money Wage Rates in the United Kingdom, 1861–1957', *Economica*, 1958

Phillips, Melanie, 'The need to defend the nation', column in the *Daily Mail*, 5 April 2004

Powell, Colin, remarks at the Development, Democracy and Security Conference, Washington DC, 30 September 2004

Priestley, J.B., *English Journey*, 1934

Raineborough, Thomas, speech in *The Army Debates About Democracy*, 1647

Rawls, John, *Theory of Justice*, 1971; *Political Liberalism*, 1993

Riddell, N., *Labour in Crisis: The Second Labour Government*, 1929–31, 1999

Rodo, José Enrique, *Ariel*, 1900

Roosevelt, Franklin D., Annual Message to Congress, 3 January 1938

Rousseau, Jean Jacques, *The Social Contract*, 1762; *Confessions*, 1782

Rowntree, Joseph, Founders Memorandum, 1904

Sacks, Rabbi Sir Jonathan, *The Politics of Hope*, 1997; *The Dignity of Difference*, 2002; *To Heal a Fractured World: The Ethics of Responsibility*, 2005

Sandel, Michael, *Liberalism and the Limits of Justice*, 1982; 'The Moral Limits of the Market', in the Tanner Lectures on Human Values, delivered at Brasenose College, Oxford, 11 and 12 May 1998

Schlesinger, Arthur, *The Disuniting Of America*, 1998

Schumpeter, Joseph A., *Capitalism, Socialism and Democracy*, 1943

Scruton, Roger, *England: An Elegy*, 2001

Sen, Amartya, *Development as Freedom*, 2000; *The Argumentative Indian: Writings on Indian History, Culture and Identity*, 2005; *Rationality and Freedom*, 2004

Shaw, George Bernard, *Man and Superman*, 1903; *Major Barbara*, 1905

Shenefield, John H., and Irwin M. Stelzer, *The Antitrust Laws, A Primer*, American Enterprise Institute, 2001

Skidelsky, Robert, *John Maynard Keynes*, 2001

Smiles, Samuel, *Self-Help*, 1859

Smith, Adam, *The Theory of Moral Sentiments*, 1759; *An Inquiry into the Nature and Causes of the Wealth of Nations*, 1776

Smith, John, Labour Party Conference speech, 1992

Social Justice Report, *Strategies for National Renewal, the Report of the Commission on Social Justice*, 1994

Stelzer, Irwin (ed.), *The Neocon Reader*, 2005

Tawney, R.H., *Equality*, 1931

Thomson, James, *The Seasons*, 1730; 'Rule Britannia', put to music by Thomas Augustine Arne, circa 1740; *The Castle of Indolence*, 1748

Titmuss, Richard, *The Gift Relationship: From Human Blood to Social Policy*, 1970

Tocqueville, Alexis de, *Democracy in America*, 1835/1840

Voltaire, François-Marie Arouet, *Letters on the English*, 1778

Walzer, Michael, *Spheres of Justice*, 1984

Webb, Sidney and Beatrice, *The History of Trade Unionism*, 1894; *Industrial Democracy*, 1897

White, E.B., on the death of John F. Kennedy, *The New Yorker*, 30 November 1963

Williams, Raymond, *Culture and Society, 1780–1850*, 1958

Williams, Rowan, Archbishop of Canterbury, Richard Dimbleby Lecture, 19 December 2002

Wilson, James Q., *The Moral Sense*, 1993

Winstanley, Gerard, *The Law of Freedom in a Platform*, 1652

Wolfensohn, Jim, speaking at Woodrow Wilson International Centre for Scholars, Washington DC, 6 March 2002

Wollstonecraft, Mary, *A Vindication of the Rights of Women*, 1792

Wordsworth, William, *England* ('It is not to be thought of. . .'), 1802

Young, Hugo, *But, Chancellor: Inquiry into the Treasury*, 1984; *One of Us: Life of Margaret Thatcher*, 1989; 'Thatcherism: Did Society Survive?', the Maisie Ward Sheed Memorial Lecture, 1992; *This Blessed Plot: Britain and Europe from Churchill to Blair*, 1998; *Political Lives*, 2001; *Supping with the Devils*, 2004

A NOTE ON THE AUTHOR

Gordon Brown was born in Kirkcaldy in 1951 and educated there. He studied at Edinburgh University from the age of sixteen and graduated with Master of Arts at nineteen with First Class Honours, later gaining a Doctorate of Philosophy. He was elected Rector of Edinburgh University by the student body and from 1972 to 1975 was Chairman of the University Court. From 1976 to 1980, he lectured at Edinburgh University and then Glasgow College of Technology, before taking up a post at Scottish TV. From 1983 to 1984 he was Chair of the Labour Party Scottish Council and in May 1983 became MP for Dunfermline East. He was Opposition spokesperson on Treasury and Economic Affairs (Shadow Chancellor) from 1992. With the election of the Labour government in May 1997, Gordon Brown became Chancellor of the Exchequer and is now the longest-serving Chancellor for 200 years. He is currently Chairman of the International Monetary and Finance Committee, which monitors the International Monetary Fund, and is a member of Kofi Annan's Panel for the Reform of the United Nations. His books include *Maxton, The Politics of Nationalism and Devolution, Where There Is Greed* (co-author), *John Smith: Life and Soul of the Party* (editor). He is married to Sarah Macaulay and they have two sons.

A NOTE ON THE EDITOR

Wilf Stevenson, a former Director of the BFI, is the Director of the Smith Institute, an independent think tank set up to undertake research and education in issues that flow from the changing relationship between social values and economic imperatives.

A NOTE ON THE TYPE

The text of this book is set in New Baskerville, which is based
on the original Baskerville font designed by John Baskerville
of Birmingham (1706–1775). The original punches he cut for
Baskerville still exist. His widow sold them to Beaumarchais,
from where they passed through several French foundries
to Deberney & Peignot in Paris, before finding their
way to Cambridge University Press.

Baskerville was the first of the 'transitional romans' between
the softer and rounder calligraphic Old Face and the
'Modern' sharp-tooled Bodoni. It does not look very different
to the Old Faces, but there's a crisper differentiation between
thick and thin strokes, and the serifs on lower-case letters
are closer to the horizontal with the stress nearer the
vertical. The R in some sizes has the eighteenth-century
curled tail, the lower-case w has no middle serif, and
the lower-case g has an open tail and a curled ear.